Bibb Falk

ALSO BY WILLIAM A. COOK
AND MCFARLAND

Big Klu: The Baseball Life of Ted Kluszewski (2012)

Jim Thorpe: A Biography (2011)

King of the Bootleggers: A Biography of George Remus (2008)

August "Garry" Herrmann: A Baseball Biography (2008)

The Louisville Grays Scandal of 1877: The Taint of Gambling at the Dawn of the National League (2005)

Waite Hoyt: A Biography of the Yankees' Schoolboy Wonder (2004)

Pete Rose: Baseball's All-Time Hit King (2004)

The Summer of '64: A Pennant Lost (2002)

The 1919 World Series: What Really Happened? (2001)

Bibb Falk
*The Man Who
Replaced Shoeless Joe*

WILLIAM A. COOK

McFarland & Company, Inc., Publishers
Jefferson, North Carolina

LIBRARY OF CONGRESS CATALOGUING-IN-PUBLICATION DATA

Cook, William A., 1944–
    Bibb Falk : the man who replaced Shoeless Joe / William A. Cook.
      p.   cm.
    Includes bibliographical references and index.

    ISBN 978-0-7864-9691-4 (softcover : acid free paper) ∞
    ISBN 978-1-4766-1857-9 (ebook)

    1. Baseball players—United States—Biography. 2. Baseball coaches—Texas—Biography. 3. Chicago White Sox (Baseball team)—History. 4. University of Texas at Austin—Baseball—History. 5. University of Texas at Austin—Alumni and alumnae—Biography. I. Falk, Bibb August, 1899–1989. II. Title.

    GV865.F25C66 2015   796.357092—dc23   [B]   2015008754

BRITISH LIBRARY CATALOGUING DATA ARE AVAILABLE

© 2015 William A. Cook. All rights reserved

No part of this book may be reproduced or transmitted in any form or by any means, electronic or mechanical, including photocopying or recording, or by any information storage and retrieval system, without permission in writing from the publisher.

On the cover: Bibb Falk (National Baseball Hall of Fame Library, Cooperstown, New York)

Printed in the United States of America

McFarland & Company, Inc., Publishers
   Box 611, Jefferson, North Carolina 28640
     www.mcfarlandpub.com

To a special niece,
Sabrina A. Cunningham

Table of Contents

Introduction 1

1. From the Forty Acres to Chicago   7
2. The 1919 World Series   17
3. Breaking In with the Black Sox   26
4. Replacing a Legend   46
5. Touring the Orient   66
6. Bibb Falk Establishes Himself as a Big Leaguer   73
7. Another Post-Season Tour   81
8. Traded to Cleveland   85
9. Falk Joins the Army Air Corps   102
10. Bibb Falk Becomes a Longhorn Legend   113
11. Looking Back   147

*Afterword: College Baseball Coaches;
No Ticket to the Show*   164

Appendices—A, B, C, D, E, F, G, H   183

Chapter Notes   189

Bibliography   193

Index   195

Introduction

Recently ESPN selected its list of the "Fifty Greatest Chicago White Sox" players. In the opinion of the network, Bibb Falk ranked as number 37. After looking over the remarkable major league career statistics and college coaching record of Bibb August Falk, I was greatly surprised to discover that the story of this extraordinarily gifted athlete and most talented coach had yet to be told in print. Immediately I decided that it was inevitable that his story would be told, and the time was now for Falk to get his due. I am confident that after one reads the story presented here of Falk's sensational baseball life, it will be hard to accept that ESPN ranking as being high enough.

Born in Austin, Texas, in 1899, standing six feet in height, Bibb Falk was a classic stereotype of a tall Texan, a man who brimmed with confidence and played the game of baseball with a swagger. He played three years of varsity football and baseball at the University of Texas before being signed by Chicago White Sox following graduation in 1920.

Texans have had a long love affair with the game of baseball. The Texas League originally formed as the Texas League of Base Ball Clubs in 1888. In fact, the University of Texas and Texas A&M were battling on the diamond before they began to battle on the gridiron. If one is talking baseball history in the Great State of Texas, whether about the Texas League, Houston Astros, Texas Rangers, Nolan Ryan, Ross Youngs, Norm Cash, TCU, Rice, Texas A&M, the University of Texas, whomever or whatever, it is impossible not to get around to mentioning Bibb Falk in that conversation.

A superb college athlete, Falk was a pitcher and first baseman for

Introduction

the Texas Longhorns baseball team in the late years of the second decade of the twentieth century. He went undefeated in three seasons on the mound while hitting for averages of .369 and .462 and .400. As a member of the Longhorns football squad, Falk was chosen as an All-Southwest Conference tackle in 1919.

In the summer of 1920, Falk reported to the Chicago White Sox without playing one game in the minor leagues. Little did Falk know or could fathom that just a couple of months after arriving on the south side of Chicago that summer, he would be called upon to replace the legendary Shoeless Joe Jackson in the White Sox lineup. Joe Jackson was one of baseball's all-time greatest players, but in late September that year he was suspended for complicity in the scandal surrounding the infamous 1919 World Series. For Bibb Falk, the aftermath of the 1919 World Series controversy was a circumstance that would become his window of opportunity in major league baseball, and he skillfully took advantage of it.

In September 1920, as the nation entered the "Roaring Twenties" and New York Yankees right fielder Babe Ruth held the baseball world's collective attention by hitting home runs at a pace never accomplished before in major league history, rookie Bibb Falk sat on the White Sox bench waiting patiently for any opportunity to play. Suddenly rumors of a fix in the 1919 World Series began to swirl about the sporting world like a buzz saw. Late in the month it was revealed in a grand jury hearing in Chicago that eight White Sox players had allegedly accepted bribes to fix the 1919 World Series for the Cincinnati Reds to win.

In an attempt to protect the integrity of his franchise and the value of his investment, White Sox owner Charles A. Comiskey immediately suspended all eight players named in the scandal. At the time, the White Sox were attempting to repeat as American League champions and were locked in a heated stretch drive battle with the Cleveland Indians and New York Yankees. With outstanding outfielders Shoeless Joe Jackson and Oscar "Happy" Felsch suspended by Comiskey, Bibb Falk, an untested rookie, was one of the reserves chosen to fill the impossible void in the White Sox lineup. In the wake of the scandal, as the White Sox saw their pennant hopes crash and burn in the final games of the 1920 season, Falk started the final three games. He batted .294 and immediately began to etch a place in major league baseball history for himself.

In the 1921 season, Falk was called upon to replace Jackson as the regular left fielder. A conspiracy trial would be held in the summer of

Introduction

1921 for seven of the eight White Sox players accused of throwing the 1919 World Series. It resulted in a not guilty verdict. But none of the seven players implicated, including Shoeless Joe Jackson, nor one other player who had charges dropped against him for lack of evidence, would ever play major league baseball again. Following the trial, the newly installed commissioner of major league baseball, Judge Kenesaw Mountain Landis, permanently banned all eight players, thereby overriding any chance of their reinstatement by Charles Comiskey.

The banishment of eight prominent players decimated the Chicago White Sox team that prior to the scandal had been acknowledged as one of the best in baseball. Bibb Falk would confront the daunting challenge—replacing legendary Shoeless Joe Jackson—with determination and stunning style. During the pitiful string of seasons the White Sox endured following 1920, between the loss of Shoeless Joe Jackson and the arrival of future Hall of Famer Luke Appling in the 1930s, Falk would be one of only a few players who would provide some genuine excitement and hope for the faithful at Comiskey Park.

In 1924, for the first time in the history of the franchise, the Chicago White Sox finished last in the American League. Nonetheless Falk had a hallmark year, hitting .352, third-best in the American League behind Babe Ruth's .378 and Charlie Jamieson's .359.

In 1929, Falk was traded to the Cleveland Indians and continued to play outstanding ball, hitting .309. He would play two more years for the Indians. Although he was removed from the Indians' starting lineup in 1930 in favor of younger players that the Indians wanted to develop, Falk met the challenge head-on and reinvented himself as one of the best pinch-hitters in the American League, hitting .325 overall in 1930 and .304 in 1931.

While Falk's major league career statistics are borderline at most for Hall of Fame consideration, his career achievements are superior or similar to notable contemporaries including Bob Meusel, Irish Meusel, Casey Stengel, Riggs Stephenson and Joe Vosmik.

It should also be noted that while Falk's nine years in a Chicago White Sox uniform are not superior to the six years that Shoeless Joe Jackson played for the White Sox, they do compare favorably. For the White Sox, Falk had an on-base percentage of .370 and a slugging average of .442. Playing on the White Sox, Shoeless Joe Jackson had an on-base percentage of .407 and a slugging average of .499.

Introduction

Currently Bibb Falk ranks fourth in career batting average among Chicago White Sox players. His career average of .315 with the White Sox ranks him behind Joe Jackson's .340, Eddie Collins' .331 and Zeke Bonura's .317. Also he currently ranks 14th in extra-base hits in White Sox history.

Though Falk retired as a player from major league baseball after the 1931 season, his legacy in the game was just beginning. He managed in the minor leagues for a season, then became a scout for the Boston Red Sox. In 1940, Falk returned to the University of Texas in Austin as head baseball coach and proceeded to become a Longhorns legend in baseball.

However, shortly after his return to Texas, Falk's tenure was interrupted by World War II. Although beyond the age of eligibility for the draft at 43, Falk volunteered for military service and joined the Army Air Force. Assigned to Twelfth Base Headquarters and Air Base Squadron at Randolph Field near San Antonio, in January 1943 Falk was promoted to the rank of corporal and later sergeant.

Falk's primary duties on the base were as a physical training instructor for military personnel. He also became the coach of the baseball team, the Randolph Field Ramblers. The Ramblers were no bunch of "bushers" and in fact would have competed favorably in the wartime AAA leagues or perhaps even the major leagues. Falk was familiar with the Ramblers as his University of Texas team had played them the past two years. In 1942 the Ramblers had claimed the unofficial title of Texas champions, having defeated Camp Barkley in a two-game series following the annual tournament. The Ramblers played in the San Antonio Service Baseball League. Under Bibb Falk's leadership, the Ramblers were Service League champions one year and runners-up the next.

Following the war, Falk returned to the University of Texas campus, commonly known as the "Forty Acres," and resumed his coaching duties with the Longhorns. He retired after the 1967 season. During his 25-year stint as coach of the Texas Longhorns, Falk's teams won two national championships, 15 Southwest Conference titles and four co-championships. Eighteen players who played on Falk's teams at Texas went on to play major league baseball.

Honors have been slow in coming for Bibb Falk. In the early 1960s, he was inducted into the Texas Sports Hall of Fame and the University of Texas Hall of Honor. In 1995, the current college ballpark at Texas,

Introduction

although completed in 1975, was dedicated as Disch-Falk Field honoring Falk and his legendary predecessor as Texas baseball coach, "Uncle Billy" Disch. However, baseball historians and MLB seldom if ever give a footnote to Bibb Falk's accomplishments in the game.

In June 1989, when Falk died at the age of 90, he was the last surviving member of the 1920 Chicago White Sox, leaving only countless legends and rumors of that tumultuous time in major league baseball history to remain in infamy.

In acquiring material for this work, I drew upon many sources, among which I should like to acknowledge in particular the collections of the Dolph Briscoe Center for American History at the University of Texas at Austin, the National Baseball Hall of Fame and Museum in Cooperstown, New York, and the H. J. Lutcher Stark Center for Physical Culture and Sports e-Archives.

1

From the Forty Acres to Chicago

Bibb August Falk spent 50 years of his life on a baseball diamond. Falk was the epitome of a stereotypical tall Texan. He walked with a swagger, was braggadocious and brash, and wore his baseball cap with the same pride as any cowboy wears his Stetson. Legends of Falk's prowess in the game at the University of Texas and in the major leagues are considerable.

Bibb Falk was born January 27, 1899, in Austin, Texas, the capital of the Lone Star State. The city lies near the geographic center of the state and at the time of Falk's birth had a population of about 22,258. West of the city is hill country, 32,000 square miles of limestone outcroppings greened with live oaks, scrub cedar and mesquite. East of the city lie rich blackland farms of cotton and sorghum.[1]

Falk's parents, Gustav (Gus) Harald Falk and Christine Falk, were both born in Sweden. Christine was a twin. They met after both had emigrated to the United States. They moved to Austin in 1891.

Bibb had three brothers, Arthur, Collie (christened Carl) and Chester, and two sisters. One sister was Elsie. The other sister, Nellie Falk Englom, died in 1918, leaving a two-day-old infant son Arthur, who died in 1964.

The family lived for 40 years in a house built for them by Mr. Oscar Kuns on a lot at 1408 East 2nd Street in Austin's Hyde Park neighborhood.

Gus and Christine's house contained many memories of their native land. In the living room was a small mirror that once hung in

Bibb Falk

the Falk home in Sweden and had been sent to the family in Austin. Among other keepsakes from Sweden were pieces of silver, exquisite linen pieces, candlesticks and pictures of the old home place and members of the family in the old country.

Gus Falk had always longed to make a return visit to Sweden, while Christine had no interest in returning. Gus Falk, a railroad man and sometimes machinist, had considerable setbacks and he simply was never able to manage the trip.

All the Falk children were baseball fans. Chester (Chet) Emanuel Falk, born on May 15, 1905, in Austin, like Bibb would play in the major leagues, with the St. Louis Browns. Chet Falk died on January 7, 1982, in Austin at the age of 76.

Bibb Falk's life was baseball; it gave him a sense of purpose. While he never married, he nonetheless had a strong sense of family obligation. For years his mother and father, and later his sister, were dependent upon him. He was the one that kept the home going and he did it tirelessly, with no regrets.

By 1942 Gus was still attempting to make a living as a fireman on the Texas Central Railroad and a railroad inspector. At that time Bibb's sister Elsie was employed as an office secretary and stenographer for insurance adjustment bureaus in Austin.

With Bibb employed as the baseball coach at the University of Texas, together with his parents and Elsie, they bought a house at 4213 Avenue D in Austin where they would live for several decades. The house would eventually be placed on the National Register of Historic Places. In 2009, zoning changes were recommended.

As a boy, Bibb Falk developed an interest in baseball watching the local Texas League team in Austin. The Falks lived in the Tenth Ward, and the ball park was down in the 1900 block of East First Street inside the fairgrounds. The baseball playing field was located in the middle of the race track. The grandstand was situated across the track. Boys could gain admission by returning foul balls hit over the fence, so Falk saw a lot games doing that. Later he sold peanuts and worked as a batboy in the ballpark. Falk considered being around a lot of professional ball players at an early age an educational experience.

Falk attended high school and played on the baseball team at Samuel F. Austin High School in Austin. He graduated in 1916. Known commonly as Austin High School, its alumni include Barbara and Jenna

1. From the Forty Acres to Chicago

Bush, daughters of President George W. Bush, and Don Baylor, who played 19 years in the major leagues with several teams while participating in seven League Championship Series and three World Series, finishing his career with 2,135 hits.

Also included among the illustrious Austin High alums are professional basketball player Xavier Silas, professional golfer Ben Crenshaw, two-time winner of the Masters (1984 and 1995), and Richard "Kinky" Friedman, noted country singer, songwriter, novelist, comedian and politician.

Bibb Falk began playing baseball in high school in 1914. He had intended to follow his father after graduation and work on the railroad, but Longhorns coach Billy Disch saw Falk play in high school and convinced him to enroll at the University of Texas and play both football and baseball. Falk readily admitted that without Billy Disch intervening, he would never have entered college.

At six feet tall and 175 pounds, Bibb Falk became a multi-sport athlete, playing both baseball and football at Texas in an era when college sports were still being formalized as campus activities. While college football and basketball are the most popular college sports with fans today and the ones most strongly supported financially by alumni, historically speaking, college baseball pre-dates both football and basketball.

The first organized college baseball game was played on July 1, 1859, when Amherst defeated Williams, 73–32, in a 25-inning game. The first organized college football game was played ten years later on November 6, 1869, when Rutgers defeated Princeton, 6–4. College basketball didn't get started until 24 years after baseball began when the University of Toronto took the hardwood against the Toronto YMCA in 1893 and won the game, 2–1. The first intercollegiate basketball game occurred in 1897 with Yale defeating the University of Pennsylvania, 32–10.

Baseball actually made its debut at the University of Texas when students organized a baseball team in 1885 only a year after the first classes had begun. One of the earliest known accounts of a baseball game involving the University of Texas reported a game played against a pick-up team from Southwestern University on April 21, 1885. The account from the files of the *Williamson County Sun* in Georgetown, Texas, stated the following in part:

Bibb Falk

Two extra coaches formed part of Tuesday's train from Austin, these coaches containing the select nine of the State University base ball club and a large number of visitors, including several ladies, who came to witness the match between the State University nine and the picked nine of the club of Southwestern University. About half-past three o'clock the game began and was witnessed by a good many of our citizens and the visitors mentioned.

[The players on both clubs were then named.]

The players on both sides exerted themselves strenuously, evidently determined that the best of their skill should be used to achieve success on the Southwestern campus, on the forty-ninth anniversary of the decisive battle of San Jacinto (the decisive battle for Texas independence where Sam Houston's volunteer army defeated the Mexican Army led by General Santa Anna).

The game lasted until about six o'clock and was watched with intense interest, cheers frequently rending the air, as one side or the other would make a score.

Each side was entitled to play nine innings. The Austin nine played their full number, while the Georgetown nine played only eight innings. When the game closed, the record showed that the Austin nine had six scores, and that the Georgetown nine had twenty-one scores. Of course the result was very gratifying to the winners, who however, conducted themselves with moderation, while the departed nine seemed to think that the victory had been fairly won.[2]

The official college baseball team at the University of Texas was formed in 1894. That was right after the Texas Longhorns football team was organized in the fall of 1893 by the team captain, James Morrison. There was no coach, and the squad played its first game on Thanksgiving morning that year, defeating the Dallas football club, 18–16.

In 1894, Texas hired R. D. Wentworth of Williams College to be the first Longhorns football coach. That season Texas won nine straight games before losing to the University of Missouri, 26–0, in the season finale.

Two years later, the Texas Longhorns football team would make international history when they traveled with the Missouri State Tigers to Monterey, Mexico, to play a game on December 24, 1896. It was the first football game ever played in Mexico. The Longhorns defeated the Tigers, 10–0.

The University of Texas sports teams' colors of orange and white were chosen in 1900, and in 1903 *The Eyes of Texas,* written by John Sinclair, was performed for the first time.

1. From the Forty Acres to Chicago

Bibb Falk arrived on the University of Texas Austin campus, popularly known as "The Forty Acres," in the fall of 1916. That was the same year that the first "Bevo," the Longhorns' steer mascot, was introduced. So all the diamond and gridiron traditions of University of Texas were in place by the time Falk started his college career. Bibb Falk would study civil engineering and graduate in 1920.

In June 1917, with the United States' entry into the World War, American colleges with a few exceptions decided to continue with their athletic programs. A few of the Southwestern Conference schools—Arkansas, Oklahoma and Texas—had voted to discontinue athletics, then reconsidered. But President Woodrow Wilson urged the colleges to attempt to keep their programs operating as a diversion from war and also as a method to keep the young men in shape for possible service in the military. So the Texas athletic programs remained in operation throughout the war.

In order to fulfill his military obligation while attending college during the World War, Bibb Falk served in the Naval Reserve stationed at the University of Texas.

The head football coach at the time of Falk's enrollment at Texas was William Juneau, who had come to Austin from Wisconsin. In 1917, Falk's first year on the squad, the Longhorns finished with a record of 4–4–0.

In 1918, the Texas Longhorns were Southwest Conference co-champions in football along with Oklahoma. Texas finished with a season record of 9–0–0 (6–0–0 in the SWC). The powerful Longhorns scored 194 points while allowing only 14. Texas held six teams scoreless including TCU, Penn Radio School, Camp Mabry, Rice, SMU and Texas A&M.

When Bibb Falk came to the Forty Acres, William J. "Uncle Billy" Disch was the baseball coach of the Longhorns. Disch was born in a log cabin in Benton County, Missouri, on October 20, 1875. When Disch was 12 years old, his family moved to Milwaukee, where he would eventually graduate from Southwestern High School in 1894.

Billy Disch pursued a baseball career and as a member of the Waupun, Wisconsin, team in 1898 and 1899, he played with Ginger Beaumont, who would become the first man to go to bat in a World Series, playing in 1903 with Pittsburgh against Boston. Disch would play a few years in the minor leagues with Ft. Worth and Galveston. Returning to

Bibb Falk

Milwaukee, he coached one year at a high school. Then he went to Sacred Heart Academy in Watertown, Wisconsin, to become baseball coach.

When the priest at Sacred Heart was transferred to St. Edwards in Austin, Disch came along. A Methodist and a man of firm moral character, Billy Disch brought with him to Texas a strong code of conduct that included no smoking, no drinking, no chewing tobacco and no exceptions. Fans and sportswriters started to refer to him as "Uncle Billy." But what made Disch such a great coach was that he knew how to deal with youth.

At St. Edwards University in Austin, Disch was a crosstown rival coach of the University of Texas. Following an academic scandal at Texas, Disch was hired on January 1, 1911, to reinstate credibility in the program. At least that was the official reason given for his hiring. In reality, it was more of a "if you can't beat 'em join 'em" scenario as Texas officials were also keenly aware of the fact that Disch's teams regularly beat the Longhorns.

Surprisingly, during Disch's first two years at Texas, the team did not do well. But that was partly because baseball and football weren't well organized in the southwest. To remedy the situation, on May 6, 1914, Disch, representing Texas, along with representatives of seven other southwestern educational institutions, got together in Dallas at the Oriental Hotel and began organizing the Southwestern Conference, or SWC. Later that year, on December 8, in Houston at the Rice Hotel, the conference was officially formed. Originally known as the Southwest Intercollegiate Athletic Conference, a constitution was agreed on by the eight original member schools: Texas, Texas A&M, Baylor, Arkansas, Oklahoma, Oklahoma A&M (now Oklahoma State), Southwestern University and Rice, which was admitted provisionally.

"Uncle Billy" Disch, like his big league counterpart, Philadelphia Athletics manager Connie Mack, was quite formal in his approach to players and did not address Falk as Bibb. He thought it was a frivolous nickname, so he called him August.

Reminiscing about Billy Disch, Falk remarked, "Mr. Disch didn't drink, and you didn't smoke around him and you didn't chew tobacco around him. He'd search the uniforms and if there was any chewing tobacco in them, he'd take up the uniform. He was just a clean cut man like that."[3] Aside from Disch's personal values, Falk emphasized that the coach knew the fundamentals of the game, he taught you how to

1. From the Forty Acres to Chicago

bunt, how to field and everything else, and you learned the game being around him.

D. C. (David) Bobby Cannon was recruited by Billy Disch off the high school ball field of his hometown of Crocket, Texas, in 1915 to play both baseball and football at Texas. Cannon, a speedy outfielder and third baseman, would eventually be a perennial leader in stolen bases and runs scored, and become an All-SWC player. He would play for the Longhorns in 1916 and 1917, then miss the 1918 season while serving in the Naval Air Corp during the World War. Cannon would return to the Longhorns for the 1919 season and be elected captain of the 1920 baseball squad by his teammates.

Speaking about Billy Disch in 1991, Cannon remarked, "When I came to the University old Uncle Billy Disch met me at the train station and said, 'I've got a job for you washing dishes and waiting tables for your room and board.' That was my introduction to the university."[4]

Billy Disch would coach the Texas Longhorns baseball team for more than a quarter of a century (1911–1939) and win 512 games with 180 defeats. From the time the Southwest Conference was formed in 1914, Texas teams coached by Disch would win 15 of the first 16 conference baseball titles.

After winning successive SWC titles in 1915, 1916 and 1917, Billy Disch saw most of his Longhorns enlist in the service as America's formal commitment to the World War began. Still, in 1918, with just two returning lettermen, outfielders Red English and Lamar Hart, along with first-year player Bibb Falk, who pitched, played first base and the outfield, they won their fourth successive SWC baseball title.

In 1919, Billy Disch's Texas Longhorns would win their fifth successive SWC title and do it in grand style.

The 1919 campaign opened with two straight loses to San Antonio of the Texas League, 3–2 and 2–0, in the first games of a seven-game series. Two days later, Bibb Falk would square off on the mound against San Antonio's Howard Payne and defeat him, 12–1. Falk had eight strikeouts and gave up only four hits. At bat he slammed a two-run home run. Lamar Hart also had a big day at the plate with a double and triple. From there the Longhorns went on to win the series with San Antonio, four games to three.

Next up for Disch's Longhorns were the Chicago White Sox, who were holding spring training in Texas. Manager Kid Gleason's team

Bibb Falk

combined speed with power to create an unpredictable offense, which was balanced by superb pitching.

The White Sox featured such stars such as Eddie Collins, Ray Schalk, Eddie Cicotte, Red Faber, Buck Weaver and Shoeless Joe Jackson. Faber, the hero of their 1917 World Series win over John McGraw's New York Giants, had returned from military service.

It turned out to be a "bad day at Black Rock" for the Longhorns as they made six errors and were crushed by the White Sox, 14–1. Still, Bibb Falk got himself noticed in the game. He played first base, had a single and double, and also pitched a couple of innings.

As SWC play began, Texas split a two-game series with TCU, winning the first game, 17–0, while getting 17 hits, and then losing the second game by a score of 3–2. But that would be the last loss of the season for the Longhorns and the only one that they would lose to a college team. Bibb Falk pitched in both games.

With Bibb Falk back on the mound as a starter, the Longhorns then beat Texas A&M, 6–1. Falk gave up six hits and at bat had two doubles and a triple. Both the Longhorns and Falk kept getting better as next they defeated Austin College, 14–0 and 12–3, before leaving on a six-game road trip to Oklahoma and North Texas.

Texas proceeded to collar Oklahoma, 8–0 and 4–0. It should be pointed out that in the 1919 season, Oklahoma had several ineligibility problems with its players. Nonetheless, in one of the games Bibb Falk had four hits including two home runs.

At Stillwater, Oklahoma, Texas beat Oklahoma A&M, 5–2 and 2–0. Then, in a non-conference game, Falk pitched and beat TCU, 2–1, on a three-hitter.

The next day in Dallas, Falk hit a home run and two singles, while scoring three runs, as Texas defeated the SMU Mustangs, 8–5. It was Falk's fifth SWC win.

Facing Oklahoma again, the Longhorns crushed the Sooners, 11–4, as Bibb Falk went 4-for-5 with two home runs.

Texas clinched the 1919 SWC championship at College Station, defeating Texas A&M, 1–0, as Falk pitched a four-hitter against the Aggies. However, Texas got only one hit. The Longhorns scored the winning margin in the fourth inning when Jimmy Greer was issued a base on balls, advanced to second on a hit batsman, and scored when Swanie Robertson stroked a single inside the foul line.

1. From the Forty Acres to Chicago

For Billy Disch and the Texas Longhorns, it was their fifth consecutive title. They finished with an overall record of 22–3–1 and an intercollegiate record of 20–1–1, and were undefeated in SWC play, going 12–0.

The big power factor for the 1919 Texas Longhorns was the performance of Bibb August Falk. He hit .462 with five home runs, three triples, 14 doubles and 14 singles. A few other players made significant contributions to the success of the team; D. C. Bobby Cannon hit .355, Swanie Robertson hit .346 and Jimmy Greer played third base the entire season without making an error.

A big left-hander, during his days on the mound for the Longhorns Bibb Falk attracted the attention of several major league teams. But interest peaked during the summer of 1919. Falk was pitching in a semi-pro game in the Rio Grande Valley for Donna, Texas, against their hated rivals from McCall. He pitched 16 innings, striking out 30 batters and winning, 2–1.

The Chicago White Sox didn't have any scouts covering University of Texas games. But the White Sox front office knew Billy Disch from his days in Wisconsin. So they wrote to him, asking about Bibb Falk. It was on the recommendation of Disch that Falk signed a contract with the White Sox with the understanding that he would receive a bonus if he did not play football in the fall of 1919. Falk also wanted to try to complete his education, so White Sox owner Charles Comiskey said it would be all right for him to report to the White Sox after the 1920 college baseball season.

Over the years, the stories of Bibb Falk's prowess on the diamond—like many legends of the game—have evolved from some being truthful to half-truths to complete fabrications.

One of the more lasting tales has it that while playing against Texas A&M with the crowd harassing him all afternoon, Bibb Falk boldly announced to his antagonists that he was going to hit a triple. There was no fence surrounding the ball park. For almost a century now the story, still on occasion carried in the press, has it that Falk hit a ball so far that the Aggies fielders refused to chase it. But when Falk pulled up at third base, he refused to go any further, just folded his arms and stared at the Aggies pitcher. As the stunned crowd became still he bellowed, "Whatsa' matter with you mugs, haven't you ever seen a big leaguer hit?"[5] While it is true that in a short time he would fulfill that

Bibb Falk

prophecy and be a big leaguer, years later Falk didn't recall the event exactly like it has been reported. In a 1967 interview Falk said the incident was a complete fabrication. "I never played baseball that way,"[6] snapped Falk. "All I did," said Falk, "was tip my hat when I got to third base after hitting a three-bagger. But I don't remember what I said."[7]

In regard to that particular incident, Dana X. Bible, the Texas A&M baseball coach at the time, said that the Aggies started to refer to Falk as "Big Noise." However, Bibb was to earn another more lasting nickname of "Jockey" because of his merciless riding of opponents from the bench.

Another Falk fable has it that following a Longhorns victory, coach Disch was addressing the team. "Men," Disch said, "The Lord was with us today." From the back of the room Bibb Falk yelled out, "Yeah, but old Falk took over in the ninth."[8]

Whatever the whole truth or half-truth may be in these stories, the salient point is that the enduring self-confidence manifest in Bibb Falk's personality was the driving force that would take him onward in achieving excellence in multiple roles in baseball over the next five decades. In the end, while Bibb Falk did not have a Hall of Fame career, he certainly had a Hall of Fame attitude about the game.

2

The 1919 World Series

Having made a commitment to Charles Comiskey to forego playing football in the fall of 1919, Bibb Falk sat in the stands as the Texas Longhorns began their season by defeating two overmatched opponents: Howard Payne, 26–0, and Southwestern Texas, 39–0. In the next two games Texas was defeated by Philips, 10–0, in Austin, and Oklahoma, 12–7, in a game played at Dallas.

Phillips was a small, unheralded school which offered to come to Austin for a guarantee of $200 and entertainment to play the Longhorns. The Phillips squad was loaded with ringers such as Steve Owen and Toby Greene.

In 1922, Steve Owen, playing with the Oklahoma All-Stars, would become one of the fledgling NFL's first defensive stars. He later coached the New York Giants, introducing his famous "umbrella" defense. Toby Greene would eventually become baseball coach at Oklahoma A&M.

The Texas vs. Oklahoma game was played at Fair Park in Dallas. The two schools put up $500 each and asked the State Fair to erect additional permanent bleachers.

With the defending SWC co-champion Longhorns' season record even at 2–2, Bibb Falk could no longer bear to watch from the stands as teams such as Phillips humiliated Texas. So he broke his pledge to Charles Comiskey and donned his football gear. With Falk back on the squad, Texas won its next game, defeating Baylor, 29–13.

The season continued to be a hard-fought one for the Longhorns, and in the next-to-last game, in which they survived a near scalping by the Haskell Indians, winning 13–7, D. C. Bobby Cannon was knocked unconscious and couldn't return to the field for two quarters. In the end, Texas finished the 1919 season with a record of 6–3, and went 4–1 after the return of Falk.

The 1919 football season would be last for Texas mascot Bevo I. In the 1915 Texas vs. Texas A&M game played at College Station, the Longhorns had lost to the Aggies, 13–0. In the 1919 game, Texas A&M defeated Texas, 7–0. During the game, some overzealous Aggies fans crept up on Bevo with a hot branding iron and permanently memorialized the score of the 1915 Texas A&M victory over the Longhorns in Bevo's hide.

After the 1919 season was concluded, the Texas Athletic Council voted that Bevo, bearing the embarrassing work of the Texas A&M pranksters, should be slaughtered and fed to the football team. Bevo's defaced hide was cut into two pieces; one part was hung in the Texas Athletic Department, where it remained until the early 1950s, and the other part was donated to Texas A&M. Beginning in the 1920 football season, a well-protected Bevo II appeared on the field.

Although Bibb Falk had been on the gridiron during the fall of 1919, completely ignoring his commitment to Charles Comiskey, up in Chicago the farthest thing from the White Sox owner's concerns was whether or not Bibb Falk was playing football down in Austin. Comiskey's White Sox had just lost the 1919 World Series to the Cincinnati Reds, five games to three, under a dark cloud of suspicion that his team had conspired with gamblers to fix the Series.

In 1919, in the aftermath of the World War, the major league team owners were uncertain as to the continued fan interest in baseball, so they shortened the season to 140 games. As it turned out, 1919 was a banner year for attendance. So in an effort to recoup some of the revenue lost as a result of the season being shortened, the owners expanded the World Series from the traditional seven games format to nine games.

The 1919 Chicago White Sox were a very good ball club, and the oddsmakers, in deference to their victory in the 1917 World Series, when they defeated the New York Giants, made them 8–5 favorites to win the 1919 World Series over the Cincinnati Reds.

Nonetheless, before the Series began in Cincinnati on October 1, experts were stating in the press that they considered the Cincinnati Reds strong enough because of their pitching to force the Series to the limit of nine games. The Reds pitching staff had led the National League with a team ERA of 2.23 and had pitched 23 shutouts and 89 complete

2. The 1919 World Series

games during the season. Furthermore, the Reds had six strong, healthy starting pitchers available for the series in Hod Eller, Dutch Ruether, Slim Sallee, Jimmy Ring, Ray Fisher and Dolf Luque. Those pitchers had won a combined 93 games, and Hod Eller had thrown a no-hitter against the St. Louis Cardinals in May.

For the White Sox, Eddie Cicotte had won 29 games in the 1919 season. Among the unsubstantiated claims made by author Eliot Asinof in his book *Eight Men Out* is that Cicotte was promised a $10,000 bonus by Charles Comiskey prior to the beginning of the season if he won 30 games. Asinof further alleges that after Cicotte won his 29th game, he was held out of the lineup during the final games of the season by manager Kid Gleason at the insistence of Comiskey, who didn't want to pay the pitcher any bonus money. Consequently, it is suggested by Asinof that Cicotte was motivated to fix the Series as a result of Comiskey's greed. Such a scenario makes good literature, but unfortunately it is historically inaccurate. No hard evidence exists to support such a claim. In fact, Cicotte's salary for the 1919 season was $9,075, well above the league average and equal to $124,292 in 2014 money value.

The facts are that Urban "Red" Faber, the White Sox's spitball-throwing number three starter, had suffered on-and-off ailments most of the season, appearing in just 25 games and pitching 162⅓ innings. So White Sox manager William J. "Kid" Gleason, locked in a tight pennant race with the Indians and Yankees, had overworked both Eddie Cicotte and Lefty Williams in 1919. Cicotte had pitched 306⅔ innings and Williams 297. They finished first and third in the American League in innings pitched. Together the two pitchers had started 54 percent of the White Sox games, with Cicotte making 35 starts and Williams 40. After Cicotte and Williams swept a doubleheader against Detroit on September 1, down the stretch Cicotte won a couple of games but didn't pitch well.

Now the White Sox were starting the World Series without Red Faber, out with an injury. Faber had been the hero of the 1917 World Series, winning three games against the New York Giants. So the White Sox went into the 1919 World Series with a serious pitching deficit against a superior Reds staff. Cincinnati center fielder and future Hall of Famer Edd Roush believed that the Reds' pitching staff was the best in the major leagues.

The Reds were a better fielding club than the White Sox, had led the National League with a .974 fielding average, and also made the fewest errors in the league, 153. The White Sox's fielding average was .969 and they had made 176 errors. However, the White Sox had the edge in hitting, finishing with a team batting average of .287 as opposed to the Reds' team batting average of .263.

Still, manager Kid Gleason was extremely confident almost to point of exaggeration that the White Sox would win the World Series. "I said last June that the Sox would win the pennant with only Cicotte and Williams in the box, and I'll say right here that my ball club will beat the Reds without being greatly extended."[1]

John I. B. "Toney" Marsh was oracular as he wrote in the *Boston Herald*, "I think it will be one of the closest World Series in a long time, as well as one of the best, but if I were asked to make a wager I would be compelled to put money down on the Reds."[2]

When the dust settled after the eighth game was played in Chicago on October 9, the Reds had won the 1919 World Series five games to three over the White Sox.

Although the Reds have been maligned by writers and myths that have grown out of the 1919 World Series over the past century, they were a very good team and capable of beating the favored White Sox by virtue of their own ability on the field. Nonetheless, at that time the Reds' capabilities did not preclude a few sportswriters and some fans from suspecting that something didn't seem right about how the Series had been played, and the fact is that a conspiracy had been hatched.

As the stage was set in Cincinnati for Game One of the 1919 World Series, the place to be was the Sinton Hotel, located at 4th and Vine Streets. The spectacular hotel had 600 rooms. Charles Comiskey and the Chicago White Sox had checked in. So had American League president Ban Johnson. Sportswriter Hugh Fullerton was rooming with Christy Mathewson, who was writing a column for *The New York Times*. U.S. Senator and presidential hopeful Warren G. Harding was there too, and also a large number of gamblers were occupying rooms, including Abe Attell, former featherweight boxing champion and associate of New York gambling kingpin Arnold Rothstein.

Rumors were circulating in the Sinton that the Series was going to be fixed. Years later in an article in *The Sporting News*, Hugh Fullerton would remark that on the morning of Game One, he and Joe Jackson, a Detroit sportswriter, had gone to a speakeasy about a half-block

2. The 1919 World Series

away from the Sinton Hotel. According to Fullerton, he was approached by a gambler in the establishment, and he introduced Jackson to him. The gambler was confused, not sure if Jackson was Shoeless Joe Jackson, the White Sox left fielder. So he pulled Fullerton aside and quietly asked him if he had talked to Joe about the fix.[3] At the time, Fullerton just laughed it off.

That evening in Eddie Cicotte's room, it is alleged that "Sleepy Bill" Burns, gambler and former major league pitcher, introduced Abe Attell to seven members of the Chicago White Sox as the man handling the money for the fix provided by Arnold Rothstein. Burns was supposedly told to stagger the payments to the players from the lump sum of $100,000 to payments of $20,000 a game. Shoeless Joe Jackson is reported not to have been in Cicotte's room during the discussion with Burns. However, third baseman Buck Weaver was there.

The next morning in the Sinton lobby, Bill Burns ran into Shoeless Joe Jackson. Assuming that Jackson was in on the fix, Burns began talking with him about some of the details of how the fix was supposed to go down. Jackson had heard rumors of a fix and suddenly realized that he was being implicated as part of a possible conspiracy. He immediately went to White Sox owner Charles Comiskey's room and begged to be benched for Game One. He urged Comiskey to say that he had been drunk and was therefore held out of the lineup. But Comiskey would not consider it.

In Game One at Redland Field in Cincinnati, the Reds' leadoff hitter, Morrie Rath, took the first pitch from White Sox starting pitcher Eddie Cicotte, a fastball, for a strike. Cicotte's second pitch hit Rath square in the back. According to the unsubstantiated story that has now been passed down for several generations, Cicotte hitting Rath with the second pitch was supposedly the signal to the gamblers that the fix was in. The Reds went on to route the White Sox, 9–1, in the first game. The Reds' starting pitcher, Dutch Ruether, threw just 88 pitches, allowing six hits and one run. At bat Ruether had two triples, a Series record that still stands, to go along with a single and walk.

That evening, back at the Sinton Hotel, it was total chaos. Scalpers roamed the hotel corridors attempting to sell tickets under the watchful eye of the federal undercover officers who were put in place to make sure the government got its share of the 50 percent war tax.

In the lobby, White Sox manager Kid Gleason lambasted a few of his players—Eddie Cicotte, Chick Gandil, Swede Risberg and Joe Jackson—in full view of other hotel guests. Gleason was angry at the display of good spirits shown by his players following a game in which they were beaten so convincingly.

Meanwhile, Abe Attell was standing on a chair clutching a wad of large denomination bills, seeking to make bets on the Reds with anyone who would take his money.

Eight days later at Comiskey Park in Chicago, the Series ended as the Reds beat the White Sox in Game Eight, 10–5. From the moment that Reds first baseman Jake Daubert gloved the final out, a dark cloud has hung over the outcome of the 1919 World Series.

Immediately a subtle suspicion prevailed about the sincerity of the on-field efforts of the White Sox in the Series. *Collyer's Eye*, a Chicago sporting publication, published an article alleging a fix in the Series and named eight White Sox players, including Eddie Cicotte, Joe Jackson, Lefty Williams and Chick Gandil, who were alleged to be part of the conspiracy.

American League president Ban Johnson had some doubts about the Series too. In fact, following Game One in Cincinnati, Johnson had been woken at 4:00 a.m. in his room at the Sinton Hotel by National League president John Heydler, who confronted him about rumors of a fix in the Series. Heydler had been asked by Charles Comiskey to speak with Johnson because the White Sox owner had been feuding with Johnson over the reinstatement of pitcher Carl Mays.

In May, while pitching for the Red Sox against the White Sox, Carl Mays suddenly left the mound, went to the locker room, got dressed, and went on a fishing trip. Soon after, Red Sox owner Harry Frazee traded Mays to the Yankees. Mays stated his reason for leaving the team was that he felt his teammates were not supporting him. Johnson ruled that Mays had jumped his contract and ordered him suspended indefinitely. The battle lines were drawn, and when the American League owners met in August they ruled that Johnson's suspension of Mays was unauthorized. After the Yankees filed an injunction in court against the league from interfering with Mays, owners Harry Frazee of Boston, Jacob Ruppert of New York, and Charles Comiskey of Chicago attempted to remove Ban Johnson as president of the American League, alleging that he had failed to keep gambling in check in American League parks.

However, the story has it that when John Heydler went to Johnson's

2. The 1919 World Series

room that night he was attempting to sleep off a heavy night of alcohol imbibing following Game One, was reluctant to consider the concerns of Comiskey, and famously blurted out, "That's the yelp of a beaten cur."[4] Heydler tried to console Comiskey by telling him that perhaps they had underestimated the strength of the Reds.

But following the Series, Johnson was quite suspicious, so he asked former Cincinnati policeman Cal Crim, an old acquaintance from his days as a sports reporter in the Queen City, to open an investigation into the Series. Later he would follow the trail of "Sleepy Bill" Burns to his hide-out in Mexico and convince him to return to the United States to testify before a grand jury in Chicago.

White Sox owner Charles Comiskey continued to have doubts about the legitimacy of his team's play in the Series and offered a $20,000 reward (later reduced to $10,000) for information on gambling activity in the 1919 World Series that could have influenced any of his players.

There certainly were some reasons to suspect questionable play in the Series by the White Sox. In Game One, the ace of the White Sox pitching staff, 29-game winner Eddie Cicotte, didn't seem like himself on the mound and the Reds battered him for six runs and seven hits in 3⅔ innings, eventually winning, 9–1. Also, in Game Four, won by the Reds, 2–0, Cicotte was involved in two critical plays that cost the White Sox runs. One was when he cut off a perfect throw from Joe Jackson from left field that allowed a run to score, and earlier in the inning he had made a wild throw to first on a ball hit back to him on the mound.

Furthermore, Lefty

Eddie Cicotte (Sports Story Reprints).

Williams, who had won 23 games during the season, never looked sharp and lost all three games he started, finishing with a Series ERA of 6.61.

Over the years, a lot of myths have been created in an attempt to add unnecessary suspense to the 1919 World Series scandal. There were well-documented incidents on the playing field that raised suspicions, such as Chick Gandil hesitating on the baseball paths in Game Three while running from second to third. But the White Sox won that game, 3–0. Shoeless Joe Jackson was accused of slowing down on balls he should have caught, and even though he hit .375 in the Series, he was accused of not hitting when it counted. Also, shortstop Swede Risberg, who had made 34 errors in 119 games in the regular season, made four errors in the eight-game Series. In Game Five, won by the Reds, 5–0, on a ball hit into the gap by Reds pitcher Hod Eller, center fielder Happy Felsch made a perfect peg that would have cut down a runner at third base if Swede Risberg had not deflected the throw. In all, there were about ten plays in the Series that critics such as sportswriter Hugh Fullerton thought were inconsistent with the White Sox's normal level of play and would form the inventory of suspicious play.

There are some film clips of the 1919 World Series, but none of them captures the controversial events that could substantiate a conspiracy. So just how much the 1919 World Series was fixed depends on the written reports of sportswriters and the oral history of those who participated in the Series.

Most of the Cincinnati Reds, including team owner August "Garry" Herrmann, believed they had beat the White Sox because they were a better team.

Hall of Fame center fielder Edd Roush was adamant until he died at age 94 on March 21, 1988, that the Reds won the 1919 World Series over the White Sox because they were a superior team. Roush stated, "Cicotte had everything on the ball when he pitched to me and I did not make a safe single off him at any time in the games he worked in. His pitching was just as hard to connect with as any other pitcher during the season."[5]

Reds third baseman Heinie Groh maintained that the Reds were a very good team:

> I still don't see why the White Sox were supposed to be such favorites to beat us in the 1919 World Series. I know how good Joe Jackson and Happy Felsch were in the outfield, but they weren't any

2. The 1919 World Series

better than Eddie Roush. And our pitching was just as good as theirs, for sure. Well, maybe the White Sox did throw it. I didn't see anything that looked suspicious. But I think we'd have beaten them either way, that's what I thought then and I still think so today.[6]

But following the Series, rumors of a fix were circulating in gambling communities like a cyclone. Joe Gedeon, who played second base for the St. Louis Browns in 1919, got in touch with Charles Comiskey and offered to take him up on his $10,000 reward offer for information revealing a Series fix. Comiskey and his lawyer, Alfred Austrian, met with Gedeon and he told them of a secondary plot to fix the Series arranged by St. Louis gamblers, Ben Frankel and the Levi brothers, Ben and Lou. However, Comiskey was already aware of this accusation.

Harry Redmon, a St. Louis theatre owner, met with White Sox manager Kid Gleason following the Series. But when Gleason offered Redmon $5,000 for information connecting the gamblers to a plot to fix the Series, he balked, telling Gleason that if he went any further it might cost him his life.

Charles Comiskey and his attorney reasoned that these gamblers from St. Louis were small potatoes and lacked the money and connections necessary to fix a World Series. Also, the tight-fisted Comiskey didn't want to part with the $10,000 reward money.

By early November of 1919, most American sports fans had turned their attention to the events of the college football season, and speculation of a fix in the World Series had disappeared from most of the newspapers.

The Texas Longhorns football squad finished the 1919 season with a 6–3–0 record, far behind SWC champion Texas A&M's 10–0–0. Nonetheless, Bibb Falk had made significant contributions to the Longhorns' comeback and was chosen as an All-Southwest Conference tackle. Now Falk was turning his attention to events of the coming year of 1920, ready to play his last baseball season with the Longhorns, graduate and begin his major league career with the suspicion-laden Chicago White Sox.

3

Breaking In with the Black Sox

As the new year of 1920 began, August "Garry" Herrmann resigned as chairman of the National Commission, organized baseball's ruling body since 1903. Later in the year the commission was scrapped by the owners in favor of an autocratic, one-man commissioner of baseball. The man chosen for the job was federal Judge Kenesaw Mountain Landis.

Meanwhile, as the 1920 season approached, on the advice of attorney Alfred Austrian, Charles Comiskey decided to push the matter of a possible fix in the 1919 World Series to the back burner on the White Sox operational agenda. There has been historical speculation that perhaps Austrian had quietly advocated a cover-up. After all, Comiskey had a million-dollar investment in the White Sox to protect and spring training was right around the corner.

Following the World Series, there had been some cursory, independent investigations of a possible fix, but no one was talking or willing to talk other than Joe Gedeon, and no formal action had been taken by the National or American Leagues or the National Commission.

However, in mid–December Chicago sportswriter Hugh Fullerton was still writing stinging columns questioning whether the 1919 World Series had been played on the square. While his Chicago newspaper refused to carry his stories, a column Fullerton wrote was published in *The New York World* on December 15, 1919, in which he named names of people with whom an investigating committee might want to speak. While he didn't name any players in his column, Fullerton named gamblers like Abe Attell, Carl Zork, the Levi brothers, and most compelling of all, New York gambler Arnold Rothstein. He also boldly predicted

3. Breaking In with the Black Sox

that seven White Sox players would not be at spring training. His source for the information was "Sleepy Bill" Burns. Two years later in 1922, without going into detail, Fullerton would say that during the time he was writing these columns he had suffered two attempts on his life.

Perhaps there was a bit of after-the-fact drama in Fullerton's allegation or perhaps there was a smidgen of truth to it. Only Fullerton knew for sure. Nonetheless, the gamblers he had named in his column had little to fear; the money had already changed hands, no federal law had been violated in a Series fix, and the gamblers he had implicated as part of the plot were staying far out of the judicial jurisdiction of Illinois.

In the late teens and early twenties, a lot of major league teams made Texas their spring training home. The Chicago White Sox trained at Waco, the St. Louis Cardinals at Brownsville, and the New York Giants, who had previously trained at Marlin, moved their facility to San Antonio.

On March 14, 1920, at a little past the noon hour, White Sox manager Kid Gleason and most of his players rolled into spring training camp in Waco. As the players stepped off the train, there was a warm southwestern breeze blowing and hardly a hint of the stench of a World Series scandal hanging in the air.

Pitchers Lefty Williams, Grover Lowdermilk and Hervey McClellan were already there. Williams said that he expected Joe Jackson to arrive any time. The only other player not in camp was Chick Gandil, who was holding out in a contract dispute with Charles Comiskey.

As soon as Kid Gleason arrived in Waco he began to hear stories about Bibb Falk, who was set to join the White Sox in June following the University of Texas baseball season.

Each spring the New York Giants made a trip to Austin to play the University of Texas. When Giants manager John McGraw saw Bibb Falk play, he remarked that in his opinion he was ready to play in the big leagues immediately. In fact, some big league coaches and scouts were sure that Bibb Falk was going to be another George Sisler.

In June 1915, George Sisler graduated from the University of Michigan and, in a controversial action by the National Commission, in a 2–1 vote was made a free agent over the protests of Pittsburgh Pirates owner Barney Dreyfuss, who claimed that he had bought Sisler's contract from Columbus of the American Association.

Bibb Falk

George Sisler signed with the St. Louis Browns, who were managed by Branch Rickey, his former college coach. In four out of his first five years in the major leagues (1915–1919) Sisler hit over .300, and in 1920 he would get 257 hits and bat .407. Sisler's 257 hits remained a major league record until 2004, when Ichiro Suzuki of the Seattle Mariners got 262 hits.

The previous spring, when the St. Louis Browns played the University of Texas Longhorns in a game at Taylor, Texas, Bibb Falk hit a home run, a triple and a double in four trips to the plate. Following Falk's performance, Browns scout Bill Friel rushed out of the stands and into the outfield to try to sign him. However, he was informed by Falk that he had already committed to the White Sox.

During the 1919 football season, when Falk had broken his commitment to Charles Comiskey not to participate on the gridiron, he had injured his left shoulder and arm. Consequently, in the 1920 collegiate baseball season Falk struggled a little on the mound early in the season, but had the fortitude to help the Longhorns win the conference championship with his bat.

In 1920, Billy Disch's Texas Longhorns were in pursuit of their sixth straight SWC title and would face some stiff competition. The 1920 roster included D. C. Bobby Cannon, captain, Dudley English, Bibb Falk, Howard Fitzgerald, Irwin Gillett, Maxey Hart, Ferdinand (Rube) Lessiner, George McCullough, Maxey Moore, Albert Penn, Swanie Robertson and Ralph Barry. The team included six lettermen with a total of 12 seasons' experience. Three other lettermen, English, Hart and McCullough, had returned from military service in the World War. Rounding out the team were two newcomers.

While Bibb Falk was considered the star on the squad, the Longhorns had a few other players with remarkable skills. Left-hander Irwin Gillett was an excellent pitcher. Then there was George McCullough, who Bobby Cannon said was the best hit-and-run batter he had ever seen. Furthermore, Dudley English had a great arm that enabled him to throw perfectly to home plate from any position in the outfield.

The season started with a couple of loses to major league teams. At Taylor, the Longhorns lost to the St. Louis Browns, 11–8. Then the Chicago White Sox handed Texas a 2–1 loss despite the fact that Irwin Gillett and Ralph Berry yielded only six hits in a game that took only one hour and 11 minutes to play. Maxey Moore and Howard Fitzgerald

3. Breaking In with the Black Sox

parlayed two of Texas' four hits into the Longhorns' only run. While Bibb Falk went hitless in the game, it would be the only game in the 1920 season in which he did not have a least one hit.

The Longhorns tied San Antonio of the Texas League, then reeled off four consecutive victories before losing to Trinity. Successive victories followed as the Longhorns defeated the 37th Infantry and Simmons. In the Simmons game, Irwin Gillett threw a one-hit, 8–0 shutout. Dudley English led the offense with three hits, including two triples.

Texas A&M was next up, and they fell to the Longhorns by a score of 14–5. Bibb Falk's arm problems seemed to have healed and he had a huge day on the mound with 17 strikeouts. At bat, he tagged the Aggies' ace, Roswell Higginbottom, for three hits including a home run, triple and single.

The following day, the Aggies were shut out, 5–0, by Irwin Gillett. The red-hot Longhorns continued to roll over their opponents as Rube Lessiner and Bibb Falk teamed up on the mound at Clark Field to defeat Rice, 12–2.

But the following day, Rice, behind the pitching of Eddie Dyer, defeated Texas, 4–2. It was Rice's first victory over the Longhorns in six seasons. Gillett started for Texas and gave up two home runs in the sixth inning. It was Gillett's first loss in two years. Dyer, the Rice ace, would go on to pitch six years for the St. Louis Cardinals, finishing his career in 1927 with a record of 15–15.

Later Dyer would become a manager in the Texas League with Houston. Then he would manage the Cardinals from 1946 to 1950. In 1946, under Dyer, the Cardinals would win the National League pennant and defeat the Boston Red Sox in the World Series.

In the 1946 World Series, Eddie Dyer employed the controversial infield shift on Ted Williams with great success. First used by Lou Boudreau of the Cleveland Indians, the shift was based on the assumption that Williams would not bunt the ball or pop it into left field, that he was certain to hit the ball to right field. Whether or not the shift had any influence on Williams' ability at the plate is up for debate. Nonetheless, the end result was that Williams failed miserably with the bat in the 1946 World Series, hitting a paltry .200 with no home runs.

As the collegiate season progressed, the Longhorns began an extended road trip in Waxahachie, where they swept two games from Trinity. But in Fort Worth the TCU Horned Frogs defeated Texas

Bibb Falk

behind Pete Donohue's three-hitter. The Longhorns would get strong competition in the early part of the 1920 season from TCU, featuring a future major league battery of pitcher Pete Donohue and catcher Astyanax Douglass. Both Donohue and Douglass would be signed by the Cincinnati Reds for a bonus of $5,000 each.

Pete Donohue's college career as a pitcher was without parallel. He pitched eight no-hitters at TCU and lost seven of them. He lost four no-hitters to SMU by scores of 1–0, 2–1 and 3–2 twice. Errors by Donohue led to the losses. Overall Donohue had a college pitching record of 45–10.

Douglass' first name of Astyanax was taken by his parents from Greek mythology. Astyanax was the son of Hector and Andromache who was thrown by the Greeks from the walls of Troy so that he could not restore the kingdom as predicted. While Douglass was a consistent .300 hitter in the minors, he played only 11 games in two years for the Cincinnati Reds. If he is remembered for anything in his time in the major leagues, it is for his periodic public and clubhouse brawls with his teammate, pitcher Jimmy Ring.

On the other hand, while Pete Donohue would develop arm trouble later in his career, he still had a solid 12-year major league career, winning 20 games three times for the Reds. As part of the Reds' big three, Donohue, along with future Hall of Fame left-hander Eppa Rixey and Dolf Luque, won a combined 363 of Cincinnati's 646 victories from 1922–1929.

Texas headed to Dallas, where SMU handed the Longhorns a 2–1 defeat. The Longhorns then rolled into Waco to square off against the Baylor Bears, coached by Frank Bridges. At that point in the season, Baylor was leading the SWC with 8–1 conference record. Texas had a 3–2 SWC record.

Bibb Falk pitched the first game against Baylor and won a 14–2 decision as Texas chased a future Hall of Fame pitcher, young Ted Lyons, from the mound after two innings. The following day, as Lyons had pitched only a couple of innings, he started again. This time Lyons and the Bears fell to the Longhorns, 2–0, as Irwin Gillett tossed a two-hit shutout.

The sweep of Baylor gave the Longhorns a 5–2 SWC record and left the Bears at 8–3. In order to win the SWC championship, Texas had to beat Baylor twice and defeat SMU and Texas A&M one game each.

3. Breaking In with the Black Sox

While Texas had defeated Ted Lyons twice at Waco in 1920, a new era would soon begin for the Bears' right-hander; beginning in the 1921 season, Lyons would become a perpetual nemesis to the Longhorns for the rest of his collegiate career.

On May 6, Baylor came to Austin and lost, 7–1, with Rube Lessiner pitching a four-hitter for Texas. Bibb Falk and Maxie Hart each had two hits. In the next game, Ralph Barry squared off against Ted Lyons and Baylor lost for the fourth straight time to Texas, 5–1. Both Bibb Falk and Bobby Cannon contributed to the win, driving in runs off Lyons during a fourth-inning rally. The loss eliminated Baylor from SWC contention. The Bears had started the 1920 season 12–2 overall and were 8–1 in conference play before losing four straight games to Texas.

The Longhorns were now smoking as they defeated SMU behind another four-hitter by Lessiner. The final score was 8–2 as Texas scored five runs in the fifth inning.

Bibb Falk closed out his college career by pitching a 2–0 victory over Texas A&M at Clark Field to win the SWC championship. In the game, he had 12 strikeouts and allowed just five hits.

It was also the final game in the Longhorns careers of Bobby Cannon, George McCullough and Swanie Robertson. Bobby Cannon went on to have a successful career as a high school coach and administrator. McCullough and Robertson remained close friends into their 80s.

At the plate, Bibb Falk hit .400 for the 1920 season and hit safely in every game but one. He had also pitched 50 innings and had a 6–0 record. In the field he made only two errors.

Adding to the Longhorns power pack were Swanie Robertson, who hit .364, Irwin Gillett at .360, and Dudley English at .326. On the mound, Longhorns pitchers Bibb Falk, Irwin Gillett, Ralph Barry and Rube Lessiner, threw six shutouts and held the opposition to two runs or less in 11 other games.

The Longhorns finished the 1920 season with a record of 18–7–1, a collegiate record of 17–5 and a conference record of 9–2. The Baylor Bears finished third in the SWC with an overall record of 13–7 and a conference record of 8–5.

During the three years that Bibb Falk played baseball for the Texas Longhorns, the team had an overall record of 57–14–1 and was 29–3 in Southwest Conference play, winning three conference championships. As a pitcher, Falk went undefeated in three years of varsity competition.

Bibb Falk

He was a consummate pitcher; he gave hitters a lot to think about at the plate as his repertoire on the mound included a fastball, curve, change-up and knuckleball. In addition, he had endurance, control and pitching sense.

When Falk wasn't pitching, he played first base and in the outfield. A contact hitter, Falk batted at least .400 in two of his three varsity seasons. His batting averages for his three years of varsity ball were, in succession, .369, .460 and .400.

Bibb Falk still had one year of eligibility left in football at Texas. But hoping to make a few quick dollars, he decided to join the Chicago White Sox. Falk was signed by Charles Comiskey for $2,500 and a $1,000 bonus. He was told to report following his graduation in June. While the White Sox offered to send Falk to the minors to get some professional experience, he was in a hurry for a taste of big league life and went straight from the campus of the University of Texas into the American League without playing in the minor leagues.

The 1920 edition of *The Cactus, The Year Book published by the Student Body of University of Texas, Vol. XXVII,* said of Bibb Falk,

> Bibb, the handsomest athlete in the school, according to some authorities, is the hardest hitter in the colleges of the Southwest. On the trip up to Oklahoma, all the players of the opposing teams wanted to shown the big "Swede," so they could remove to a respectful distance when he batted. Bibb had a poor year last year and did not bat as high as .500. He missed this by forty percent, however. The 1920 season will be his last also as he reports to the Chicago White Sox at the end of the school year.

In June, with his degree in civil engineering in hand, Bibb Falk reported to the Chicago White Sox. It was apparent immediately that with his football injury not having enough time to heal properly and his taking the mound for the Longhorns in the spring, his days on the mound had come to an end. But White Sox manager Kid Gleason was well aware of Falk's ability with the bat and decided to make an outfielder out of him.

Although no longer on the mound, Falk still found it necessary to go through the motions of a pitcher before every game. For years after joining the White Sox, before each game Bibb would religiously go to the bullpen, find an extra catcher and warm up.

The American League pennant race in 1920 had been a close,

3. Breaking In with the Black Sox

three-team battle since Opening Day. On July 17, a few weeks after Bibb Falk joined the team, the defending American League champion Chicago White Sox were in third place in the American League, two games behind the second-place New York Yankees and 3½ games behind the first-place Cleveland Indians.

The White Sox were in New York to play the Yankees at the Polo Grounds, with 30,000-plus fans on hand to see Eddie Cicotte face off against Carl Mays. However, the game turned into a route as the Yankees scored early and often. With the game out of reach, manager Kid Gleason sent Bibb Falk up to the plate to pinch-hit for Cicotte. So at the age of 21, Bibb Falk made his major league debut, but he failed to get a hit as the Yankees pounded the White Sox, 20–5. It would be nearly two months before he got in another game.

Many analysts considered the defending champion Chicago White Sox the best team in baseball in 1920. Red Faber was now healthy and, along with Eddie Cicotte, Lefty Williams and Dickie Kerr, the foursome were hands down the best starting rotation in the major leagues. The White Sox were also pounding the ball and five hitters—Joe Jackson, Buck Weaver, Happy Felsch, Shano Collins and Eddie Collins—were hitting well above .300.

Bibb August Falk (National Baseball Hall of Fame Library, Cooperstown, New York).

Bibb Falk

As the dog days of August arrived, the American public was transfixed by the hand-to-hand battle for the American League pennant taking place, and no one seemed to care about the rampant rumors of the past fall that a fix had taken place in the 1919 World Series.

On August 16, the Cleveland Indians were tied for first place with the Chicago White Sox. That day Cleveland was playing the New York Yankees at the Polo Grounds when Indians shortstop Ray Chapman was hit in the head by a pitch by Carl Mays. Chapman died the next day as a result of complications from a fractured skill.

Between 1876 and 2014, there have been over 100,000 hit batsmen in major league baseball. Hughie Jennings was hit by a pitch 287 times in his career, Craig Biggio 285 times, and 82 players have been hit more than 100 times. But Ray Chapman remains the only player to have died from an on-field injury of any type on a major league diamond.

A few years later, in an effort to exonerate himself in Chapman's death, Carl Mays told Yankees teammate Waite Hoyt, "Hell, I threw him a curve ball. You don't throw a curve when you're trying to hit somebody."[1]

The death of Chapman had a demoralizing effect on the Indians' team psyche and they proceeded to lose eight out of the next 11 games. By August 30 the Indians were in third place, 2½ games behind the White Sox.

In late August, the White Sox completed a 15-game road trip. On August 26, after beating the Yankees 16–4, they were in first place with a 3½ game lead. Shockingly, they dropped seven games in a row. Immediately there was renewed suspicion that gamblers were pressuring some of the suspect White Sox players from the 1919 World Series to lose games down the stretch.

Eddie Collins was becoming suspicious of some of his teammates, and in early September voiced his concerns to Charles Comiskey. It was just what Comiskey didn't want to hear. He had attempted to sweep away, go into denial about, or perhaps cover up his own suspicion about the legitimacy of the 1919 World Series. So Comiskey simply told Collins he would look into the matter.

As the White Sox battled the Indians and Yankees for the pennant, there wasn't much opportunity for Bibb Falk to play. He batted left-handed, and Kid Gleason had Amos Strunk and Eddie Murphy available to pinch-hit from the left side of the plate and play occasionally in the

3. Breaking In with the Black Sox

outfield. Amos Strunk was a 13-year veteran and had played in three World Series with Connie Mack's Philadelphia Athletics. Eddie Murphy was a nine-year veteran who had also played in three World Series with the Athletics and White Sox. In 1919, playing in just 30 games, six in the outfield, with 35 at-bats, Murphy had hit .486. So rookie Bibb Falk continued to ride the bench throughout the late summer of 1920.

Finally, on September 14, Falk got his second chance to pinch-hit. The White Sox had fallen into third place, 1½ games behind the league-leading New York Yankees and one game behind second-place Cleveland. The White Sox were at home at Comiskey Park, hosting the Washington Nationals. Falk pinch-hit for pitcher Shovel Hodge and stroked a single off Jose Acosta for his first major league hit as the White Sox lost to the Senators, 7–0.

By then the winds of scandal were starting to blow harder. On September 7, 1920, a grand jury had been convened in Chicago and was hearing testimony in regard to an alleged fix of a game between the Chicago Cubs and Philadelphia Phillies played on August 31. William Veeck, Sr., one of the owners of the Chicago Cubs, had presented to the grand jury a stack of reports written by private detectives stating that the game had been fixed.

On September 22, the grand jury abruptly changed its focus when American League president Ban Johnson testified that he believed that some players had thrown games in last year's World Series but had no evidence.

The following day, Rube Benton, a pitcher for the New York Giants with a jaded past, told the grand jury that during the season, Hal Chase, Buck Herzog and Heinie Zimmerman had offered him a bribe to lose a game. Benton also told the Grand Jury of a possible fix in the 1919 World Series. In a separate statement, Benton told the panel that a gambling ring leader in Cincinnati had told him he had knowledge of four White Sox players—pitchers Eddie Cicotte and Lefty Williams, first baseman Chick Gandil, and center fielder Happy Felsch—being involved with fixing the 1919 World Series.

On September 25, Harry H. Brigham, foreman of the Cook County Grand Jury, told newspaper reporters that the name of the man who fixed the 1919 World Series for Cincinnati to win had been given to the grand jury. That man was Arnold Rothstein, a New York gambler.

As the 1920 baseball season entered the final week on the schedule, the White Sox continued to battle the Indians and Yankees for the lead in the American League pennant race. But September 27 was to be a fatal day. The White Sox defeated the Detroit Tigers, 2–0, in their final home game, and then all hell broke loose.

That evening a deputy from the State attorney's office appeared at the home of Eddie Cicotte with a subpoena. To make matters worse, in the evening edition of *The Philadelphia North American*, Billy Maharg, a former boxer who had pitched two games in the major leagues, revealed in detail the story of the 1919 World Series. Maharg stated that Abe Attell had headed up the gambling ring that fixed the Series, and he had connected Eddie Cicotte with the plot. He stated that Attell double-crossed the White Sox players and they never received the $100,000 promised to them. Attell told Maharg that he was withholding the players' payments because he needed the money to bet.

Maharg also stated in the paper that he had knowledge that in a pre-grand jury hearing held by National League president John Heydler, New York Giants pitcher Rube Benton testified that he had seen a telegram sent to another Giants pitcher, Jean Dubuc, from "Sleepy Bill" Burns tipping him off that the 1919 World Series would be fixed. Maharg also said that Benton had told Heydler that he had seen Hal Chase bet $100 on the Series.

Hal Chase is the only left-handed-throwing and right-handed-hitting player to win a major league batting title. In 1916, while playing for the Cincinnati Reds, he led the National League with an average of .339. It has long been believed that Chase had profited far greater on the Series than simply making a $100 bet. Many unsubstantiated reports estimate that Chase may have won as much as $40,000 on the Series and was much more involved in the fix. In fact, there is speculation that it may have been Chase who convinced "Sleepy Bill" Burns to approach Arnold Rothstein in an attempt to finance a Series fix.

There had been speculation that Hal Chase and Heinie Zimmerman had made errors on purpose as the Giants were locked in tough battle for first place with the Reds in late summer 1919. A lot of the Giants players and manager John McGraw had become suspicious, and Hal Chase was removed from the Giants roster. National League president John Heydler had obtained a cancelled check for $500 paid to Chase by a known gambler. When Chase failed to appear at the Polo Grounds one day, John McGraw was asked about his disappearance. McGraw

3. Breaking In with the Black Sox

stated, "He's sick. He hasn't been feeling well for a long time. I doubt he will play again this year."[2] A few days later Heinie Zimmerman was gone, never to return to the major leagues.

A year later, during the investigation of the 1919 World Series, McGraw would say that he booted both players from the team because they had thrown games and attempted to bribe pitcher Fred Toney and outfielder Benny Kauff, offering them $250. While Zimmerman angrily denied McGraw's accusations, Chase, playing in an outlaw league near the Mexican border, remained silent. Although Chase's name would continually surface in the grand jury hearings, he was not indicted.

Hal Chase had a controversial career on and off the field. He had been suspected of throwing games as far back as 1913, when he played first base for the New York Highlanders. Still, in the first Hall of Fame balloting in 1936, Chase received 11 votes, eight more than Shoeless Joe Jackson received.

As the grand jury hearings continued in late September, the forthcoming conclusion to the exciting 1920 American League season suddenly seemed like a bloody mess. American League president Ban Johnson had become worried that the White Sox were going to win the pennant again and feared a repeat of another scandal in the World Series. According to Johnson, rumors were becoming more prominent that gamblers were attempting to bribe the White Sox to lose the 1920 pennant by threatening to expose their involvement in the 1919 World Series fix.

White Sox owner Charles Comiskey was livid. He and Johnson were still not on speaking terms, and now he was accusing Johnson of attempting to prevent the White Sox from winning the pennant.

On September 28, both Eddie Cicotte and Joe Jackson appeared before the grand jury, and their testimonies caused the scandal to become forever etched into major league baseball history. A few moments after taking the witness stand, Cicotte broke down emotionally, began to shed tears and told a story of utter betrayal, saying over and over again, "I wished I wasn't mixed up in it."[3] He told the grand jury that he, Joe Jackson and six other teammates had conspired to fix the 1919 World Series.

The other six players implicated by Cicotte were pitcher Claude "Lefty" Williams, first baseman Arnold "Chick" Gandil, outfielder Oscar "Happy" Felsch, shortstop Charles "Swede" Risberg, reserve infielder Fred McMullin, and third baseman George "Buck" Weaver.

Babe Ruth and Shoeless Joe Jackson (Sports Story Reprints).

 Cicotte alleged in his testimony that the amount of the bribe money that each accepted was the following: Chick Gandil $20,000, Fred McMullin $15,000, Swede Risberg $10,000, Lefty Williams $10,000, Happy Felsch $5,000, Buck Weaver $5,000, Joe Jackson $5,000 and himself $10,000.

 Cicotte told the grand jury,

3. Breaking In with the Black Sox

"I played a crooked game and lost. Risberg, Gandil and McMullin were at me for a week before the series started. They wanted me to go crooked. I needed the money. I had the wife and kids. I had bought a farm. There was a $4,000 mortgage. I paid that off with the crooked money. The eight of us got together in my room three or four days before the series started. Gandil was master of ceremonies. We talked about throwing the series, and decided we could get away with it. We agreed to do it."[4]

Eddie Cicotte's testimony had been corroborated the night before by Billy Maharg in his Philadelphia newspaper interview.

Later that day, Shoeless Joe Jackson took the witness stand. While Jackson shed no tears, he hung his head and covered his face as he talked about being double-crossed. He stated that Lefty Williams had drawn him into the plot. He was told that all he had to do, when hits meant runs, was either strike out or just tap the ball for an easy out.

Jackson testified, "When Claude Williams unfolded the plan to give the series to the Cincinnati Reds, I demanded $20,000 for my share. We had several conferences and squabbles over the amount, but I finally consented to take the $5,000. Williams told me that we were all getting the same. Had I known some of the others were getting $10,000, I would have held out for $20,000."[5] When the Series began in Cincinnati, according to Jackson, he found $5,000 on his bed in the Sinton Hotel that had been left for him by Lefty Williams.

Jackson testified before the grand jury for nearly two hours, and when his testimony was completed, he left the grand jury room smiling and walking erect. He left the courthouse in the custody of bailiffs. He had asked for protection as he was fearful of a reprisal by Swede Risberg for testifying. Later Joe Jackson stated to reporters that the reason he had bailiffs surround him and escort him from the courthouse was because "Risberg threatens to bump me off if I squawk."[6]

Legend has it that as Jackson walked out the door of the courthouse, he was confronted by a disbelieving newsboy who pleaded with him, stating, "Say it ain't so, Joe!"

Unfortunately, this is one of those cases of classic American mythology, right up there with such tales as George Washington throwing a silver dollar across the Potomac and the Santa Claus portrayal in *The Miracle on 34th Street.* Actually the incident of the skeptical youth was penned by sportswriter Hugh Fullerton in an article published in the *New York Evening World*, and it has become ingrained in the American lexicon.

The facts are that the bailiffs surrounding Joe Jackson that day hustled him out the door of the Cook County Court House and refused to allow him to talk with the press or anyone else. He was immediately pushed into a taxi that quickly drove off, carrying the legend of Shoeless Joe Jackson into infamy.

The following day, Lefty Williams testified before the grand jury. Prior to testifying, Williams had told Alfred Austrian in a sworn statement that Chick Gandil first approached him about fixing the World Series in front of the Hotel Ansonia in New York. Asked if Shoeless Joe Jackson was in on the meeting at the Ansonia, Williams stated he was not.

After returning to Chicago, Williams said, he was called to the Warner Hotel, where several members of the White Sox involved in the plot were gathered—Eddie Cicotte, Chick Gandil, Buck Weaver, and Happy Felsch—and two fellows introduced as Brown and Sullivan who were gamblers from Boston. He said they wanted them to throw the Series for $5,000 each. Williams said that wasn't enough money. He said that Gandil told him that either with him or without him the Series was going to be fixed. Williams testified that he told Gandil, "Anything they did would be agreeable with me; if it was going to be done anyway, that I had no money and might as well get what I could."[7]

Williams further testified that after pitching and losing the second game, he was supposed to receive $10,000. However, he didn't receive that payment. "I figured then that there was a double-cross some place," said Williams. "On the second trip to Cincinnati, Cicotte and I had a conference. I told him that we were doubled-crossed and that I was going to win if there was any possible chance. Cicotte said he was the same way."[8]

Buck Weaver had considered voluntarily testifying in front of the grand jury and stating that he had been present at the meeting in Chicago in Cicotte's room at the Warner Hotel when the decision was made to fix the Series, but did not join in the talk. But after being advised that he could be indicted for perjury, he remained silent. Instead, Weaver took a defensive stance. "What can I confess? Look at my record in the World Series. I fielded 1.000 and batted .333. That doesn't look much as if I was fixed, does it? I'm going to hire the best lawyer in Chicago to defend me and I'm going to be cleared."[9]

3. Breaking In with the Black Sox

On the morning of September 29, 1920, the roof blew off in the scandal, as nearly every newspaper in the United States carried the story of the grand jury hearing and printed the leaking testimonies of Eddie Cicotte and Shoeless Joe Jackson. In addition, the pictures of all eight named players were on the front pages.

Charles Comiskey had surmised that Eddie Cicotte would be a weak link in the actual chain of events. So some time before his grand jury testimony (the actual date is not clear) Comiskey arranged a meeting at his office with Cicotte and the team's attorney, Alfred Austrian. At the meeting, legend has it that Comiskey brow-beat Cicotte into a confession. Then he met with Joe Jackson and did the same.

Furthermore it is alleged that Comiskey, with Austrian present, coerced both Eddie Cicotte and Shoeless Joe Jackson, without benefit of counsel, into signing waivers of immunity prior to each testifying before the grand jury.

A short time after the season ended, as the grand jury hearing continued, St. Louis Browns second baseman Joe Gedeon was summoned and voluntarily came from his home in California to testify. Gedeon testified that he was a friend of Swede Risberg and, on a tip, presumed to have come from Risberg, he bet on the Reds in the Series and pocketed $600 to $700 in winnings. Gedeon also mentioned a group of St. Louis gamblers he had approached for a loan to make his bet on the Series. It is believed that without knowing it, Joe Gedeon may have given a group of St. Louis gamblers a reason to suspect something was up in the Series, causing them to attempt to establish a secondary fix.

Gedeon testified that he didn't really know that the World Series was crooked until the third game. He said that he attended a meeting at the Hotel Sherman in Chicago at the suggestion of his two gambler friends from St. Louis, where an effort was being made to raise an additional $25,000 for the White Sox players involved in the plot. This admission would come back to haunt Joe Gedeon.

While Joe Gedeon was exonerated by the grand jury, following his appearance he told reporters outside the courtroom that he feared he was through in baseball.

Arnold Rothstein, the man everyone wanted to hear from, came from New York to testify before the grand jury and stated that Abe Attell and "Sleepy Bill" Burns had approached him with a proposal to fix the World Series. They told him that the Series could be fixed for

$100,000. But he turned them down as he was convinced that the Series could not be fixed. He concluded his testimony by stating that he lost $6,000 in the Series betting on the White Sox. Furthermore, he was convinced that Abe Attell had used his name to put the whole thing over.

On October 29, 1920, the grand jury concluded its work. Its final report would be presented to Chief Justice Charles McDonald on November 26. Seven of the White Sox players and several of the gamblers were indicted. Charges against Fred McMullin were dropped for lack of evidence. Arnold Rothstein was exonerated by the grand jury of any wrongdoing.

At first, the State's Chief Prosecutor, Maclay Hoyne, had been reluctant go forward with the investigation, saying it was engineered by persons antagonistic to Charles Comiskey. Rather than conduct the gambling investigation himself, he had assigned Assistant State Attorney Hartley Replogle to present the state's evidence to the grand jury. Then Hoyne resigned to return to private practice. Shortly after Hoyne left office, it was revealed that all the papers relating to the White Sox gambling case had disappeared from the prosecutor's office, including the confessions of Eddie Cicotte, Joe Jackson and Lefty Williams.

Someone informed American League president Ban Johnson of the missing confession. He notified Judge Landis, newly installed as commissioner, who was outraged and said that if those persons responsible for tampering with the evidence were found, federal action would be taken. Still, copies of the indictments were circulating. *The New York Herald* had copies and offered them to *The Chicago Tribune* in eight installments for $25,000.

With the grand jury records somehow winding up in New York, Ban Johnson charged that Arnold Rothstein had paid $10,000 for them. Rothstein denied the allegation and said he would sue Johnson for $100,000. But the suit was never filed.

Chicago police chief John J. Garrity was calling the grand jury probe of the 1919 World Series and an investigation launched by Ban Johnson a joke. Garrity stated, "Baseball gambling in Chicago is no more under official prosecution than the stick-up business, burglary or any other form of crime. In the present circumstances, it cannot be stopped. I would have to put a policeman in every building in Chicago. I had better say in every room in Chicago, in order to eradicate gambling on baseball games or in the horse races."[10]

3. Breaking In with the Black Sox

Chief Garrity proved to be clairvoyant. By 1949, 30 years after the 1919 World Series had the potential to destroy the national pastime, baseball gambling was alive and well in Chicago. *Sports World Magazine*, in its September 1949 issue, estimated the daily take by bookies in Chicago from baseball betting at between $750,000 and $1,000,000. Nationally, by 1949 baseball betting was a $12,000,000-a-day enterprise spanning the country coast to coast. In the downtown gambling parlors and smoke shops in almost every American city, baseball bets were being handled by bookies right along with horse racing wagers. In many ballparks, betting even took place in the grandstands and bleachers.

In 1967, Detroit Tigers pitcher Denny McLain was engaged in a bookmaking operation using the clubhouse telephone as a vehicle to take wagers. After the operation was exposed, McLain attempted to rationalize his activity by stating, "It was hardly any kind of major operation. It was a bunch of guys having fun. We got in trouble when the Pepsi truck guy told the wrong people. And I got out of the business when we got taken for 40 grand."[11] The so-called 40-grand incident allegedly involved Detroit mobster Tony Giacalone, later implicated in the mysterious disappearance of former Teamsters union president Jimmy Hoffa.

By 1988, as revealed in the Dowd Report, soon to be banished Cincinnati Reds manager Pete Rose was so brazen as to place his $2,000-a-game bets on baseball from the clubhouse and dugout telephones at Riverfront Stadium with his small-time bookie and drug dealer friend Ron Peters.

Following the testimonies before the grand jury of Eddie Cicotte, Joe Jackson and Lefty Williams, Charles Comiskey refused to meet with reporters. He dictated a telegram and sent it to all the eight players named in the scandal, suspending them. In the communication, Comiskey stated, "If you are guilty, you will be retired from organized baseball for the rest of your lives if I can accomplish it."[12] In tears, knowing that his team was in ruin and was not going to win the 1920 American League pennant, Comiskey announced that pay due for the eight players would be sent immediately.

Nonetheless, White Sox secretary Harry Grabiner was defiant to admit defeat and announced that "the club would play out the schedule to the end if it had to employ Chinamen to fill the vacancies on the team."[13]

On October 1, the Chicago White Sox were in second place, 1½ games behind the first-place Cleveland Indians. They got ready to play

Bibb Falk

the final three games of the 1920 season against the St. Louis Browns with a makeshift lineup. For Bibb Falk, it was an opportunity to get off the bench, and he was inserted in right field as Amos Strunk moved from right field to left field to replace Joe Jackson, while Nemo Leibold went to center field to replace Happy Felsch.

Bibb Falk went 3-for–5 in the game and had an RBI, but the White Sox were defeated by the Browns, 8–6. The following day, the White Sox defeated the Browns, 10–7, as Falk went 0-for–3.

With one game remaining on the schedule, the White Sox remained two games behind the Indians and the pennant race was over. Had the White Sox somehow stumbled across the finish line and repeated as American League champions, it would have been even a bigger embarrassment for major league baseball than just the revelation of the World Series fix, so many insiders in the game were relieved.

On the final day of the 1920 season, just for good measure, the Browns pounded the White Sox, 16–7. Bibb Falk went 0-for-5 finishing the 1920 season having appeared in seven games, getting five hits in 17 at-bats for an average of .294.

Joe Gedeon played second base for the St. Louis Browns in the final series of the 1920 season against the White Sox. But October 2, 1920, would be Joe Gedeon's final game in the major leagues. Gedeon gave credibility to the old adage "there is no honor among thieves" as it was a bit ironic that as Swede Risberg's friend, he had been the one who had tried to sell his knowledge of a fix in the 1919 World Series to Charles Comiskey.

As the scandal involved with the 1919 World Series broke, Bibb Falk quickly and conveniently distanced himself from the controversy, claiming he was taken by surprise. Stories kept appearing in the newspapers, and Falk said that he asked Eddie Cicotte what it was all about. Cicotte replied it was a lot of bull.

> "I never really knew much about it," said Falk. "I had been with the club all season but I really didn't associate with the older players. Then we went to St. Louis the last week of September and it broke wide open. Suddenly half of our team was gone. That's when I got my chance to play. I went into left field in place of legendary 'Shoeless Joe' Jackson."[14]

> "I had one good break in pro ball ... that was it. We had to rebuild the club. Otherwise, I would have been down in the bush league trying

3. Breaking In with the Black Sox

to work myself up from Wheeling. Jackson was a great ball player, and I really don't think he knew how to throw a game. He just went in because of some of those guys that he knew. He just followed the leaders."[15]

The 1920 White Sox had been divided between two groups of players who hardly spoke to each other off the field. According to Eddie Murphy, "There were cliques on the club, and the eight who were thrown out always hung around together, even at the batting cage. And there cliques within cliques. Weaver and Felsch were very close, and Felsch would do anything Weaver wanted. Eddie Cicotte and Lefty Williams were close, and so were their wives. Cicotte was a clean-living fellow who had never been in trouble before."[16]

The demise of the 1920 Chicago White Sox was a true tragedy. It was a very talented team and one of the best ever to finish in second place. Four White Sox pitchers won 20 games (Red Faber went 23–10, Lefty Williams 22–14, Eddie Cicotte 21–10, and Dickie Kerr 21–9). There would not be another major league team with four 20-game winners until 1971, when the Baltimore Orioles staff accomplished the feat with Mike Cuellar, Pat Dobson, Jim Palmer and Dave McNally.

Also, the 1920 Chicago White Sox had three hitters with more than 200 hits in the season, Joe Jackson 218, Buck Weaver 210, Eddie Collins 204). The only other team in the modern era to equal this feat would be the 1921 St. Louis Browns with George Sisler, Jack Tobin and Baby Doll Jacobson.

4

Replacing a Legend

Charles Comiskey had suspended the eight White Sox players awaiting trial in Cook County Criminal Court. Without such stars as Shoeless Joe Jackson, Eddie Cicotte, Buck Weaver, Happy Felsch and Lefty Williams, the core of the great team no longer existed. Consequently, a new lineup for the 1921 season would have to be built. Regardless, Comiskey was glad to be done with the renegades.

In 1921, the Chicago White Sox held spring training at Waxahachie, Texas, the home town of Paul Richards, who would become a catcher in the major leagues for eight years and a manager for years for the Chicago White Sox and Baltimore Orioles.

Waxahachie is located deep in the cotton country, and as soon as the White Sox arrived they hung the "HELP WANTED" sign outside the ballpark. About 50 college players, career minor leaguers and sandlot players were in camp, hoping to land a job. Manager Kid Gleason wasn't accepting any sympathy and went to work crafting his "New Sox." He still had three future Hall of Famers—second baseman Eddie Collins, catcher Ray Schalk and pitcher Red Faber—to build the team around. Ray Schalk, Red Faber, Dickie Kerr and Roy Wilkinson were resolved to work with the younger pitchers coming aboard to replace the 20-game winners, Cicotte and Williams, lost in the scandal. Among those hopefuls were 6'4" Clarence "Shovel" Hodge, who joined the team at the end of the 1920 season, and Lum Davenport, a southpaw with a good fastball from the University of Arizona.

But with three-fourths of the White Sox infield awaiting trial, Kid Gleason had his work cut out for him. Shano Collins played first base

4. Replacing a Legend

in the 1920 season when Chick Gandil held out all year in a contract dispute with Comiskey. To replace Swede Risberg at shortstop, veteran Ernie Johnson took over. Johnson had broken into the major leagues in 1912 with the White Sox. At third base, Eddie Mulligan, a former Pacific Coast League player, was inserted to take over for Buck Weaver.

Veteran Harry Hooper took over in right field. Hooper had been acquired over the winter in a trade with the Boston Red Sox that saw Shano Collins and Nemo Leibold depart. Amos Strunk and Johnny Mostil replaced Happy Felsch in center field, and Bibb Falk was chosen to replace the legendary Shoeless Joe Jackson in left field.

But there was some concern about Falk. He had been ill over the winter and reported to spring training underweight. Kid Gleason was sure that the former college slugger could hit big league pitching, but he needed work on his fielding and running the bases. If the scandal hadn't deprived the White Sox of some of their biggest stars, Bibb Falk would have continued to languish on the bench and regret his decision to jump from college ball directly to the big leagues without minor league experience.

Joe Jackson's shortened career of 13 seasons saw him finish with a .356 lifetime batting average, third highest in major league history. In 1911, playing with Cleveland, Jackson had hit .408 and finished second to Ty Cobb, who won the American League batting crown with an average of .420. Bibb Falk knew it would be a nearly impossible task to replace one of the greatest hitters in baseball history,

Bibb Falk, Chicago White Sox (National Baseball Hall of Fame Library, Cooperstown, New York).

even for a seasoned veteran. Still, Falk was resolved to prove to everyone that he belonged in a major league uniform. The tight-fisted Charles Comiskey was counting on him and even raised his salary to $3,000 for the 1921 season.

Throughout the history of the game, there have been numerous occasions when both young and seasoned players have been called upon to face the challenge of replacing legends. One of the more memorable challenges occurred in 1927 when Frank Frisch was faced with the daunting task of replacing Rogers Hornsby at second base following a blockbuster trade sent him from the New York Giants to the St. Louis Cardinals. Three times in the previous five seasons, Hornsby had hit over .400. He would wind up his major league career with a .358 lifetime batting average, second only to Ty Cobb in major league history. Frank Frisch went on to have a remarkable career with the Cardinals. A sportswriter of the era wrote that Frisch didn't make the Cardinals fans forget Hornsby, but he made them remember Frisch.

However, the difference in the challenge faced by Frank Frisch as opposed to that faced by Bibb Falk was that Frisch was a veteran of eight major league seasons in which he had consistently batted over .300. Falk had just seven games major league experience.

The White Sox opened the 1921 season on the road, playing two games at Detroit and two at St. Louis, winning one and losing three. On Opening Day at Comiskey Park, Thursday, April 21, more than 25,000 fans showed up to cheer for the New Sox. None was blaming Charles Comiskey for the scandal; it had been the eight players who had betrayed their trust.

The White Sox defeated the Tigers, 8–3, behind the pitching of Dickie Kerr. Two days later, the White Sox again defeated the Tigers, 3–2, in an 11-inning game. Red Faber pitched the first eight innings, squaring off against Detroit's Dutch Leonard, with Shovel Hodge taking over in the ninth. Both Eddie Collins and Bibb Falk went 3-for-5 in the game. Falk's two singles and a double raised his batting average to .318.

The 1919 World Series scandal was still a pile of smoldering rubbish for major league baseball that needed to be extinguished. During mid-winter 1921 in Chicago, the new Cook County District Attorney, Robert Crowe, informed American League president Ban Johnson that without the missing confessions of Cicotte, Jackson and Williams there was nothing for him to do but dismiss the indictments. With no evi-

Urban "Red" Faber (Sports Story Reprints).

dence, the state had no case. Crowe also made it clear to Johnson that according to Illinois law, an indictment must be returned within 18 months of the time the crime was committed. As the alleged crime had been committed in October 1919, that meant the time limit for indictments was a few weeks away in April 1921.

So the clock was ticking. Now Ban Johnson was accusing Judge

Landis of doing nothing to pursue the case. Concerned about the commissioner's procrastination, Johnson went into action, spending his own money and that of the American League to reopen the investigation. He traveled 10,000 miles, talking with suspects who had knowledge of the conspiracy, and even induced "Sleepy Bill" Burns to return from his self-imposed exile in Mexico and talk.

By March 26, aided in Chicago by the investigation of Assistant Attorney Crowe and his assistant John Tyrell, Johnson submitted enough evidence to re-indict seven of the eight players and several of the gamblers.

As the 1921 baseball season progressed, on July 21 Red Faber won his 20th game of the season for the White Sox. The game went 14 innings and Faber gave up 16 hits before Chicago defeated the Philadelphia A's, 2–1, on Bibb Falk's leadoff home run in the 14th inning off Rollie Naylor. While Falk was playing hard and making contributions, Kid Gleason's "New Sox" weren't doing so well in the American League standings, holding down seventh place with a record of 40–49.

With new prosecutors in place in Cook County in the persons of Assistant State Attorneys Edward Prinville and George Gorman, on July 18, 1921, a conspiracy trial began in Chicago for the seven indicted former Chicago White Sox players: Eddie Cicotte, Happy Felsch, Chick Gandil, Joe Jackson, Swede Risberg, Buck Weaver and Lefty Williams; and two gamblers, Carl Zork and David Zelser, all who allegedly conspired to fix the 1919 World Series.

The formal charges were stated as the case of *State of Illinois vs. Eddie Cicotte et al.* Seven players and two gamblers faced charges of: (1) conspiring to defraud the public; (2) conspiring to defraud White Sox catcher Ray Schalk; (3) conspiring to commit a confidence game; (4) conspiring to injure the business of the American League; and (5) conspiring to injure the business of Charles Comiskey.

It took two weeks to examine roughly 600 prospective jurors before a panel was seated. Charles A. Comiskey was the first witness called by the prosecution. The prosecution presented to the jury a lengthy chronology of Comiskey's career in major league baseball from his days as a player beginning in the American Association in 1882 to his ownership of the Chicago White Sox. Then the prosecution attempted to establish as fact that Charles Comiskey had been financially harmed by the players' conspiracy.

4. Replacing a Legend

At once the defense pointed out that the 1920 season had in fact been the most profitable year in the history of Comiskey's ownership of the White Sox. Comiskey's secretary, Harry Grabiner, was called to the witness stand and verified the defense's contention. The facts were that in 1919 the Chicago White Sox, for 70 home games, had an attendance of 627,186, the second highest figure in the American League. In 1920, for 77 home games, the White Sox had a total home attendance of 833,492, the third highest total in the league. Therefore the defense had established that gross revenue was higher in 1920 than in 1919, when the players had allegedly defrauded Charles Comiskey.

Then it was formally revealed that somehow the official grand jury confessions of Eddie Cicotte, Joe Jackson and Lefty Williams had disappeared from the district attorney's files.

On Monday, July 25, the presiding judge in the case, 38-year-old Hugo Friend, removed the jury from the courtroom. Judge Friend heard testimony from Eddie Cicotte, Shoeless Joe Jackson and Lefty Williams, each of whom admitted that he had made a confession, but had done so under duress. Furthermore, all three players said that they had made their confessions with a promise of immunity before signing some piece of paper that actually turned out to be a waiver of immunity.

With the issue of immunity raised, Judge McDonald and former district attorney Hartley Replogle were called to testify, and both swore that there was no promise of immunity made to Cicotte, Jackson or Williams.

Judge Friend ruled that the confessions of Cicotte, Jackson and Williams could be used against them, but not the others named in their statements. With the actual confessions missing, the judge ordered that a transcript be given to the jury.

At this point, the prosecution was convinced that they would prove their case against all the players. Out in the halls during recess, the prosecutors were telling the press that nothing less than sentences to the penitentiary for all the players and gamblers would be satisfactory to them.

On July 28, several of the active White Sox players were called to testify, including Red Faber, Ray Schalk, Eddie Collins, Dickie Kerr, Roy Wilkinson and Harvey McCellan, along with the team's trainer. The White Sox were on the road in Washington, and Kid Gleason asked Nationals owner Clark Griffith to postpone the game. Griffith refused, the game was played, and the White Sox lost, 8–5. Bibb Falk was hitting

.300 and attempted to fill the void by going 2-for-5 in the game. But with the White Sox mired in seventh place with a record of 40–53, Griffith's strong refusal to postpone the game would not have any significant impact on the 1921 American League pennant race and amounted to little more than a subtle snub of Charles Comiskey.

Back at the witness stand, the defense asked each of the non-indicted players, Schalk, Faber, Kerr, Wilkinson, etc., whether they thought the indicted players had played the World Series to the best of their ability. Each time the question was raised, it was met with shouts of objection from the prosecution. Judge Friend sustained the objections on the grounds that the defense was asking for opinions. Nonetheless, it was curious that Ray Schalk, who had been so adamant that the indicted players had thrown games, literally recanted his allegation.

The prosecution had intended to put Joe Gedeon on the stand to testify that Carl Zork of St. Louis had been responsible for setting up a secondary fix in the Series. However, as the trial proceeded, the prosecution became concerned that Gedeon might turn out to be an unreliable witness. So the prosecution turned to Harry Redmon to make their case for a secondary fix in the Series.

According to Redmon, the fix instigated by Abe Attell and Curley Bennett, a confidential go-between for Arnold Rothstein, fell apart when the players decided to double-cross the fixers by winning a game they were supposed to lose. Redmon also testified that in still another fix, St. Louis gamblers Carl Zork and Ben Franklin arranged for the White Sox to drop the last two games of the Series for $20,000. Redmon stated that Zork had told him that he had the players under his thumb and that he had also fixed games during the regular season. However, evidence of other games being fixed by Zork was not allowed since only the games in the 1919 World Series were involved in the trial.

The Cook County Grand Jury had indicted Abe Attell on charges of bribing the players. In fact, when the scandal broke in September 1920, in New York Attell was boasting that he would tell the names of all the fixers and blow the scandal wide open. Then Attell had a change of heart and went on the lam, hiding out in Montreal. When he returned to New York in early 1921, Illinois sought to extradite him. But Attell filed a writ of habeas corpus in New York Supreme Court and fought extradition, claiming he was not the Abe Attell indicted in Illinois in connection with the 1919 World Series.

4. Replacing a Legend

On June 6, 1921, a hearing on Attell's writ was held in the New York Supreme Court. During the grand jury hearing in Chicago in 1920, a resident named Samuel W. Pass had complained that he had been bilked by Attell in the 1919 World Series scandal. So the Illinois District Attorney sent Pass to New York for the purpose of identifying Attell. But when Pass took the stand and was asked to identify Attell, he stated that he had never seen him before. He called his testimony in front of the Cook County Grand Jury hearsay.

Other witnesses brought to New York by the district attorney failed to show up in court. Then the justice who had been hearing the case announced that he would be going on vacation for a month, thereby causing a delay in the hearing. The attempt to extradite Attell fell apart when his attorney informed the new justice assigned to the case that because of the change in jurist, he would need to delay the hearing a month.

Meanwhile, all of the indicted White Sox players kept a safe distance from New York so as not to be subpoenaed as witnesses in the Attell hearing.

The prosecution called "Sleepy Bill" Burns to the stand. Burns had been involved in the alleged plot to fix the Series, working with his cohort, Bill Maharg. Since the indictments were handed down by the grand jury in Chicago, he had been hiding out in Mexico, but at the insistence of American League president Ban Johnson he agreed to return to the United States and testify. Burns was to be the prosecution's chief witness as they needed to connect the players directly to the gamblers to have any chance of a conviction.

Burns testified that the players first approached him about fixing the Series and that he had met with Eddie Cicotte and Chick Gandil at the Ansonia Hotel in New York on September 16, 1919, with the players informing him that the White Sox were going to win the American League pennant and had decided to dump the World Series.

In a follow-up meeting with Cicotte and Gandil at the Ansonia on September 18, Burns said, he was told by Gandil that if he could arrange for $100,000 to be paid to the players, then the White Sox would throw the World Series to the Reds.

The morning before the World Series began in Cincinnati on October 1, Burns said, he met at the Sinton Hotel with Cicotte, Gandil, McMullin, Felsch, Weaver and Williams and told them he had the

$100,000 players' share to cover the fix. He said that the financiers were Arnold Rothstein, Abe Attell and a man named Bennett, who was actually David Zelser of Des Moines, an alleged confidential go-between with Rothstein. When Burns was asked if Joe Jackson was at that meeting, he replied that he didn't remember seeing him. Burns said that the payoff plan was that the White Sox needed to lose five games to lose the Series, so players would receive $20,000 from Abe Attell after each loss to Cincinnati. Burns would act as the go-between of the players and fixers.

The defense, led by Michael J. Ahern (later lawyer for Al Capone in his tax fraud trial), was skillful in not putting any of the accused players on the witness stand where the prosecution could cross examine them. Nonetheless, historically it can be argued that some of the players on trial, namely Joe Jackson and Buck Weaver, may have done themselves a huge disservice by not taking the witness stand. They had an opportunity to contradict or disagree with the state's star witness, "Sleepy Bill" Burns, who had described in detail how they had agreed with the plot to fix the series for $100,000. In the long run, their silence at the trial would become interpreted as guilt. Burns indicated that Weaver was present at the meeting when the Series fix was planned, and he never took the witness stand to deny the charge. That would be the smoking gun on Weaver's culpability that would be used by Judge Landis to keep him out of baseball. In denying Weaver's petition for reinstatement, Judge Landis said in part, "If the incriminating evidence was false, the baseball public had a right to Weaver's denial under oath. Of course, it is true that a verdict of not guilty was rendered in Weaver's favor. It was also likewise true that the same jury returned the same verdict in favor of Cicotte, Claude Williams and Joe Jackson, each of whom had confessed his guilt."[1]

The defense instead called Alfred Austrian, Charles Comiskey's lawyer, whom they sought to establish as an unreliable witness. The defense asked Austrian if he had called Harry Redmon a blackmailer when Redmon told him of what he knew of Comiskey's plot to cover up the Series scandal. Austrian denied doing so. Then Austrian was questioned about his alleged promise to get the players off easy in return for their confessions. Once again Austrian denied it. Then the defense charged that Austrian had acted as an attorney for Arnold Rothstein when he came to Chicago to testify before the grand jury.

The Black Sox in court 1921 (Shoeless Joe Jackson, second from left, Buck Weaver, third from left).

Austrian also denied this charge. But during the course of questioning Austrian, it was revealed that the missing confession of Lefty Williams had been in his office, not in the possession of the state's attorney.

In its summation, the prosecution stated that a criminal conspiracy had taken place and that the players' intention was to defraud the public. They stated that Cicotte, Jackson and Williams had sold out the Series for a paltry $20,000, and when the scandal broke, their consciences forced them to seek out the state attorney's office to make their confessions which they repeated to the grand jury. State's attorney Edward Prindville stated that the defendants had worked a con game and swindle on the American people. He called for convictions and penalties of five years in the penitentiary and a fine of $2,000 for each defendant.

The defense in its closing arguments, presented by St. Louis attorney Morgan Fromberg, representing gambler Carl Zork, repeatedly questioned why Arnold Rothstein had not been indicted. He told the jury to consider that a State's witness had named Rothstein as the financier of the alleged conspiracy. He also questioned why Abe Attell and others who had been named ringleaders in the case were never brought to trial.

Fromberg stated that when Rothstein came to Chicago to testify before the grand jury, he was chaperoned by Alfred Austrian, the White Sox lawyer. "What bowing and scraping must have taken place when 'Arnold the just' entered the sanctum of 'Alfred the Great.'"[2] Later Austrian boasted that he had prevented Rothstein from being indicted.

Fromberg also said that the state, having let the instigators of the baseball scandal go free, was "trying to make the goats of underpaid ball players and penny-ante gamblers. Why were these underpaid ballplayers, these penny-ante gamblers from Des Moines and St. Louis, who bet perhaps a few nickels on the world series, brought here to be the goats of this case?"[3] In conclusion, Fromberg stated, "Ask Ban Johnson, who pulled the strings in this case. Ask him who saved Arnold Rothstein."[4]

Defense lawyer Michael Ahern, in his summation, stated that Ban Johnson had hired "Sleepy Bill" Burns and Bill Maharg to gather evidence, and that Johnson used his money to send Maharg to Mexico to find Burns. Ahern said that Maharg came into the courtroom as an auto worker, but was sporting enough diamonds on his fingers to buy a fleet of autos.

Ahern went for the knockout punch as he characterized the state's chief witness, "Sleepy Bill" Burns, as a liar. He said that Burns had said that he had talked to the players on the morning of the first game, but had not. He accused Burns of lying about meeting with Chick Gandil in Chicago after Game Two. In conclusion, Ahern compared Burns' testimony to moonshine, stating that it looks good, but when one drinks it, the result is a stomach ache.

With weak evidence presented by the prosecution against the seven White Sox players and the two gamblers, on August 2 they were all acquitted of any wrongdoing.

As a wild scene of jubilation erupted in the courtroom, Arnold "Chick" Gandil bellowed his immortal epithet at the top of his lung capacity: "Boys, I want to give you a sailor's farewell. Goodbye; good luck; and to hell with Ban Johnson."[5] The exonerated players, their attorneys and members of the jury retreated to an Italian restaurant and made merry long into the night.

Immediately following the not guilty verdict, rumors began to circulate that Arnold Rothstein, who had been exonerated by the grand jury, had paid a former Illinois attorney general $10,000 to steal the incriminating documents. But four years later the documents would be discovered in the files of White Sox owner Charles A. Comiskey,

4. Replacing a Legend

and he would be forever suspected of a cover-up of the conspiracy to fix the 1919 World Series.

About the same time that the indictments had been handed down against the White Sox players, the old governing body of major league baseball, the three-man National Commission, which consisted of American League president Ban Johnson, National League president John Heydler, and chairman August "Garry" Herrmann, president of the Cincinnati Reds, was scrapped and replaced by a commissioner who was given sweeping autocratic powers by the major league team owners. On November 20, 1920, Judge Kenesaw Mountain Landis, a jurist with a friendly reputation towards organized ball and a long-time fan, was appointed the first commissioner of major league baseball.

Judge Landis was greatly disturbed by the alleged fix in the 1919 World Series and was concerned about the integrity of the game. On August 4, 1921, two days after the not-guilty verdicts had been delivered for the seven White Sox players, Judge Landis exercised his power as commissioner and issued a lifetime ban from organized ball for all seven players who had gone to trail and unindicted alleged conspirator Fred McMullin.

In the case of Fred McMullin, his part in the fix had been incidental. He had actually forced himself upon the conspirators when he happened to eavesdrop on a locker-room conversation between Chick Gandil and Swede Risberg about the possibility of fixing the Series and demanded to become part of the plot. His actual participation on the playing field was minimal as his total playing time amounted to two pinch-hitting appearances in which he got one hit.

So if was official—the brilliant 13-year career of Shoeless Joe Jackson, a player who had hit .408 in his first full season in the major leagues with Cleveland in 1910, was over. Bibb Falk was now the White Sox left fielder and would play in Jackson's shadow for years to come.

Following his ban from organized ball, Joe Jackson returned to his native Greenville, South Carolina, and continued to play ball at the semi-pro level. Playing in the semi-pro Million Dollar League at Waycross, Georgia, Jackson hit .535 in 100 games. In 1933 he played for the Wentz-Only team of Philadelphia.

In 1934 Joe Jackson applied for reinstatement to organized ball. The people in Greenville, South Carolina, wanted to start up a minor league team and wanted Jackson to manage the club. In his petition to the commissioner, Jackson wrote, "The people of my town are trying to put professional baseball back and they want me to manage the club. At my age of 45 years I do not think I can play big league baseball, but I think I could do a lot for minor league ball."[6]

In denying Jackson's petition for reinstatement, Judge Landis pounced on the implication that Jackson felt that there was a different standard applied to the minor leagues as opposed to the major leagues. Landis stated, "The game played in a small town in a Class D league is no less important to the spectators and players than is the game played in the large city in the highest class league."[7]

In 1924, Joe Jackson sued Charles Comiskey for his back pay due on a three-year contract he had signed in February 1920. A jury held that since Jackson had not been convicted of conspiring to throw the 1919 World Series, he was entitled to his back pay and awarded him $16,700. When Jackson's attorney demanded $119,000 in punitive damages from Comiskey, his case fell apart when suddenly Jackson's long-lost confession surfaced. It was a total mystery how these documents had surfaced after being presumed missing since 1920.

Jackson eventually operated a barbeque stand, a dry cleaning business and a liquor store, all in Greenville, and at one point went broke, even though his capable wife Kate handled his financial affairs.

While Jackson had admitted that he accepted $5,000 in bribe money from his roommate Lefty Williams, he would forever maintain that he had played his best in the 1919 World Series, hitting .375. He stated that the only thing he was guilty of was being Lefty Williams' roommate.

The *Reach 1920 Official Guide* attempted to blame the White Sox's 5–0 loss in Game Five in the 1919 World Series on Jackson. The publication made an unsubstantiated accusation that Jackson was daydreaming when Reds pitcher Hod Eller hit a fly in his direction that began a four-run rally in the sixth inning.

However, the documented facts show a much different scenario that suggests Swede Risberg's play was the reason for the Reds' rally. It was well known by scouts and in game summaries that Eller hit the ball to left often. Coming down the pennant stretch, Eller had even hit a three-run home run far up into the left field stands at the Polo Grounds.

What actually happened was that with Hod Eller leading off the sixth inning, White Sox manager Kid Gleason waved center fielder Happy Felsch over towards right field. Then Eller hit the ball into left-

4. Replacing a Legend

center, between Felsch and Jackson. Felsch chased the ball down as it rolled toward the wall, then made a high throw to Swede Risberg, who deflected the ball. It rolled away, allowing Eller to reach third base. Eller was credited with a double and took third on the throw, with an error charged to Felsch. In regard to the play, sportswriter Grantland Rice wrote, "Had Risberg not deflected the throw and left the play alone the ball would have traveled directly to Buck Weaver waiting on the bag."[8] As it turned out, the next Reds batter was Morrie Rath, who really shook things up hitting a single to right, scoring Eller, and then the floodgates opened with the Reds scoring three more times. But the fact is that the play of Joe Jackson had little or nothing to do with creating the Reds rally.

Jackson's struggling legacy will eternally be in a tug-of-war between brilliance and improbity. In an interview with reporters in New York at the McAlpin Hotel in 1940, Ty Cobb named both Shoeless Joe Jackson and Buck Weaver to his all-time baseball team, along with such greats as Babe Ruth, Eddie Collins, Honus Wagner, Tris Speaker, Lou Gehrig, Mickey Cochrane, Walter Johnson, Grover Cleveland Alexander, Ed Walsh and Christy Mathewson.

In February 1951, the South Carolina Senate and House of Representatives drafted a resolution on Jackson's behalf, attempting to clear his name. That same year, Jackson was invited to make a television appearance on Ed Sullivan's "Toast of the Town" program in December. Sullivan was going to provide a forum for Jackson to tell his side of the story in regard to the 1919 Series scandal before a national audience. But ten days before his scheduled appearance on the show, Joe Jackson suffered a massive heart attack. He died on December 5, 1951.

All of the other seven White Sox players banned for life from organized ball faced their exiles in scenarios similar to Joe Jackson.

Eddie Cicotte, in an effort to protect his family, took an assumed name. At first he played some outlaw ball with some of his banned White Sox teammates. Then he went back to his native Detroit and went to work for the Ford Motor Company, retiring in 1944. He raised strawberries on a farm near Farmington, Michigan, while answering letters sent to him by baseball fans around the country wanting to know if he actually threw the Series. Cicotte passed away at the age of 85 on May 5, 1969.

In a bit of irony, Morrie Rath, the Cincinnati Reds second baseman and leadoff hitter in the 1919 World Series whom Eddie Cicotte hit with his second pitch that supposedly was the signal to the gamblers that the fix was in, committed suicide in his Philadelphia home in 1945. He was 58 years old.

Claude "Lefty" Williams, following his ban from organized baseball, played with some of the other banned players in the Frontier League in Douglas, Arizona. For a time, he operated a pool room in Chicago. Eventually he moved to California and started a nursery business in Laguna. Williams passed away on November 4, 1959. He had remained silent about the scandal, refusing to talk about it until the day he died.

Arnold "Chick" Gandil, later reported to have received as much as $35,000 in the alleged World Series conspiracy, remained in California. For a while he played in the Frontier League with Lefty Williams. Then he became a plumber, working in the San Francisco Bay Area for 14 years before retiring in 1952. Later, noted criminal attorney Melvin Belli was contacted in regard to representing Gandil in a suit to clear his name with organized ball. But the matter never seriously moved forward. Gandil died of complications from emphysema and heart disease in Calistoga, California, on December 13, 1970.

Oscar "Happy" Felsch continued to play amateur ball and in 1925 played on a team with Swede Risberg in Scobey, Montana, where he made $600 a month. Felsch raised six children in his hometown of Milwaukee while working as a crane operator and grocer, and later running a tavern. Flesch died in Milwaukee on August 17, 1964.

Fred McMullin moved to Los Angeles and became a carpenter. After a while he became the traffic manager with the Thomas Haverty Company. In 1941, he entered law enforcement as a Los Angeles County Deputy Marshall. His duties included acting as a bailiff in municipal court and serving arrest warrants. He died in Los Angeles on November 21, 1952.

Charles "Swede" Risberg settled in Minnesota and became a dairy farmer. However, after he lost his house, his automobile agency and the dairy farm in the stock market crash of 1929, he signed to play for the Sioux Falls, South Dakota, Canaries of the Northern League. Later he went back to his native northern California and operated a tavern. However, he continued to be problematic for Judge Landis and major league baseball.

In 1927, Risberg made accusations that at the end of the 1917 season the White Sox had bought a four-game series with the Detroit Tigers

Oscar "Happy" Felsch (Sports Story Reprints).

to ensure they won the American League pennant. Judge Landis investigated the matter, even summoning the entire 1917 rosters of players of both teams to his office. However, the charges could not be substantiated and the matter was dropped.

In the early 1930s, Risberg sought reinstatement to organized ball in order to accept a coaching job with a team in the American Association, but was turned down by Judge Landis. When Risberg died a bitter man on his 81st birthday on October 13, 1975, he was the last survivor of the eight banished White Sox.

One of Risberg's four children, Robert Risberg, claims that for a while his father played in the Negro Leagues, disguising his identity by applying shoe polish to his face and hands.

George "Buck" Weaver continued to play semi-pro ball and fight for a reversal of his banishment by Judge Landis. When the Masonic Lodge in Chicago presented a petition on Weaver's behalf with 20,000 signatures to Landis, he turned the other way. Even teammate Eddie Collins' signature was on the petition. Weaver, still fighting to distance himself from the scandal, died on January 31, 1956, in Chicago.

On November 23, 2005, then U.S. Senator Barack Obama of Illinois, along with fellow Democratic Party senior Senator from Illinois Dick Durbin, sent a letter to Commissioner of Baseball Bud Selig requesting that Buck Weaver be posthumously reinstated into baseball. The letter stated in part, "I respectfully request that your office conduct a posthumous investigation and hearing of the claims of Mr. Weaver's family and those interested Chicagoans and others who believe that this honorable man was treated unjustly."[9]

Actually the popular refrain "eight men out" is not accurate. There were nine players banished by Judge Landis. Joe Gedeon was also banned for life by Landis based on "guilt by association." As a friend of Swede Risberg, he was alleged to have had knowledge of the conspiracy and didn't report it.

Following his banishment from baseball, Joe Gedeon went back to his native California and dropped out of sight. In 1924, he was arrested in Sacramento on violating the Prohibition laws. In 1933, he was arrested in Seattle with $400 in counterfeit bills in his possession. A heavy drinker, Gedeon died of complications from cirrhosis of the liver and bronchial pneumonia on May 18, 1941, at the age of 47.

In 1939, Gedeon's nephew Elmer Gedeon would play in five games for the Washington Nationals. Inducted into the Army Air Corps in January 1941, almost a year before the Japanese attack on Pearl Harbor, Elmer was commissioned a lieutenant, later promoted to captain; he would die in combat when his plane was shot down over France in 1944. He would be one of only two men who played major league baseball to die in combat during World War II.

4. Replacing a Legend

Rube Benton, the man who had opened the whole can of worms about the alleged fix of the 1919 World Series with his testimony before the grand jury in 1920, despite the fact that he had direct first-hand knowledge of the fix was spared by Judge Landis and continued to pitch in the major leagues through 1925.

As for Arnold Rothstein, AKA "A. R., last of the gentleman racketeers," the alleged mastermind and financier of the conspiracy in the 1919 World Series, he died with a bullet in his stomach on the morning of November 7, 1928, at New York's Stuyvesant Polyclinic Hospital.

Rothstein died without revealing who had shot him. It was not known if Rothstein had been shot by a hired hit man from Chicago or a hot-headed creditor. All that was known was that Rothstein and five big-time gamblers had been in a card game several weeks before in September.

Jimmy Meehan was a gangster with both New York and Chicago ties. Meehan had met a trio of California gamblers and invited them to New York. One of them was "Nigger Nate" Raymond. When Raymond came to New York, Meehan introduced him to Rothstein, telling Rothstein, "Here's a good kid, good pay, and a hot sport. Take him and his crowd on in your game. I'm backing them with my word and my cash."[10]

It is theorized that Rothstein welshed on a bet and was shot. An autopsy performed at Bellevue Hospital suggested that he was shot under the table as the bullet ranged upward from the point it entered the body in the groin. Rothstein is thought to have lost $340,000 to Raymond playing a card game called "high spade." Early in the evening Raymond had lost $19,219 playing the same game and he didn't even get that back before the game changed from cash to chips. That money went to some of the small winners. Also in the game were George "Humpy" McManus who lost $51,000, along with Myer Boston from St. Louis and Clarence "Titanic" Thompson, both of whom broke about even.

When the game ended, all Raymond got was a verbal promise from Rothstein to pay him the $340,000 he had lost to him. However, Rothstein believed that he was cheated in the game and withheld payment.

For a few days following the game, Raymond appealed to Rothstein to pay up. On November 4, a creditor's meeting with Rothstein, Jimmy Meehan and others who had played in the game was held at the Park Central Hotel. Rothstein still withheld payment. Rothstein told them about his belief that he had been cheated and said he would pay up

Bibb Falk

after he won bets on the coming presidential and New York gubernatorial elections, in which he believed that he would win several hundred thousand dollars. It is believed that Rothstein was shot at the follow-up meeting. He staggered out of the side entrance of the Park Central Hotel before being taken to the hospital where he died three days later.

Complicating the matter was that police were aware of a visit to New York, at about the same time as Rothstein was shot, by a Chicago racketeer identified only as Al Capone's brother. The NYPD said that fit with stories of a Chicago mob being called in to collect from Rothstein. Furthermore, with Rothstein being branded a welsher, the gambling community in New York quickly forgot the matter, complicating the investigation.

Police found a coat in the hotel room where the meeting had been held with George "Humpy" McManus' name it. McManus was charged with the murder of Rothstein and brought to trial. But when a chambermaid recanted her story about seeing him at the hotel, the case fell apart and McManus was not convicted.

Left in disarray by the loss of Joe Jackson and the seven other banned players, the Chicago White Sox would finish the 1921 season in seventh place with a record of 62–92, 36½ games behind the pennant-winning New York Yankees.

Bibb Falk accomplished what he set out to do in the 1921 season, establishing himself as a big league player. He played in 152 games and finished with 82 RBI, 167 hits and a batting average of .285.

Despite a losing record, there was a consolation in the 1921 season for the Chicago White Sox as they shut the door on any hopes that the Cleveland Indians had of repeating as American League champions. The Indians arrived in Chicago on September 29 for the final four games of the 1921 season trailing the league-leading New York Yankees by 1½ games. The White Sox dashed the hopes of the Indians by winning three out of the four games.

Despite the fact that Bibb Falk had played in more games (149) in the outfield than any other player on the White Sox roster (Amos Strunk played 111, Harry Hooper 108, and Johnny Mostil 91) over the course of the 1921 season, he was not in the starting lineup the final four games, only being used to pinch-hit twice and as a late-inning replacement in left field in the game of October 1 in which the White Sox defeated the Indians, 8–5.

4. Replacing a Legend

Meanwhile, the New York Yankees swept a four-game series from the Philadelphia Athletics to win the pennant by 4½ games over the Cleveland Indians to set-up the first-ever "subway series" against the New York Giants and the first inter-city World Series since 1906, when the Chicago White Sox defeated the Chicago Cubs.

The Yankees' Babe Ruth, hitting .378 with 59 home runs in the 1921 season, had captured the imagination of the nation, and the scandal of the 1919 World Series was quickly fading in the memories of most baseball fans outside of Chicago. Furthermore, most fans in Cincinnati were convinced that the Reds had simply been a better team than the White Sox and won the Series fair and square—a debate that lives on today.

5

Touring the Orient

As a result of the Black Sox scandal, most of those writers and historians who chronicle baseball history have treated the 15 seasons following the scandal as if the Chicago White Sox had fallen into a black hole. While it is a fact that after the 1920 season the White Sox would not finish higher than fifth place in the standings until 1936, there was hardly a string of silent springs on the south side of Chicago. With the coming of every April following the 1920 season there was the same eager anticipation and excitement of the White Sox fans in regard to the coming pennant race as could be found in any other ballpark in any other city in the major leagues.

The 1922 season was no exception as 602,860 fans went through the turnstiles of Comiskey Park to root for their White Sox. That year on the north side of Chicago, only 542,283 fans showed up for Cubs games. In the wake of the scandal, the White Sox were still the hot ticket in Chicago baseball and had outdrawn the Cubs every season since 1919.

The 1922 White Sox fielded a mature team with an average age of 29.2. The starting lineup included catcher Ray Schalk (29), first baseman Earl Sheely (29), second baseman Eddie Collins (35), shortstop Ernie Johnson (34), third baseman Eddie Mulligan (27), right fielder Harry Hooper (34), centerfielder Johnny Mostil (26) and left fielder Bibb Falk (23), the youngest of the starting eight.

The opening game at Comiskey Park in the 1922 season was played on April 12 with the White Sox losing to the St. Louis Browns, 3–2. Red Faber started for the White Sox against the Browns' Urban Shocker.

A little over two weeks later, on April 30, White Sox rookie pitcher

5. Touring the Orient

Charlie Robertson pitched a perfect game, defeating Ty Cobb and the Tigers. The game was witnessed by 25,000 fans at Navin Field in Detroit. In was the first perfect game pitched in the major leagues since October 2, 1908, when Addie Joss of the Cleveland Indians blanked the White Sox, 1–0. Bibb Falk did not play in the game as Johnny Mostil patrolled left field. There was an overflow crowd in the ballpark and fans were permitted on the field, separated by mounted police. The only ball hit hard in the game was caught on the fly by Mostil, fighting off both fans and mounted police.

Charlie Robertson (Sports Story Reprints).

About a month later, on May 27 at Comiskey Park, the White Sox were nearly on the receiving end of a perfect game pitched by Urban Shocker. Bibb Falk's single with one out in the bottom of the eighth inning broke up Shocker's bid for a perfect game. Ray Schalk followed with a double to tie the game. Ultimately the White Sox would score an unearned run in the tenth inning to win 2–1 on a RBI by Falk.

The rebuilding White Sox were marginally competitive most of the 1922 season and occupied third place until August 2. After being three games over .500 with three games left in the season, they finished in fifth place with a record of 77–77, 17 games behind the pennant-winning New York Yankees.

Part of the problem with the White Sox was that they seemed incapable of winning on the road. At home they finished with a record of 43–34, but on the road they were 34–43. Just a couple more victories on the road would have resulted with the White Sox finishing in third place.

While the 1922 White Sox featured four players who hit above

Bibb Falk

.300 for the season, Bibb Falk batted .298, hitting a career-high 12 home runs, tops on the club, and driving in 79 runs, third highest on the team, while playing in 131 games. On the mound, Red Faber finished the season with a record of 21–17.

Perhaps the White Sox may have finished higher in the standings if Charles Comiskey had not stubbornly refused to give left-hander Dickie Kerr a three-year contract, thereby prompting him to sit out the season. In 1921, Kerr had finished with a record of 19–17.

Still it could not be denied that the White Sox starting lineup had been decimated by the Black Sox scandal. Comiskey was spending lavishly for young players, attempting to build the team for the future. Despite the loss of Shoeless Joe Jackson and Happy Felsch, the outfield replacements of Harry Hooper, Johnny Mostil and Bibb Falk were doing a creditable job. But the infield needed considerable attention.

On May 29, 1922, Charles Comiskey acquired third baseman Willie Kamm from the San Francisco Seals for $100,000, infielder Douglas McWeeney and two players to be named later, pitcher Shovel Hodge and third baseman Eddie Mulligan. The purchase price for Kamm was at that time the largest amount ever paid for a minor league player and was surpassed in organized ball only by the $125,000 that Jacob Ruppert of the New York Yankees paid to Harry Frazee of the Boston Red Sox in 1920 for Babe Ruth.

Willie Kamm was 22 years old and hands down the best fielding third baseman in the Pacific Coast League. While he was a very capable player, Kamm had a lot of insecurities and was terrified of playing in the major leagues. So an agreement was made in the deal to allow Kamm to finish the season with the Seals and report to the White Sox in the spring of 1923 so he could transition into major league baseball more at ease.

Willie Kamm stated that he found out about being traded to the White Sox from newsboys in San Francisco. In June of 1922, Kamm experienced a bad charley horse and the Seals left him at home to rest when they traveled to Los Angeles. One evening he didn't have anything to do so he decided to take a walk and get some fresh air. Kamm said, "I was walking up Market Street, at Powell, when suddenly I hear the newsboys yelling, 'Willie Kamm sold to White Sox for a hundred thousand dollars!'" So he stopped, walked over to get one of the papers, and one of the newsboys recognized him. Kamm didn't know what to do and he panicked. "Completely. I started running as fast as I could go

5. Touring the Orient

up Market Street, charley horse and all, with that pack of newsboys at my heels. 'Hey it's Willie Kamm.'" He finally ducked into a movie theatre and began to ponder the circumstances, telling himself over and over, "It can't be true. I'm not that good. But suppose it is true. It must be.... I won't go, I'm no Big League player."[1]

Willie Kamm did report to the White Sox the following spring and proceeded to have an outstanding 13-year major league career with the White Sox and Indians.

Judge Landis had suspended Babe Ruth and two other New York Yankees for the first 39 days of 1922 season for violating Major League Baseball's ban on barnstorming following the World Series. The suspension of Ruth was met with strong protest by major league owners and fans alike.

Following the 1922 season, Judge Landis decided to loosen up on the anti-barnstorming edict. The new rules permitted barnstorming as long as no more than three players from one club were on the same team. To that end, Herb Hunter, who had played in the major leagues sporadically between 1916–1921 with the Giants, Cubs, Red Sox and Cardinals, and had done some coaching in Japan, decided to organize a tour of the Orient. Judge Landis gave his approval for the tour to be organized. The tour was to play games in Japan, Korea, China, Hawaii and the Philippines.

In addition to being the tour organizer, Hunter would also play second base. In order to show the people of the Orient the best quality of American baseball, the players going on the tour had to be of All-Star caliber and had to pass the scrutiny of Judge Landis in regard to their moral fitness. Free-spirited Babe Ruth was conspicuous by his absence on the list of players asked to participate.

Chosen to represent the Chicago White Sox on the tour were Bibb Falk and Amos Strunk. They would be joined by Waite Hoyt, Fred Hofmann and Leslie "Bullet Joe" Bush of the Yankees, Herb Pennock of the Red Sox, Bert Griffith of the Brooklyn Robins, George Kelly, Emil "Irish" Meusel and Casey Stengel of the Giants, Luke Sewell and Riggs Stephenson of the Indians, and others, 23 players in all. All the players' wives were also invited. Herb Pennock even brought his daughter along. Bibb Falk and Casey Stengel were bachelors, so they traveled alone. Also joining the tour were Dr. John Lavin, the St. Louis Cardinals' team trainer, and Frank "Buck" O'Neil, a correspondent for the *New York*

Sun. O'Neil was charged with keeping score and writing stories about the tour.

Baseball commissioner Judge Landis warned the players to behave well on the junket and assigned umpire George Moriarty, a rather pious man, to go along, umpire the games and send reports back to his office on the tour's activities. Moriarty also took along his 15-year-old son to act as the bat boy.

Some of the owners, including Charles Comiskey, fearing injuries, decided to withhold contract negotiations with the players on tour until spring training in 1923. Comiskey's concerns were hypocritical considering that following the 1913 World Series he, along with John McGraw and several Giants players, had made a world tour that included several of his White Sox players and his top minor league pitching prospect, Red Faber. Both Comiskey and McGraw had profited handsomely from the tour.

Before embarking on the tour from Vancouver, B.C., on October

Casey Stengel (center), New York Giants.

5. Touring the Orient

19, 1922, several of the players made a promotional appearance at a new Spalding's sporting goods store in that city. Later in the day the tour entourage left Vancouver aboard the *R.M.S. Empress of Canada* en route to Yokohama, where they would continue on to Tokyo.

For 14 years in the big leagues, Casey Stengel would achieve a lifetime batting average of .284. But in the fall classic Stengel would swing a big stick, compiling a lifetime World Series batting average of .393 while playing in three World Series. In the 1916 World Series, Stengel played for Brooklyn against the Boston Red Sox. Although the Robins lost the series four games to one, Stengel hit .364. In the 1922 World Series, the New York Giants swept the New York Yankees. As the Giants' fourth outfielder and playing part-time, Casey Stengel hit a robust .400 in the Series. The following year, in the 1923 World Series, the Giants fell to the Yankees, four games to two. Stengel, then 33 years old, hit .417 with two home runs for the Giants.

Bibb Falk's most enduring memory of the trip across the Pacific to Japan was that of Casey Stengel doing daily battle with the rough seas to avoid seasickness. According to Falk, someone had told Stengel that the best way to battle seasickness was to keep walking. So each morning, as several members of the tour lay groaning in their cabins, Stengel would bound up on deck and begin walking, while pounding his chest, waving his fist and challenging the Pacific Ocean. As he walked around the deck, Stengel would yell at the Ocean, "Rare up, Mr. Pacific. Give us some action. I thought you wuz tough."[2]

As the only bachelors on the tour, Falk and Stengel would become buddies and seek recreational activity together, going out at night in Tokyo. "He liked to cabaret it," recalled Falk. "He was one of those champagne guys, and he would go dancing on the roof gardens until dawn. He used to say, 'Hell, ordinary champagne isn't good enough for Casey. I've got to have the best.' He was a free spender."[3]

The American team won every game on the tour but one. That was a 9–3 loss to the Mita Club on November 19. The loss infuriated Judge Landis, as he was suspicious that the Americans had thrown the game to promote future tours.

Waite Hoyt pitched a no-hitter in one game, but he was also the losing pitcher in the team's only loss. In a game played in Seoul, Korea, to entertain the students of the University of Seoul, the Americans won, 21–3. However, the game was played in temperatures as low as two below zero. In fact, when the tour reached Manchuria in January, it was so cold that Bibb Falk purchased ear muffs. When he stepped into the batter's box wearing them, umpire George Moriarty, by now fed up with Casey Stengel's antics, asked Falk when he had become a clown.

On Thanksgiving Day, November 22, the tour was enjoying an off-day in Osaka, Japan. "Bullet Joe" Bush's 30th birthday was on November 27, so some of players decided to celebrate and have a combined Thanksgiving and birthday celebration. The hotel where the tour was staying acquired a turkey from an American ship. The party was to begin at 4:00 p.m. in Waite Hoyt's room. The celebration was kept quiet so as to not alert the pious George Moriarty. Drinks were going to be served, and even though the sale and distribution of alcohol was legal in Japan, Moriarty was a flaming Prohibitionist.

As the frolicking commenced, suddenly there was a loud knock on the door and outside a booming voice proclaimed, "Let me in—stop that, I say."[4] The door was opened and there stood Moriarty with his hands on his hips. A bitter exchange ensued with pushing and shoving, and several of those celebrating, including Hoyt and Joe Bush, challenged Moriarty to fight. This may have not been the wisest thing to do. George Moriarty was no pushover. In 1919, following a game in Boston, he had fisticuffs with both Ty Cobb and Harry Heilmann under the grandstand and held his own with both combatants.

After the occupants of the room had finally shoved Moriarty back in the hall and closed the door, it was noticed that newspaper correspondent Frank "Buck" O'Neil had been hiding behind a door so Moriarty could not see him. Joe Bush became so inflamed by O'Neil's fear of Moriarty that he broke a cane over his head. O'Neil promptly left the gathering and the party resumed with all the celebrants signing *The Star-Spangled Banner.*

On the way home, the tour stopped in Manila for a game and played a final game in Honolulu. After barnstorming for three and a half months, the tour arrived back in San Francisco on January 30, 1923.

6

Bibb Falk Establishes Himself as a Big Leaguer

Bibb Falk returned from the tour of the Orient unscathed, and Charles Comiskey signed him for the coming 1923 season to a contract calling for $4,800. That was after Comiskey offered to trade him to the New York Yankees.

For several weeks following the 1922 season, Charles Comiskey had been pursuing Yankees outfielder Bob Meusel. Comiskey was even willing to part with Eddie Collins and Amos Strunk in exchange for Meusel and one of the Yankees' pitchers, namely Waite Hoyt or Sam Jones. The Yankees wanted Collins but rather than part with Hoyt, they offered pitcher Carl Mays, who they considered incorrigible, along with Meusel and infielder Aaron Ward. Comiskey was willing to buy Mays from the Yankees, but the pitcher he wanted in the trade was Hoyt. The deal fell apart when Charles Comiskey and Kid Gleason reconsidered trading Collins.

In early December, with the annual baseball meeting scheduled to begin in New York, the trade talk began again. This time the White Sox were reported to be offering Collins along with Bibb Falk and pitcher Charlie Robertson, who had pitched a perfect game for the White Sox against Detroit the previous season, for Meusel, Hoyt and Ward.

Nothing was accomplished in New York but the trade talks continued hot and cold into February, when Yankees co-owners Col. Jacob Ruppert and Col. Tillinghast Huston, who had given the deal due consideration, decided to put the kibosh on it. Ruppert told the press, "Two weeks ago when I was in Chicago, the White Sox management

Bibb Falk

was willing to give us Collins and Falk and another player. They demanded in return, however, a man we felt we could not afford to let go. We are willing to do business on a reasonable basis, but will not kill our chances for the pennant just to get one man."[1]

Looking at the unfinished deal from a historical perspective, Col. Ruppert and Col. Huston exercised some incredibly bad judgment in not becoming the benefactor of Charles Comiskey's generosity. Comparing Bibb Falk and Bob Meusel, Falk would achieve a lifetime batting average of .314 for 12 years as opposed to Meusel's .309 for 11 years.

Acquiring Eddie Collins would have put a future Hall of Fame player on second base for the Yankees, replacing Aaron Ward, who would wind up his 12-year major league career in 1928 with a batting average of .268, as opposed to Collins' .333. In 1926, Aaron Ward would be replaced in the Yankees lineup by Tony Lazzeri and eventually be traded to the White Sox.

In regard to the pitcher Comiskey was seeking, the Yankees had plenty of pitching with Bob Shawkey, Herb Pennock and Bullet Joe Bush, so the loss of either Waite Hoyt or Sam Jones would have mattered little.

Nonetheless, Col. Ruppert got his pennant in 1923 with the Yankees finishing 16 games ahead of Detroit. Bob Meusel hit .313 with nine home runs and Aaron Ward hit .284. Sam Jones had a record on the mound of 21–8, and Waite Hoyt went 17–9.

The Chicago White Sox arrived at spring training at Seguin, Texas, in 1923 full of optimism about the coming season. The club featured speed on the bases and had a starting lineup filled with .300 hitters.

But the optimism of spring training would rapidly turn into a day-to-day struggle to advance in the standings. On Opening Day, April 18, 1923, at Cleveland, with 20,373 fans in attendance, the White Sox lost 6–5. A week later on April 26, in the first game of the season at Comiskey Park with 30,000 on hand, the White Sox lost to the Indians again as Stan Coveleski outdueled Red Faber, 3–0. After the first eight games of the season, the White Sox were in last place in the American League with a record of 1–7.

On the night of April 22, a pipe bomb exploded outside of Comiskey Park near the main entrance. The night watchman was thrown out of his chair by the explosion, the windows in the offices upstairs were blown out, and a portable hot dog stand at street level was blown to

6. Bibb Falk Establishes Himself as a Big Leaguer

smithereens. There were several theories as to the perpetrators. One was that it was a retaliatory strike against both the White Sox and Cubs, who were working with the Chicago Police Department to bring a halt to bookmaking in the stands. Another theory was that the bombing had been the work of organized labor agents who were disturbed by the fact that Comiskey Park had recently been painted by non-union workers. As it was with scores of other Prohibition era bombings in Chicago, no suspects were ever charged.

By June 15, the White Sox were still steeped in last place with a record of 19–27. That day in Washington, Bibb Falk hit a pinch-hit three-run home run off Walter Johnson, pitching in relief in the seventh inning. But the Nationals held on to win the game, 8–6, with Cy Warmoth getting the win.

The major league-phobic Willie Kamm made his debut playing third base for the White Sox in 1923 and quickly established himself at the hot corner as one of the best fielding third sackers in the league. Nonetheless, Kamm said that the greatest play he ever saw in his career occurred in 1923 at Yankee Stadium, and the player who made it was Bibb Falk. This was surprising because Falk had never been known for his glove. What he lacked in ability to cover the outfield he attempted to make up for with hustle and his bat.

The White Sox were on the road in New York. There were two men on base and the Yankees' Bob Meusel was at the plate. Sloppy Thurston was pitching for Chicago when Meusel hit a screaming line drive over third and down the left field line. It looked like a sure double. According to Kamm,

> "Bibb was away at the crack of the bat, and he came in fast. No one thought he could possibly get there. I don't think he thought so himself. But he kept coming. And when it seemed the ball would surely hit the ground he left his feet in an old fashioned football dive. Watching from third, it seemed to me he slid a full twenty feet and then stretched out his hand and took the ball. The stands rocked with applause as he walked to the bench. Even the Yankees rushed out their dugout to pat him on the back."[2]

Willie Kamm wasn't the only player impressed with Falk's catch. Babe Ruth stated in his autobiography that Falk's catch was one of the three greatest catches he had ever seen.

It was a case of mutual admiration between Falk and the Bambino;

Eddie Collins and William "Kid" Gleason.

although Bibb Falk played against and with some of the greatest names in the history of the game—Ty Cobb, Eddie Collins, Home Run Baker, Lou Gehrig, Harry Heilmann, Ray Schalk, Lefty Grove, Walter Johnson, Joe Cronin, Tris Speaker, George Sisler and many others—he always maintained that Babe Ruth was the best player he ever saw.

6. Bibb Falk Establishes Himself as a Big Leaguer

In the early 1920s, the New York Yankees were experiencing unparalleled success with Babe Ruth's power hitting, so they were quite concerned about his health. Yankees pitchers throwing batting practice were warned that if they hit the Babe, they're likely going to be out of here. The Yankees management was also concerned with the health of Ruth's eyes. Therefore Ruth seldom played the sun field. So when the Yankees played at Comiskey Park, Babe Ruth and Bibb Falk would be in their respective lineups playing the same position in left field. Falk would use the situation to rattle Ruth. "In those days," recalled Falk, "you left your gloves in the field when you came in. I would get his glove and stuff the fingers with a dead bird or something, and when he would pick it up, I would see him cussing me."[3]

In the spring of 1923, a publicity stunt had been arranged where a photographer brought White Sox catcher Ray Schalk from the Chicago spring training camp to a Baylor Bears practice to catch their hard-throwing 22-year-old right-hander, Ted Lyons. After Schalk caught Lyons for a brief time, he doffed his catching gear and quickly returned to the team's hotel, where he sought out manager Kid Gleason and urged him to sign Lyons. Later Lyons was to remark that he was surprised by the White Sox's interest in him. Lyons felt that the day Schalk caught him he didn't have much on the ball.

The Philadelphia Athletics had attempted to sign Ted Lyons following his first season at Baylor, when he went 10–2. Connie Mack offered Lyons a deal including a tuition-free education at Baylor. But Lyons rejected the deal, concerned that signing it might affect his amateur status.

In the 1923 collegiate season, Ted Lyons led the Baylor Bears to their first SWC baseball championship. A couple of days later, he signed a contract with the Chicago White Sox calling for a $1,000 bonus and $300 a month. Lyons went directly from the Baylor campus to the big leagues, making his debut with the White Sox on July 2 in relief against the St. Louis Browns and retiring all three batters he faced. It was the beginning of a 21-year major league career with the White Sox in which he would lead the American League in wins twice—1925 (21) and 1927 (22)—finish his career with 260 wins and 230 loses, and be elected to Hall of Fame in 1955. Ted Williams would later say that Ted Lyons was the toughest pitcher for him; he just could not figure him out.

At the time that Lyons joined the White Sox, they were moving up in the standings. After sweeping the St. Louis Browns in a July 4 doubleheader, 9–7 and 3–1, they had climbed one game above the .500 mark and found themselves occupying third place. But they didn't stay hot and after going 10–16 in August and 11–16 in September, the White Sox finished the 1923 season in seventh place with a record of 69–85.

At the age of 36, Eddie Collins hit for a .360 average and led the American League in stolen bases with 48. Bibb Falk, although he only played in 87 games due to injuries, hit .307 with five home runs. In the end, the 1923 season turned out to be a continuation of the ruination the Chicago White Sox found themselves in in the wake of the revelation of the 1919 World Series scandal. It seemed like the team had been permanently scarred by the scandal. The fact that Ray Schalk only hit .228, a dip of 53 points from his previous season's average, didn't help matters either. It was the end for Kid Gleason at the helm of the Chicago White Sox, and following the annual city series with the Cubs on October 17, he quietly resigned.

Kid Gleason had experienced serious emotional issues as a result of the 1919 scandal. For a protracted period following the 1919 World Series, he experienced difficulty eating and sleeping, and dreaded being alone. After resigning from the White Sox, Gleason would never again manage a big league club. All through the 1919 World Series, while rumors of chicanery were rampant, Gleason never gave up on his team. In the seventh game at Cincinnati, the White Sox defeated the Reds, 4–1, with Eddie Cicotte throwing a complete game. The win cut the Reds' lead in the series to four games to three. On the train headed back to Chicago for the eighth game, Gleason told reporters, "my gang played the kind of baseball it has been playing all season. Even though we are still one game behind, we will win for sure."[4] Kid Gleason died on January 2, 1933, in Philadelphia, still feeling remorse for his club's involvement in the 1919 scandal.

There was wide speculation on who would replace Gleason at the White Sox helm—Eddie Collins, Ray Schalk, or Yankees coach Charley O'Leary. The answer to the question came during the winter meetings in Chicago when Charles Comiskey hired Frank Chance, who had just been let go by the Boston Red Sox after they finished in last place in the 1923 season. But during the winter of 1923–1924, Chance contracted pneumonia and as spring training approached he was still in a very weak state and convalescing in Hot Springs, Arkansas, so he wired Comiskey and offered to resign.

6. Bibb Falk Establishes Himself as a Big Leaguer

Comiskey wanted Chance for his manager and told him to take whatever amount of time was necessary to recover. Meanwhile, as spring training began, the White Sox were being managed by a committee of coaches that included Eddie Collins, Ed Walsh and Frank Chance's old Cubs teammate, Johnny Evers.

Frank Chance attempted to rally, but his condition simply would not stabilize. In a weakened state, Chance attended an exhibition series in Chicago with the New York Giants prior to Opening Day. But the frigid climate of early spring in Chicago caused him to catch a cold, resulting in an emergency room visit. Chance never made it into the White Sox dugout during the 1924 season, and on September 14 he died in Los Angeles at the age of 47.

While Charles Comiskey held out hope for the eventual arrival of Frank Chance, he appointed Johnny Evers to be interim manager of the club. But the situation in 1924 kept deteriorating when on May 14 Evers was admitted to Mercy Hospital for an emergency appendectomy. While he recovered, Evers appointed Ed Walsh to be interim manager. But Walsh seemed to have no managerial ability whatsoever and after two games he was replaced by Eddie Collins.

After the team incurred several injuries combined with the lack of useful direction as a result of the musical chairs manager system, in August the White Sox went on a 13-game losing streak—the longest in club history. The White Sox finished the season in last place with a record of 66–87, 25 1/2 games behind the pennant-winning Washington Senators. It was the first time in Chicago White Sox franchise history that they had finished in last place.

But the 1924 Chicago White Sox were a better team than their record showed. At the plate they were a force to be reckoned with, finishing with a team batting average of .289. The powerful second-place New York Yankees hit .291.

On July 12, 1924, after getting 14 hits in his last eight games, Bibb Falk was leading the American League in hitting with a robust .373 average, tied with the Yankees Babe Ruth. Falk finished the season with a .352 batting average, good enough for third place in the American League behind the league-leading Ruth's .378 and the Indians' Charlie Jamieson's .359. Falk also had 99 RBI. However, what has become lost because of Falk's remarkable achievements at the plate in the 1924 season is the fact that he had 26 assists from left field to lead the league.

Bibb Falk

Also in 1924, Eddie Collins finished right behind Falk, hitting .349, fourth in the league. Harry Hooper hit .328, Johnny Mostil .325 and Earl Sheely .320. Although five regulars hit over .300 (same as third-place Detroit) it was not enough to pull the White Sox out of the American League cellar.

The problem was that the White Sox pitching staff that included Sloppy Thurston, a 20-game winner (20–14), young Ted Lyons (12–11) and veteran Red Faber (9–11), allowed a lot of runs. The staff ERA of 4.74 was the highest in the American League.

The White Sox were also careless in the field, compiling a team fielding average of .963, lowest in the league, while committing the most errors, 230.

Bibb Falk reasoned that as he had finished third in the American League batting race, he deserved a raise. So he wrote a letter to Charles Comiskey and forthrightly requested one. But Comiskey turned Falk down, telling him in a return letter that "they'd never heard of a player giving them a refund after he had a bad year."[5]

Falk was always of the opinion that the letter he supposedly received from Comiskey had been written by Harry Grabiner, who signed The Old Roman's signature. According to Falk, the players never saw Charles Comiskey that much. Following the Black Sox scandal, Comiskey began spending considerably more time at his retreat in Wisconsin while Grabiner virtually ran the team.

7

Another Post-Season Tour

In the fall and winter of 1913–1914, Charles Comiskey and John McGraw had made a highly publicized and successful world tour with their teams playing games in Asia, the Middle East and Europe. Eleven years later, with that tour buried in an avalanche of history that included the rise and fall of the Federal League, World War I, the Black Sox scandal, the heroics of Babe Ruth and the onset of national Prohibition, the "Old Roman" and "Little Napoleon" decided to put together another excursion following the 1924 World Series. The destination for the six-week exhibition series would be Europe.

The junket was publicized as a good will tour to develop interest in baseball in Europe. *Time Magazine* designated the White Sox and Giants as missionaries, stating, "Instead of Bibles and hymn-books, these missionaries will carry with them balls, bats, and mitts. Instead of love and light, these missionaries will shed baseball fanaticism all over Europe."[1]

Over the years, some historians have become skeptical of Charles Comiskey's motivation for the European tour as being more about cronyism and entertainment than foreign marketing of the national game. For many years during the off-season, Charles Comiskey had invited many of his favorite players, managers and sportswriters to his lodge in Wisconsin for bouts of hunting, fishing and frolicking in the woods. Participants were known as the Woodland Bards. Some have suggested that the 1924 European tour was just more of the same in a foreign setting.

Once again Bibb Falk packed his suitcase. He was included on a roster of players making the trip of whom many would eventually be

Bibb Falk

enshrined in Cooperstown: Ted Lyons, Johnny Evers, Hughie Jennings, Ross Youngs, Ed Walsh, Frank Frisch and Travis Jackson. Eddie Collins had also been invited but he declined, preferring to stay home and go hunting.

Casey Stengel, now with the Boston Braves, was nearing the end of his colorful career as a player. Still, he was invited by John McGraw to join the National League champion Giants' contingent on the tour.

According to Bibb Falk, this was a much more refined Stengel than the man who had made the tour of the Orient with him in 1922. In between the tours, Van Meusel, wife of Giants outfielder Irish Meusel, had introduced Stengel to his future wife, Edna. Now married and with Edna joining him on the tour, Stengel was a changed man. Falk, who never married, stated that in his opinion, Stengel married the right type of girl. She made a great companion for him.

While Falk and Stengel would go their separate ways and become iconic baseball managers—Falk with the University of Texas Longhorns and Stengel with the New York Yankees—they would remain friends. In the 1950s, the Yankees invited White Sox old-timers to New York to play a three-inning exhibition against some old-time Yankees. Falk said, "Casey spotted me on the bench and insisted that I go over to the box seat and visit Edna."[2]

The 1924 tour began with four games in Canada, two games each in Montreal and Quebec, with a crowd of 6,500 turning out in Montreal for the first game to witness a 13–5 Giants victory. The tour arrived in England on October 22, and an exhibition game was played in Liverpool with about 2,500 spectators in attendance. Then the tour moved to London, where the modest crowds at Wembley Stadium, which included a lot of curious cricket players, were considered disappointing. Former major leaguer Hans Lobert came along on the tour as John McGraw's assistant and would be in charge of the layout of the diamond in the various stadiums and settings where the games were played.

A game in Dublin, Ireland, on October 28 drew only 20 spectators, forcing Comiskey and McGraw to cancel a scheduled second game. McGraw was at ease speaking with Irish President William Edgar Cosgrove. However, Cosgrove was more interested in talking about American industry than baseball.

The tour returned to London where on November 6, a game was played at Stanford Bridge with King George V, Queen Mary, the Prince

7. *Another Post-Season Tour*

King George V greets players at Stanford Bridge (National Baseball Hall of Fame Library, Cooperstown, New York).

of Wales, Prince Henry, the Duke of York, as well as Frank Kellogg, the American Ambassador to the Court of St. James, and George Bernard Shaw in attendance. The Duke elected to sit right behind the press benches and chat with Harry Cross and Robert Boyd, two New York baseball writers who accompanied the teams on the tour and attempted to score the game according to their instructions.

However, the big crowd of almost 20,000 was more interested in the fielding than the hitting, and they were thrilled when White Sox outfielder Johnny Mostil made a running one-hand catch in deep center.

According to Bibb Falk, it was a great experience. He stated that they lined out a baseball diamond in that big stadium and "We all lined up before the game. The King (George V) came by every guy and we were introduced. We weren't supposed to reach out our hand or anything, just bow."[3] Falk also stated that the King's son who later married the American

(Edward VIII) was right behind him, while the Queen (Mary) was up in the stands, and she waved her hand at the players.

The tour moved on to France for games in Paris and Lyon. However, attendance was so sparse, about 1,000 for each game, that following another game in Paris on November 13, Comiskey and McGraw decided to cut their losses and cancel games scheduled for Brussels, Nice, Rome and Berlin.

In the edition of November 24, 1924, *Time Magazine* reported that

> They came, they saw, they gave it up. The New York Giants and the Chicago White Sox, seeking to acquire cash and culture simultaneously by means of exhibition baseball games in Europe, disbanded in Paris. Some headed for Berlin, others for Rome, some for the Riviera, some for the battlefields. All were agreed that the trip had gone far enough. Despatches stated no causes, but probable ones were: bored spectators, slender receipts, foul weather, diverting sights, fare, people.[4]

The tour had been poorly planned, and Comiskey and McGraw picked up the tab for their fiasco. There was hardly any mention of the tour in U.S. newspapers. Still, everyone had a good time and no one complained when they all came home. Bibb Falk and the others on the tour returned to the United States on the *Leviathan*, a German steamship requisitioned by the U.S. Government at the onset of World War I.

Later John McGraw revealed that upon arriving back in New York, he had made reservations on the Twentieth Century Limited to take him to Chicago for the baseball meetings. However, he was unable to make reservations on the steamship he preferred and was forced to come home with the rest of the tour on the *Leviathan*. Consequently, McGraw missed the train, which was wrecked at Forsyth, New York, with nine people killed.

8

Traded to Cleveland

Prior to the 1925 season, Eddie Collins negotiated a contract with Charles Comiskey for $35,000 and became playing/manager of the White Sox. With Collins at the helm, the White Sox finished in fifth place with a record of 79–75. It was the club's best finish since 1922.

On June 6, Collins got his 3,000th hit when he stroked a double off of Walter Johnson in Washington. Collins was only the sixth major leaguer to have achieved 3,000 hits.

At the start of the 1925 season, Willie Kamm had been appointed to replace Eddie Collins as team captain. The job included a benefit of an additional $3,600 a year. At the White Sox's spring training camp in Louisiana, the team demonstrated superior potential as they swept a 19-game schedule playing against less skilled Class A and Class B teams.

But near the end of spring training, the White Sox suffered another tragedy when utility infielder Harvey "Little Mac" McClellan, who had been with the team since 1919 and was going to be the starting shortstop in the coming season, suffered serious stomach problems and had to be operated on for ulcers. Following the season, on November 6, McClellan died at his home in Cynthiana, Kentucky, not far from Cincinnati.

The 1925 White Sox pitching staff included Ted Lyons, Red Faber, Ted Blankenship and Sloppy Thurston. It had promised to be the best the White Sox had put together since 1920. In fact, Lyons went on to win 21 games and Blankenship 17. Lyons just missed pitching a no-hitter on September 19, when Bobby Veach of Washington looped a Texas League single over the head of Earl Sheely with two out in the bottom of the ninth inning.

Bibb Falk

The 1925 season also saw the return of Dickie Kerr with a pregame ceremony on August 15. However, Kerr's reunification with the team turned out to be unceremonious as during his four-year hiatus he had lost his effectiveness.

Kerr retired and began managing at the minor league level. In 1940, while managing the Class D Daytona Beach Islanders, one of Kerr's players would be a young 19-year-old pitcher named Stan Musial. After Musial injured his pitching arm in a freak accident, Kerr converted him to an outfielder. Musial went on to have a Hall of Fame career with the St. Louis Cardinals. Musial was ever grateful to Kerr and as a tribute named his first-born son Richard after him.

Since Bibb Falk joined the White Sox in 1920, the club management and some fans wondered if it would benefit both him and the team to return to the mound. After all, he held the Texas Longhorns record for strikeouts. On several occasions, Kid Gleason had attempted to persuade Falk to take the mound. However, Falk would not entertain the suggestion. Eddie Collins believed that Falk was a superior outfielder, but he too was curious about what he might be able to do as a pitcher. It was confusing for the fans and the parade of White Sox managers, past and present, to continue to watch Falk warm up in the bullpen before every game.

According to Falk, the reason that he threw in the bullpen before games was "to have my arm in condition to shoot them in from the outfield. I'll last a good deal longer out there than on the mound."[1]

Falk also said that in 1924, when they wanted to make a pitcher out of him, he told them, "I didn't think my arm was good enough to stand it and one day I got the two homers and single, then walked, and that convinced them I shouldn't be pitching anyway."[2]

In 1925, Early Shelly hit for a .315 average in 153 games and Eddie Collins hit .346 in 118 games. Bibb Falk had a batting average of .301 with 181 hits, and for the second consecutive season had 99 RBI.

Following the 1925 season, Comiskey released future Hall of Fame outfielder Harry Hooper, who had hit .265 playing in 127 games, when he refused to take a pay cut. But Hooper was 38 years old and his skills were declining. Refusing requests for raises was a standard operating procedure for the "Old Roman." Some of the baseball moguls and sportswriters still blamed the crooked events of the 1919 World Series on Charles Comiskey and his frugal management style—denying players

8. Traded to Cleveland

raises, promising players bonuses for winning the 1917 World Series and never paying up, and pinching pennies on team amenities, including laundering uniforms.

Still, in 1925 Bibb Falk would receive a little extra cash when he became a benefactor of some unfinished business from the 1920 season. Following the indictments of the White Sox players accused of throwing the 1919 World Series in late 1920, the American League presidents and then Judge Landis followed suit, withholding $4,800.53 in 1920 second-place money from those named players.

Happy Felsch and Joe Jackson had filed suits in Milwaukee in an attempt to receive their shares of the 1920 second-place money, and lost. So Judge Landis decided to divide up the entire sum among all the players on the 1920 White Sox roster who were not indicted, including players who had been sent to the minors or traded to other clubs.

The scandal of the 1919 World Series was still fresh in the minds of many of the baseball moguls and most prominent in the memory and personal agendas of American League president Ban Johnson and Commissioner Landis.

Prior to and during the 1925 World Series between the Washington Senators and Pittsburgh Pirates, Johnson hired a platoon-size staff of private detectives on the west coast to follow the money being bet. Millions of dollars were bet on the 1925 World Series, and Los Angeles was the clearing house for a large syndicate operating there on behalf of the Pirates. The money trail started in Los Angeles, where money would be sent to agents all over the country for bets to be placed in Chicago, Detroit, Kansas City and smaller cities such as Scranton. Most of the so-called "sucker money" was being wagered on Washington.

The Nationals lost the 1925 World Series to the Pirates, four games to three. The Pirates had come back from a three-games-to-one deficit to win the Series. They won the seventh and deciding game when Washington manager Bucky Harris allowed sentimentality to get in the way of his managerial reasoning by allowing 37-year-old Walter Johnson to be battered for 15 hits in eight rain-soaked innings in a come-from-behind 9–7 win by the Pirates.

Roger Peckinpaugh, the Senators shortstop and American League MVP, made two errors in the eighth inning of the second game, allowing the tying run to score before Kiki Cuyler hit a home run to help the Pirates achieve a 3–2 victory. Peckinpaugh became the goat of the

Bibb Falk

1925 World Series as he made a total of eight errors, a World Series record.

In the scandalized 1919 World Series, White Sox shortstop Swede Risberg had only made four errors in eight games. Many errors made by Peckinpaugh came at crucial moments. Although Peckinpaugh was distraught over his blunders, after the early games, Judge Landis, aware of the large sums of money that had been bet on the Pirates, decided it was in the best interest of the game to have Peckinpaugh shadowed by detectives of his own.

It was also in 1925 that Bibb Falk's younger brother Chester "Spot" Falk, a left-handed pitcher, was brought up by the St. Louis Browns. When 19-year-old Chet Falk was being pursued by four other teams, including the Yankees and Red Sox, older brother Bibb did the negotiations for him. At the time Chet was attending the University of Texas, and he was eventually signed by the Browns' business manager, Bill Friel.

While Browns manager George Sisler had high hopes for the young left-hander, Chet Falk never quite lived up to his promise. He would pitch in relief for the Browns from 1925–1927 and compile a career record of 5–4 in 40 appearances. Chet Falk would finish his professional career pitching for Buffalo and Montreal before arm problems caused him to quit the game. He died on January 7, 1982, at Seton Medical Center in Austin, Texas.

In the 1926 season, Eddie Collins returned as manager and the Chicago White Sox were contenders in the first half of the season. On July 7, they were in second place. However, in the end, with injuries to several key players such as Willie Kamm, Bill Barrett and Ted Blankenship, Chicago failed to finish in the first division, ending in fifth place with a record of 81–72, nine games behind the first-place Yankees.

The 1926 White Sox would finish tied for third in batting average in the American League with an average of .289, three points behind the Washington Senators, who led the league in hitting with an average of .292. On Sunday, June 20, the White Sox were in third place, 10 1/2 games behind the New York Yankees, when the two clubs squared off at Comiskey Park before a record-breaking crowd of 43,000. That day the White Sox fielded a starting lineup with the first five hitters batting above .300: Johnny Mostil .367, Bill Hunnefield .300, Eddie Collins .346, Earl Sheely .305, and Bibb Falk .359, and the sixth hitter in the order, Bill Barrett, was hitting .296. The White Sox defeated the Yan-

8. Traded to Cleveland

kees, 4–3, and Bibb Falk drove in a key run with his 25th double of the season.

On August 21, Ted Lyons pitched a no-hitter against the Boston Red Sox. While the White Sox had 13 hits and scored six runs, Bibb Falk went 0-for-3 in the game. It would be nine years (August 31, 1935) before Vern Kennedy would pitch the next White Sox no-hitter.

While Johnny Mostil finished the season with a .328 average, Bibb Falk had the finest year in his major league career, hitting .345, with 195 hits and 108 RBI. He hit 43 doubles, which equaled a club record set the previous season by Earl Sheely. The record would stand for 37 years until Floyd Robinson set a new club record in 1962 with 45 doubles.

Speaking in a recorded interview with Eugene Converse Murdock on June 3, 1974, about his equaling the doubles record in 1926, a whiff of racism was revealed in Bibb Falk's personality. Falk told Murdock he "held the White Sox record for forty years till about five years ago when some nigger playing right field hit about 46 or 48 playing in 161 games."[3] Whether or not Bibb Falk commonly used such offensive language is not known. But in his interview with Murdock, it is very apparent that his use of the derogatory term in reference to Floyd Robinson was used in full consciousness and intent.

For his first six years in the big leagues, Bibb Falk had compiled an impressive career batting average of .308. But the most the surprising result in Falk's statistics for the 1926 season was that he had made only three errors in 155 games, leading American League outfielders with a fielding average of .992. The previous season, he had made 14 errors.

In late December 1926, another 1919 baseball scandal grabbed the headlines of the newspapers. Former pitcher Dutch Leonard alleged that two of the game's biggest stars, Ty Cobb and Tris Speaker, had conspired to fix the last game of the 1919 American League season to ensure that the Detroit Tigers would receive the third-place share of the World Series money. Incriminating letters were produced that had been written between Cobb and Leonard, and Smoky Joe Wood and Leonard.

Judge Landis held a hearing on the matter. Both Cobb and Speaker came to Chicago to protest their innocence in front of Landis. Cobb stated that for 22 years he had played the game as hard and clean as any man ever had. In a move that smacks of the modern-day case involving steroid-stained slugger Alex Rodriguez, in which Major League Baseball paid his accuser, Anthony Bosch, $150,000 for incriminating evidence documenting Rodriguez's use of PEDs, Cobb pointed out that the American League had paid Dutch Leonard $20,000 for the letters.

Speaker called himself "the goat" of the game, pointing out that he was not mentioned in either of the Leonard letters, and demanded that Leonard be brought in to face him.

Dutch Leonard refused to leave his California home to attend the hearings and alleged that a threat had been made to get him after he had been waived out of the American League in 1925.

Thousands of letters poured into the commissioner's office from fans supporting both Cobb and Speaker. Cobb and Speaker maintained attorneys and threatened organized baseball with suits if their names were not cleared. U.S. Senator Hoke Smith of Georgia boldly declared that he would get justice done for both players.

American League president Ban Johnson was of the opinion that the evidence presented against Cobb and Speaker was sufficient to convict both. But Judge Landis felt that banning the two aging superstars would be a horrific blow to baseball that would reinvigorate the whole Black Sox scandal controversy, so on January 27, 1929, he cleared both players of any wrongdoing.

At the same time that the Cobb/Speaker/Leonard matter was being considered by Landis, Black Sox shortstop Swede Risberg surfaced from exile and made new disparaging allegations. This time Risberg charged that that near the end of the 1917 season, the Chicago White Sox had bought a four-game series from the Detroit Tigers to ensure that they won the American League pennant. On January 5, 1927, Judge Landis summoned the entire rosters of both teams that had played in 1917 to his office. Testimony was heard for over five hours before Landis cleared everyone of any wrongdoing.

Prior to the 1927 season, Charles Comiskey spent $600,000 to refurbish his ballpark, adding a second deck to the outfield stands and increasing the seating to 52,000. Then he fired Eddie Collins and appointed Ray Schalk to manage the White Sox.

Out as manager, released after playing for the White Sox for 12 years, and never having been fully appreciated for his loyalty to the club or contributions on the field, Eddie Collins returned to the Philadelphia Athletics, where he had attained major league fame as part of Connie Mack's "$100,000 infield," winning four pennants and three World

8. Traded to Cleveland

Series in five years prior to being sold to Charles Comiskey in late 1914 for $50,000.

With Collins released, Charles Comiskey brought Yankees second baseman Aaron Ward to Chicago in a trade for Johnny Grabowski and Ray Morehart. Then he acquired Washington shortstop Roger Peckinpaugh in a trade for Sloppy Thurston and Leo Mangum.

On March 9, spring training in Shreveport, Louisiana, was marred by an attempted suicide by center fielder Johnny Mostil, who cut himself 13 times, trying to end his life in his room at the Hotel Youree. Mostil used a razor blade to slash his throat, legs, wrist and breast.

Charles Comiskey told the press that Mostil had been in agonizing pain from a nerve disorder diagnosed as neuritis. The affliction had caused many sleepless nights for Mostil, and he wasn't able to cope with the pain any longer. After being stabilized, Mostil was sent back to Chicago for extensive rehabilitation and would play only 13 games during the season.

In an otherwise dull season, the most exciting game for the White Sox occurred on July 1 when they engaged in a slugfest with the St. Louis Browns. The Browns won the game, 14–12, getting 18 hits to the White Sox's 16. For the Browns, George Sisler and Ken Williams each had four hits. For the White Sox, Bibb Falk had three hits, including two doubles and a home run. The Browns' Ernie Nevers, pitching in relief, was credited with the win. The game, played at Sportsman's Park, was witnessed by only 500 spectators, and despite the 26 hits took only one hour and 34 minutes to play.

On August 16 at Comiskey Park, Babe Ruth was en route to his record-setting season home run total of 60 in the 1927 season. That day Ruth would baptize Charles Comiskey's new right field upper deck by blasting his 37th home run of the year over the roof. The ball came back down to earth in an adjacent soccer field some 474 feet from home plate.

In the first game of a doubleheader on August 2, Bibb Falk helped Ted Lyons gain his 17th victory of the season with two singles, a double and a home run in four at-bats as the White Sox defeated the Philadelphia A's, 7–4. But within a week, the trade winds began to blow again and the rumor was that Bibb Falk along with Willie Kamm was headed to the New York Yankees for Bob Meusel. In the end, no one changed their address.

Bibb Falk

Bibb Falk had another outstanding season in 1927, finishing with a batting average of .327, 175 hits and 83 RBI.

While Charles Comiskey had added new seats to his ballpark, he didn't add any new fans. The 1927 season attendance was 614,423, considerably less than the 710,334 that had come out to the ballpark in 1926. The White Sox, under Ray Schalk, finished in fifth place with a record of 70–83.

As a catcher, Ray Schalk had been one of the White Sox's pillars of competitiveness on their pennant-winning teams in 1917 and 1919 and the near miss in 1920, playing in 100 games or more for 11 straight years. Charles Comiskey felt an extraordinary loyalty towards him. But Schalk's managerial style in the dugout didn't emulate his feisty style of play on the field. His lack of fire from the helm was seen as weakness, and White Sox veterans such as Bibb Falk and Bill Barrett would often undermine his authority.

Going into the 1928 season, Charles Comiskey had to rebuild his middle infield again when veteran shortstop Roger Peckinpaugh retired to become manager of the Cleveland Indians and Aaron Ward was sold to Cleveland on waivers. To plug the holes in the infield, Bill Hunnefield, who had split the shortstop position with Peckinpaugh during 1927, was moved to second base and Comiskey purchased the contract of hot-shot Pacific Coast League shortstop Chalmer "Bill" Cissell for the exorbitant price of $123,000. It was just another case of Comiskey trying in vain at any cost to re-establish the White Sox as pennant contenders.

For all the ballyhoo that preceded his arrival, Bill Cissell would play 123 games at shortstop for the White Sox in 1928 and hit .260. He would remain with the White Sox until 1932 then drift around the major leagues with four other teams, with a few stints in the minors here and there, through 1938.

In early July 1928, the White Sox were floundering more than 20 games behind the New York Yankees. Following a split of a doubleheader with the St. Louis Browns on July 4, the White Sox had a record of 32–42 and Charles Comiskey quietly asked Ray Schalk to resign.

Coach Lena Blackburne was appointed manager and took over on July 6. Blackburne's managerial style was diametrically different from that of Schalk's. Blackburne was a hard-nosed manager who advocated a fast-paced hit-and-run offense and took no criticism from his players.

8. Traded to Cleveland

In fact, upon taking over, in an attempt to neutralize potential internal critics such as Bibb Falk and other veterans, he immediately announced a policy of a $50 fine to anyone who sassed him. Quickly the White Sox began to gain some modest ground under his authoritarian leadership style.

Playing against the New York Yankees on July 18, Bibb Falk hit a three-run home run off Waite Hoyt in in the eighth inning to tie the game. But the Yankees won in the ninth inning, 9–8, on Babe Ruth's 36th home run of the season, coming off Ted Lyons with two on and two out.

Under Lena Blackburne, the White Sox would once again finish in fifth place in 1928 with a record of 72–82, 29 games behind the New York Yankees. But there was little that Blackburne could have done to change the outcome of the 1928 American League pennant race, which was a shootout between the Yankees and the Philadelphia Athletics. Every other team in the league was an also-ran; even the third-place St. Louis Browns finished 19 games off the pace.

For all intents and purposes the 1928 American League pennant race was decided on Sunday, September 9, with the largest crowd in major league history at that point in time on hand, 85,264 in New York. The first-place Athletics, led by Al Simmons and Lefty Grove, came to the Bronx to meet the Yankees, led by Babe Ruth and Lou Gehrig. The Yankees swept the doubleheader to reclaim first place and win the pennant by 2 1/2 games.

It was during the 1928 season that the White Sox brought up a young, free-spirited, flamboyant first baseman by the name of Art Shires who billed himself as "Art the Great." For Bibb Falk, Shires would take the cake as the most colorful and unusual teammate he would ever have at any level.

Art Shires had a wardrobe that included 50 suits, 100 hats, 40 pairs of spats, 300 neckties, 20 canes and a half-dozen tuxedos. He even had yachting attire. If any two cities in America epitomized the "Roaring Twenties," they were Kansas City and Chicago. Shires was a typical roaring twenties "jazz bird" and he relished the Prohibition-era night life in the bawdy city of Chicago.

Shires moonlighted as a prize fighter. He was trained by Jack Blackburn, who later would be a trainer for heavyweight champion Joe Louis. Shires would enter the ring in a crimson robe with "Art The Great" stitched in bold white letters on the back. One of his opponents was George Trafton of the Chicago Bears. Shires had about six bouts before Judge Landis gave him an ultimatum to choose between boxing and baseball.

Art Shires had been taught the fine points of playing first base by Hal Chase while playing in an outlaw league in Arizona. That circuit also featured other banned players from organized ball such as Chick Gandil, Buck Weaver and Jimmy O'Connell, formerly of the New York Giants. O'Connell had been banned by Judge Landis for allegedly offering a $300 bribe to Philadelphia Phillies shortstop Heinie Sand to lay down in a game late in the stretch drive in September 1924 as the Giants were battling for their fourth straight pennant.

Playing in his first game for the White Sox on August 20 in Boston, "Art the Great" Shires hit a triple and three singles off Red Ruffing. Shires played in 33 games in 1928 and went to bat 123 times, hitting .341.

In the habit of perpetually horsing around, Shires' shenanigans caused him to get into a brawl with Lena Blackburne in the White Sox clubhouse. Shires had borrowed a red cap from an usher and had it on during batting practice. When Blackburne ordered him to take it off, Shires made some disparaging remarks and was ordered to the clubhouse. After the game, when Blackburne entered the clubhouse, he found Shires fighting with the club's traveling secretary, Lou Barbour. Attempting to separate the two, Blackburne got into the middle of the fray and got socked in the eye. The two would have a return bout in the clubhouse during the 1929 season in which Blackburne, a bit of a roughneck himself, would knock Shires out cold.

In June 1930, the hard-playing, hard-drinking, hard-partying "Art The Great" Shires would be traded to the Washington, and following the 1932 season with Boston, he would be back in the minors, never to return to the major leagues. Later he became a professional wrestler and still later opened a steakhouse restaurant in Dallas.

Bibb Falk had not been very happy playing in Chicago since the departure of Kid Gleason. Halfway through the 1928 season, when Charles Comiskey fired manager Ray Schalk and replaced him with Lena Blackburne, Falk's troubles began to escalate. While Falk had little respect for Schalk as a manager, he didn't care for Blackburne's style of managing the team either. Blackburne believed that Falk was indifferent and began to sit him on the bench. Consequently, Falk played in only

8. Traded to Cleveland

98 games for the White Sox in 1928, hitting .290 with 83 hits. He played just 79 games in the outfield, the second lowest total in his career.

As a result of Falk's lack of production, White Sox business manager Harry Grabiner wanted to cut his salary by $2,500, and he strongly objected. So that winter, on February 28, 1929, Falk was traded to the Cleveland Indians for catcher Martin "Chick" Autry. The trade seemed like a good career move for Autry, who was playing behind Luke Sewell in Cleveland, and Falk was glad to get out of Chicago. The Indians gave Falk a contract calling for the same amount—$10,000—that he had been paid by Chicago in 1928. But Chick Autry wound up getting just about the same amount of playing time in Chicago, becoming the backup catcher behind Moe Berg.

Bibb Falk got to know Roger Peckinpaugh during his brief stint with the White Sox and was very high on the Indians manager and pleased to be playing for him. However, veteran Charlie Jamieson was playing left field, so Falk played half of the time in right.

There was considerable enthusiasm for the coming campaign among the Tribe as they filtered into spring training at New Orleans. Falk was assigned to room with first baseman Lew Fonseca. It was a great match and benefited both players; throughout the season the two constantly talked baseball. They sized up enemy pitchers, batters and fielders and devoted a lot of time to helping the younger players on the team develop.

Bibb Falk was not with the Cleveland Indians very long before he witnessed one of the ugliest fan riots in major league baseball history. The Indians would

Bibb Falk, Cleveland Indians.

draw 536,210 fans to League Park (Dunn Field) in 1929. But on Saturday afternoon, May 11, during a game between the Indians and Philadelphia Athletics, a great many of the 15,000 fans in attendance at League Park would go crazy. Falk was in slump, hitting .275, and did not start the game, but he did pinch-hit late in the game and struck out.

That day, facing the Athletics' Lefty Grove, in the eighth inning the Indians were down 4–0 and began to rally. With runners on first and second, Lew Fonseca came to bat, laid down a bunt and appeared to be safe at first, as both runners advanced. But umpire William "Bick" Campbell ruled that Fonseca had run outside of the baseline and interfered with the throw to first. He called Fonseca out and ordered the runners back to first and second.

Indians manager Roger Peckinpaugh stormed on to the field and loudly began to protest the call. At first the fans only booed the umpire. Then the booing began to reach a deafening level, and it was apparent that there was seriousness about it. When Campbell threw Peckinpaugh out of the game, all hell broke loose as pop bottles began to fly from the stands and players ran for cover. As bottles rained down on the field, a squad of police from the Perkins E. 55th precinct station was sent to the ball park.

Umpire Emmett T. "Red" Ormsby was standing on the third base line and was hit in the head by a thrown bottle. He suffered a concussion. First aid was immediately administered to Ormsby by Cleveland team physician Dr. M. H. Castle in the club's office. Umpire Campbell was escorted off the field surrounded by a police escort, but there was no attempt made to arrest any of the bottle hurlers. Ormsby could not finish the game and returned to his hotel room.

A spectator, 28-year-old Lee Porter from Akron, was also hit in the head by a flying bottle. He suffered a fractured skull and died in an Akron hospital four days later.

Indians general manager and former American League umpire Billy Evans had witnessed a riot in a game between Cleveland and Philadelphia in 1912 and had fist fights with several fans who rushed him following the game. Bravely, Evans took the field and pleaded with the crowd to stop the barrage, and they complied with his pleas. There were so many bottles on the field that it appeared that the game would have to be called. Thankfully, no bottles were permitted in the upper deck of the stands or the barrage might have continued until dark. The

8. Traded to Cleveland

debris was removed by stadium workers using wheelbarrows, the game resumed, and the Athletics defeated the Indians, 4–2.

On July 10, 1929, Indians pitcher Wes Ferrell hit the first home run of his career as the Indians defeated the Washington Nationals, 9–7. Farrell would go on to hit 38 home runs in his major league career, most ever by a pitcher.

League Park (Dunn Field) was a rectangular shaped ball park that was built to fit into the surrounding neighborhood and the Cleveland street grid. As a result, the outfield dimensions were hideous in design. The left field stands were 375 feet from home with a five-foot-high fence. To the deepest part of center at the scoreboard, the distance from home plate was 460 feet. However, to right field it was only 290 feet. To compensate for the short porch, a 40-foot-high wall was built with a 25-foot screen attached. The dimensions of right field didn't seem to bother Bibb Falk very much. Between July 4–13, he hit four home runs over the high screen.

Bibb Falk (National Baseball Hall of Fame Library, Cooperstown, New York).

In 1928, the Indians had finished in seventh place with a record of 62–92. But in 1929 the Indians were competing for a place in the first division. On August 2, they were holding down fourth place. While Earl Averill, Lou Fonseca and Wes Ferrell were individually having terrific seasons, most analysts believed that the trade that brought Bibb Falk to Cleveland was a key factor in the Indians' rise in the standings.

Early in the season, Falk had been mired in a slump. But by August 2, he was hitting a robust .331 and knocking in runs frequently. The Indians were in New York to play the Yankees, who were trailing the

Bibb Falk

league-leading Philadelphia Athletics by 10½ games. The Indians won the game, 9–8, on a three-run home run by Falk in the ninth inning. It was Falk's 11th home run of the season.

On August 11, at League Park with 25,000 fans on hand, Babe Ruth hit the 500th home run of his career off Indians pitcher Willis Hudlin. The historic homer came in Babe's first at-bat and sailed over the right field wall onto Lexington Avenue. The ball was retrieved by Jack Geiser, a young lad from New Philadelphia, Ohio, who had come to Cleveland for the game. A meeting was shortly thereafter arranged in the Yankees dugout between Geiser and the Babe, who explained to the youth that he would like to keep the ball. So Geiser gladly surrendered the ball. In return, Ruth autographed another ball for Geiser and placed a $20 bill in his hand.

The Indians won the game, 6–5, and the victory gave them sole procession of third place as the St. Louis Browns lost to Washington. The game had been a seesaw battle that saw the lead change several times. After home runs by Ruth and Lou Gehrig got the Yankees off to a 2–0 lead, the Indians took the lead in the fourth inning after Earl Averill and Lou Fonseca singled and were moved along by a key sacrifice by Bibb Falk that set the stage for Johnny Hodapp to drive them in.

In the fifth inning, the Yankees' Bill Dickey attempted to go from first base to third after Mark Koenig singled to left and Falk momentarily fumbled the ball. But Falk quickly recovered and threw Dickey out by six feet.

Experiencing a renewed spirit as a player in Cleveland after rusting on the bench in Chicago, Falk hit .312 and had 94 RBI for the season. Lew Fonseca won the American League batting crown with an average of .369, and rookie Earl Averill hit .332. Falk, Fonseca and Averill drove in a combined total of 292 runs but it wasn't enough fire power to overcome the Philadelphia Athletics, who won the pennant by 18 games over the second-place New York Yankees and 24 games over the Indians, who finished in third place with a much-improved record of 81–71.

On May 11, 1930, Bibb Falk got five hits, had five RBI, and scored five runs as the Indians defeated the Athletics, 25–7. The Indians had 25 hits, but not one home run. The 25 hits in a game without a home run tied a major league record set in the Deadball era in 1901.

In 1930, Bibb Falk's playing career started to wind down for no reason connected to his ability to play, but rather due to the sentimen-

8. Traded to Cleveland

tality of those who called the shots in the front office. The Indians had new ownership and they felt a loyalty to veteran Charlie Jamieson, who had been in the American League since 1915, and they informed general manager Billy Evans and manager Roger Peckinpaugh that they wanted Jamieson to play left field, on his own terms. Peckinpaugh felt Bibb Falk was one of the best outfielders in the game, and while he had been given fully authority to run the team, it came with a caveat—he was not allowed to bench Charlie Jamieson unless he wanted to bench himself.

As for center field and right field, the Indians had two young outfielders in Earl Averill and Dick Porter in whom they had invested over $100,000, and they needed to play in order to develop.

So in the 1930 season Bibb Falk would play in only 82 games, just 42 in the outfield. Falk accepted his role on the Indians roster with grace. He was still glad to be out of Chicago and now resigned himself to the role of a pinch-hitter. Being the competitor that he was, Falk became one of the best pinch-hitters in the American League. In 1930 Falk pinch-hit 40 times, which was almost equaled by "Fatty" Fothergill, who split the season between the Tigers and White Sox, and pinch-hit 38 times. While Falk had the most pinch hits, 13, and an average of .382 as a pinch-hitter, the American League leader in pinch-hitting average was Jimmy Reese of the Yankees, with ten pinch-hits in 20 at-bats for a .500 average.

Coming to the realization that he wasn't going to play much longer, in early January 1931, Bibb Falk signed his contract with the Indians. His early signing made news as he had brought a reputation with him from Chicago of being notoriously late in coming to terms. His contract called for the same $10,000 that he had been paid every year since 1927.

In 1931, Falk pinch hit 46 times with 14 hits for a .333 average. While Falk finished in a tie for most pinch-hits that season, Smead "Smudge" Jolley of the White Sox led the American League in pinch-hit average, .452 (14-for–31). Falk's lifetime average as a pinch-hitter was .314 (37 for 118).

On September 23, 1931, Bibb Falk played his final game in the major leagues. The Cleveland Indians were playing a doubleheader at League Park against the Detroit Tigers. In the first game, won by the Tigers, 9–7, Falk pinch-hit and singled, the last hit of his major league career. He entered the second game to replace Joe Vosmik in left field as Vosmik was moved to center to replace Earl Averill, who was taken

Bibb Falk

out of the game. Falk went 0-for–2 at bat and finished the season with an average of .304. It was the eighth time that he had hit over .300 in a season.

Bibb Falk had played for 12 years in the American League with the Chicago White Sox and Cleveland Indians. He finished his career with 1,463 hits, 69 home runs, 784 RBI and a batting average of .314. Falk credited Eddie Collins and Ty Cobb with making him into one of the American League's best hitters. Whenever the White Sox were playing the Detroit Tigers, Falk routinely approached Cobb and asked him questions about hitting. According to Falk, there were two things that Ty Cobb liked to talk about, hitting and money.

While Falk averaged just 5.75 home runs per season during his career, he acknowledged that he wasn't a home run hitter. He would often remark, tongue-in-cheek, that he hit to all fields, infield and outfield.

Of all the pitchers he hit against, Falk remarked that he enjoyed hitting against the Indians' George Uhle the most. According to Falk, he could hit a ball pitched by Uhle with the handle of the bat and get a hit. Hitting George Uhle was not easy for most hitters. He pitched in the American League for 17 years between 1919–1936, winning 20 games for Cleveland three times and finishing his career with 200 wins. Falk's overall batting average vs. Uhle was .415 (27 for 65).

One of the most telling of Falk's hitting statistics that demonstrates his development as a big league hitter is the number of times he struck out each year. In 4,652 at-bats, Falk struck out 279 times. But 124 (44 percent) of those strikeouts came in his first two full seasons in the major leagues. In Falk's last nine years in the majors, he averaged 16.7 strikeouts per season. He credited his decrease in striking out during his career with learning that you had to change your grip on the bat when you had two strikes in order to adjust to the pitchers' movement on the ball.

While Bibb Falk's playing career ended at the age of 32, had he played only a few more seasons it is highly possible his stats would have been worthy of Hall of Fame consideration. But Falk's decision to quit playing was made because he knew he was slowing down. It was beneath Falk's dignity to play at any less a level than that of a true big leaguer.

By the end of his major league career, Bibb Falk had played with and against some the greatest all-time players in the game. In 1930, a reporter asked him who he considered the best players in the American

8. Traded to Cleveland

League, and his responses were surprising and raised a few eyebrows. Falk stated that Ted Lyons was the best pitcher in the American League, with Wes Ferrell running a close second. He felt Al Simmons was the best all-round hitter. Simmons and Harry Rice had the best throwing arms, and Carl Reynolds was the best base runner.

With his playing days behind him, in 1932 Bibb Falk became manager of the Cleveland Indians' American Association Toledo farm club, succeeding Casey Stengel. Falk was offered the appointment at Toledo when retiring Indians outfielder Charley Jamieson declined it. Under Falk, Toledo finished the 1932 season in fourth place. He also played part-time for the Mud Hens and hit .321 in 79 games.

Bibb Falk, Boston Red Sox 1934.

In 1933, he rejoined the big club as a coach. On June 7, 1933, Cleveland general manager Billy Evans fired manager Roger Peckinpaugh and hired Walter Johnson to replace him. In his one-game tenure as interim manager of the Indians on July 19, 1933, the only game that Bibb Falk managed in the major leagues, the Indians defeated the St. Louis Browns, 5–2, behind the pitching of Wes Ferrell.

In 1934, Falk joined the Boston Red Sox as a coach under manager Bucky Harris. The next season, Joe Cronin was named manager and he brought Al Schacht with him. Falk maintained that that killed his coaching job. So in 1935, he went home to Austin and began scouting for the Red Sox. While not comfortable in the role, he would continue it for a few years.

9

Falk Joins the Army Air Corps

In 1940, Bibb Falk returned to the University of Texas as an assistant baseball coach. Almost immediately upon his arrival at the Forty Acres, health concerns with heart disease forced legendary Longhorns head coach "Uncle Billy" Disch to retire from on-field duties. Problems for Disch began when he attempted to help a student push his car out of the mud and the strain caused a heart ailment. When the University of Texas held a testimonial dinner for Billy Disch that April, he was so ill that his doctor advised him not to attend.

Under the leadership of Billy Disch, the Longhorns, with the exception of 1921 and 1922 when they had difficulty beating Baylor with Ted Lyons pitching, had been perennial SWC champions. Fans were still talking about how Disch's Longhorns beat the Philadelphia Phillies, 4–1, in a game in 1939.

The early days of Disch's tenure had often been stormy as his critics on the campus felt he wasn't a good fit as head coach because he didn't have a college education and lacked professional baseball experience.

Regardless, toward the end of his 29-year tenure at Texas, Disch had acquired a strong ally in university president Dr. Homer P. Rainey, who solidified his position with the program. Dr. Rainey had been a professional baseball player and had pitched for Houston in the Texas League. But it was not until 20 years after he quit the game that Houston officially gave him his release.

With the onset of his illness, Billy Disch recommended Bibb Falk as his successor. It was widely speculated that Falk's toughness was inherited from Disch. Upon accepting the job, Falk stated, "I am here

9. Falk Joins the Army Air Corps

trying to fill in for Uncle Billy; his policy is my policy, and any man would be a darn fool not to follow his advice."[1] From that point on, Bibb Falk would continue the excellence in the University of Texas baseball program that Billy Disch had built over more than a quarter of a century, while his own style of running the program evolved over time. He was intense, demanding, and often bombastic, but nonetheless caring.

Bibb Falk was glad to have the Texas job. "I didn't like scouting, and my 'money' job had run out, so I decided to do it. I needed a 'paying' job."[2]

Once again, just as circumstances had been when he joined the Chicago White Sox in 1920 and replaced Shoeless Joe Jackson in the White Sox outfield, Bibb Falk was faced with the challenge of following a legend. Uncle Billy Disch's teams at the University of Texas had won numerous conference titles. Upon taking over as the head man on the field while Uncle Billy watched from the stands, Falk felt humbled being in Disch's shadow and told a reporter, "Uncle Billy always will be coach at Texas as long as he lives."[3]

Falk took over the Longhorns' head coaching job on April 9 following the first Southwest Conference game against SMU. A review of his debut published in the *Austin American Statesman* the following day was positive.

> Bibb Falk proved himself a very astute baseball coach in his first start with the Texas Longhorns yesterday. The Bibber flashed the old home run signal twice in the first two innings and Texas came out with enough runs to beat Baylor. The Longhorns added a lot more for good measure later; however, and the final count was 14–2. That was a pretty stiff assignment they handed Bibb Falk out there yesterday, pinch hitting for the Old Master himself. There are easier jobs than filling in for Uncle Billy Disch.[4]

Falk dove headfirst into the challenge of following Disch and guided the Longhorns to their 21st Southwest Conference Championship in 1940 with a record of 20–4. At first it was cultural shock for the Texas baseball program. Replacing the refined "Uncle Billy" Disch with the outspoken Falk, schooled in the ways of the big leagues, took a little getting used to for the Texas Athletic Department, but as the wins mounted up, everyone seemed pleased and applauded his appointment.

For an encore in 1941, Falk's Longhorns again won the SWC championship when Pete Layden hit a home run in the bottom of the tenth inning to beat Texas A&M. However, in 1942 the Aggies got their revenge as they beat the Longhorns in the season's finale for the SWC crown.

The outbreak of World War II interrupted the lives of almost everyone in the United States. By the end of the war more than ten million men would be drafted into military service, including over 500 major league players and a couple of thousand minor league and Negro Leagues ballplayers.

There were, of course, those big league ballplayers with a strong patriotic streak in them who, following the Japanese attack on Pearl Harbor on December 7, 1941, immediately enlisted without question. These included All-Stars like Hank Greenberg and Bob Feller. Still, some of the draft circumstances involving major league players would be controversial.

A few months before the Pearl Harbor attack, Ted Williams of the Boston Red Sox was coming off of his epic 1941 season in which he hit .406. When Williams was drafted in January 1942, he resisted. Williams had been classified 3-A because of his sole support of his mother. Williams stated that his mother was 50 years old and in poor health, and he didn't want to see her have to seek employment. To that end, he had sent her $5,000 in the past year and wanted to keep up payments on three annuities accounts that he had established for her. Following a physical on January 8, he passed, was reclassified as 1-A, and was tentatively scheduled to be inducted on January 24.

Eddie Collins, who had served in the U.S. Marines in World War I, was now the Boston Red Sox general manager, and he remarked, "I can tell you baseball ought to be proud to have men like Ted Williams in the service. That's the way we feel about it. And he'll make a fine soldier."[5]

Williams had just signed his 1942 contract with the Red Sox calling for $30,000 and was resigned to play. So he appealed his 1-A classification asking the draft board to grant him an exception. He was denied. Then he appealed to the President's Board of Appeal and once again was denied. His request for an exemption even went as far as President Roosevelt's desk, where his appeal was successful and he was reclassified 3-A.

Controversy surrounding Ted Williams was considerable as he started the 1942 season. Many were labeling him as a draft dodger, and Williams lost lucrative product endorsement contracts such as one for $4,000 from Quaker Oats. Williams finally brought an end to it all

9. Falk Joins the Army Air Corps

when on May 22, 1942, he enlisted in the Naval Aviation Service. His enlistment permitted him to finish the 1942 season and he hit .356 and while winning his second consecutive American League batting title and his first of two Triple Crowns. Then he reported for training and served with distinction.

Although there were scores of other major leaguers who also were classified 3-A, including, Joe DiMaggio, Joe Gordon and Stan Musial, all of whom played in the 1942 season, it was Ted Williams who faced the most negative publicity over his 3-A classification. Musial continued to play ball until the war was coming to an end in 1945 before enlisting when it was apparent that he was about to be drafted. But even then Stan Musial never left American soil and served just over a year in uniform.

By the end of the war, 281 major league players had been classified 4-F. Fans sensing an inferior level of competition stayed away from games in droves until 1945. In 1941, the combined attendance of American and National League teams totaled 9,265,309. By the second year of the war, in 1943, attendance had dropped off by 20.4 percent to 7,378,058.

In some respects, major league baseball became a sideshow during the war. In Cincinnati, 15-year-old pitcher Joe Nuxhall faced the St. Louis Cardinals, giving up five runs in two-thirds of an inning, resulting in a 67.50 ERA. The St. Louis Browns signed Pete Gray, a one-armed outfielder. Babe Herman, a 42-year-old former major leaguer who had been playing in the Pacific Coast League since 1939, returned to play for Brooklyn as a pinch-hitter in 1945.

Star players well past their prime such as the Pittsburgh Pirates' famed Waner brothers, Lloyd and Paul, hung around the major leagues until the end of the war. Paul Waner later remarked that in 1944, when he was playing for the New York Yankees, one day a fan in the bleachers yelled, "Hey Paul, how come you're in the outfield for the Yankees"? Waner answered back, "Because Joe DiMaggio's in the army."[6]

The minor leagues, like the majors, were drained of players by the draft. The Texas League shut down operations from 1943 to 1945. At the end of the war only ten minor leagues were still active.

With so many major and minor league players in the armed services, Chicago Cubs owner P. K. Wrigley decided to assign the ball club's assistant general manager, Ken Sells, the task of organizing a woman's professional baseball league in an effort to raise morale of workers and sustain fan interest in baseball. The result of Sells' effort was the All American Girls Professional Baseball League that opened in 1943 and continued to operate until the mid–1950s.

Although the Negro Leagues lost many players to the draft, the teams made adaptations to conditions they faced as a result of the war. They reduced travel and targeted the large numbers of blacks arriving from the south to fill war-time defense jobs in the north to attend the games. By 1945 the Negro Leagues were a $2 million a year business. Ric Roberts, a Pittsburgh sportswriter, claimed that star pitcher Satchel Paige, with a salary of $40,000 year to go along with all his special appearance fees, was making more than any white major league player. The Negro Leagues would survive the war but face their demise with post-war complications brought about by the integration of major league baseball and the introduction of televised games.

While the quality of major league baseball was suspect during the war, the quality of baseball played by service teams was highly competitive and featured star-studded lineups. The Army Air Force team that played before tens of thousands of troops in the Pacific Theatre featured major league players such as Joe DiMaggio, Red Ruffing and Joe Gordon of the New York Yankees, Mike McCormick (Cincinnati Reds), Walt Judnich (St. Louis Browns), and Dario Lodigiani (Chicago White Sox), along with future major leaguers Ferris Fain (Philadelphia Athletics) Bob Dillinger (St. Louis Browns) and Charlie Silvera (New York Yankees).

In 1945, as the war was coming to an end, Enos Slaughter and Howie Pollet (St. Louis Cardinals), along with Joe Gordon and Birdie Tebbetts (Detroit Tigers) and some other major leaguers, toured the Pacific Theatre and played exhibition games for the troops' amusement. They played games on Guam, Iwo Jima, Tinian and Saipan.

According to Birdie Tebbetts, Enos Slaughter played ball in the service with the same relentless competitive spirit that he played games in the major leagues. Tebbetts recalled that during a softball game in the Pacific, Slaughter made a head-first slide on coral.

On Saipan, Slaughter and his teammates played an exhibition against a scrub team of Marines who had defeated the Japanese in the bloody battle. One of the opposing players who had fought in the battle was U.S. Marine and future major league second baseman Wayne Ter-

9. Falk Joins the Army Air Corps

williger (Chicago Cubs, Brooklyn Dodgers, Washington Senators, New York Giants, Kansas City Athletics).

Baseball was played on an organized level in Japan, and the Japanese people were huge fans of the game. Shinichi Ishimaru, who had been a 20-game winner in Japanese baseball before the war, died flying a kamikaze plane mission, crashing intentionally into an American warship.

The Japanese had much exposure to the American game through several major league tours dating back to 1913, including Bibb Falk's junket in 1922 and a later one featuring Babe Ruth in 1934. When Ruth took batting practice at Meiji Shrine Stadium on November 4, 1934, 65,000 fans watched. Although Ruth was a hero in Japan as well as the United States, it has been stated by American soldiers who served in the Pacific that, during lulls in close combat at night when they were within hearing distance of Japanese lines, they would occasionally hear the enemy yell out "Fuck Babe Ruth!"

Enos Slaughter remembered the exhibition game on Saipan as having some most unusual spectators. According to Slaughter, when his exhibition team got to Saipan there were still quite a few Japanese soldiers that had not surrendered holed up in the hills. "I'll be damned," said Slaughter, "if they didn't sneak out and watch us play ball. We could see them sitting there, watching the game. When it was over they'd fade back into their caves. But they could have got themselves killed for watching a ball game."[7]

Bibb Falk was 42 years old at the outbreak of World War II and was relatively immune from the draft. Still, in September 1942, Falk turned over the helm of the Texas Longhorns baseball team to Blair Cherry and enlisted in the Army Air Force as a private.

Assigned to Twelfth Base Headquarters and Air Base Squadron at Randolph Field in Texas, in January 1943, Falk was promoted to the rank of corporal, and he later became a sergeant. After three weeks of recruit drill work, he was assigned to the recreation department at Randolph Field outside of San Antonio. Randolph Field, referred to as the West Point of pilot training, was a basic flying training facility from 1941 to 1943, when the base's training mission was broadened.

Falk's primary duties on the base were as a physical training instructor for military personnel. At first the job title was slightly ceremonial in its operational intent. His duties were to see that there were enough

Bibb Falk

footballs, basketballs and equipment available for the base's recreational programs. He also looked after the bowling alley on the base. But when spring came, Falk became coach of the base baseball team, the Randolph Field Ramblers.

The Randolph Field Ramblers were no bunch of bushers. Falk was familiar with them as his Texas Longhorns team had played them the past two years. In 1942, the Ramblers had claimed the unofficial title of Texas champions, having defeated Camp Barkley in a two-game series following the tournament. The Ramblers played in the San Antonio Service Baseball League. Under Bibb Falk's leadership, the Ramblers were Service League champions one year and were runners-up the next.

The Ramblers featured several future major league players, including catcher Matt Batts (Boston Red Sox, St. Louis Browns, Detroit Tigers, Chicago White Sox, Cincinnati Redlegs), future major league pitcher Boo Ferriss (Boston Red Sox) and Leycester "Tex" Aulds, who would play three games in the major leagues in 1947 for the Boston Red Sox. The Ramblers also featured a host of minor league players such as Marty Errante, Tom Finger, Irv Fortune, Jim Morris, Clarence Pfeil and Rube Naranjo.

In 1943, the San Antonio Service Baseball League consisted of eight teams. The Randolph Field Ramblers, under Falk, with a record of 58–19–1, won the league championship by 8½ games, but lost in the playoffs.

Bibb Falk's Randolph Field Ramblers had two very good pitchers in David "Boo" Ferriss and Walter Nothe, who was considered the ace off the staff. Nothe was a hard-throwing left-hander who stood 6'2" and weighed 200 pounds. He was a Philadelphia native who had won 15 games for the Reading Chicks of the Interstate League in 1940. On January 21, 1941, Nothe enlisted in the U.S. Army and was eventually assigned to the Army Air Force at Randolph Field.

On May 16, 1943, Nothe pitched a one-hitter against Stinson Field but lost the game, 1–0. Four days later, he pitched a no-hitter against Camp Normoyle. Nothe was selected to play on the league's All-Star team and on June 7, he pitched against the Waco Field Flyers, managed by Detroit Tigers catcher and future big league manager Birdie Tebbetts (Cincinnati Redlegs, Milwaukee Braves, Cleveland Indians). Nothe gave up one run and two hits in three innings, helping the All-Stars to a 6–5 win. For the Ramblers in 1943, Nothe's won-lost record was 16–6.

9. Falk Joins the Army Air Corps

Following his discharge from the Army in 1945, Walter Nothe resumed his professional baseball career. He went to spring training with the Brooklyn Dodgers in 1946, went north with the team because manager Leo Durocher liked him, but never pitched in a game and in early May was optioned to St. Paul. He was recalled by the Dodgers in September and once again did not appear in a game.

After playing in Cuba in the winter of 1946–1947, Walter Nothe was suspended from playing organized ball by George Trautman, president of the National Association. He was finally reinstated in August and joined the Dodgers' farm club in Montreal of the International League. In 1948, Nothe returned to the Montreal Royals.

Even though Nothe pitched a no-hitter in AAA ball for the Toledo Mud Hens in 1949 against the Minneapolis Millers, he continued to languish in the minors. After he broke his pitching hand while packing a trunk for the trip to the funeral of his wife's grandmother in Michigan, rather than waiting for the hand to heal, Toledo released him.

Still relentlessly pursuing his dream of pitching in the big leagues, in 1952 Walter Nothe threw nine innings of no-hit ball for the Miami Beach Flamingos of the Florida International League against their archrival Miami Sun Sox. He had a perfect game going until the second baseman bobbled a grounder with two outs in the eighth inning. Nothe lost the game in ten innings, 1–0.

For the 1952 season, Nothe went 15–8 with an ERA of 1.79. The Miami Beach Flamingos had a record of 103–49 but actually lost the league championship by one game to the Miami Sun Sox, who finished with a record of 104–48. In 2001, in celebration of 100 years of minor league baseball, historians and SABR members William J. Weiss and Marshall Wright were asked by MiLB.com to select the 100 greatest minor league teams of all time. The men rated the Miami Sun Sox as the 40th greatest minor league team.

Walter Nothe finally gave up his dream of making the major leagues after pitching for the Macon Peaches of the Sally League in 1954. He passed away in Philadelphia in March 1985, at the age of 67.

David "Boo" Ferriss, the other star pitcher on Falk's Randolph Ramblers, would go on to have a brief, but distinguished career with the Boston Red Sox. The Red Sox first took notice of Ferriss in the summer of 1941 when his college coach in Mississippi made arrangements for him to pitch in the Northern League. On an off-day in late July, the coach

Bibb Falk

took Ferriss and a couple of his teammates down to Boston to see their first major league game at Fenway Park, where they met Ted Williams, Dom DiMaggio and Bobby Doerr. When the Northern League season ended, the Red Sox invited Ferriss to pitch batting practice for the Red Sox.

Speaking about the experience, Ferriss remarked, "They even took me to Yankee Stadium. There I was, throwing batting practice to Ted (Williams) at Yankee Stadium, while he was going for .400. It was all a thrill."[8]

At Randolph Field, Boo Ferriss would benefit greatly from the tutelage of Bibb Falk, and it would take him from having just that one summer of Class D ball in the Northern League to becoming a 20-game winner with the Boston Red Sox. Bibb Falk was sure that Boo Ferriss had the ability to play in the major leagues. "There was never any doubt about Dave; he had the natural ability plus the proper mental outlook, necessary diligence,"[9] said Falk.

Boo Ferris was 24 years old when he was discharged early from the Army after two years of service in 1945 due to a severe asthma condition. Pitching for a lackluster war-time Boston Red Sox team that finished in seventh place, Ferris went 21–10.

The following year, with the return of Ted Williams, the Red Sox won the American League pennant. Boo Ferriss posted a record of 25–6. In Game Three of the 1946 World Series, he pitched a 4–0 shutout against the St. Louis Cardinals. He would also be the Red Sox's starting pitcher in Game Seven, getting a no-decision. For six years in Boston, Ferriss had a record of 65–30 with an ERA of 3.64.

In February 1944, Bibb Falk turned down an honorable discharge because of his age. He also declined an appointment to officer's training school because he didn't want to leave the enlisted personnel at Randolph Field.

As the war took more and more players in 1944, the San Antonio Service Baseball League was cut to six teams. Bibb Falk's Randolph Field Ramblers returned to the playoffs that year and faced the Kelly Field Fliers. Boo Ferriss beat the Fliers in the first game. Walter Nothe started the second game and the Fliers beat him, 3–1. Then Ferriss came back to win Game Three and send the Ramblers to the finals for the second straight year. Ferriss also won the league batting crown that season with an average of .417.

9. Falk Joins the Army Air Corps

The Ramblers would face the San Antonio Aviation Cadet Center in a best-of-five series. The SAAC Warhawks were the class of the league and perhaps all of service ball. The Warhawks were managed by infielder Dutch Meyer of the Detroit Tiger and led by two St. Louis Cardinals, outfielder Enos Slaughter and pitcher Howie Pollet. In 1943, Enos Slaughter had led the team in hitting with an astounding .498 average in 75 games. The Warhawks also featured catcher Del Wilber, who would go on to play for three major league teams following the war.

Unfortunately for Bibb Falk, his Ramblers were swept by the Warhawks in three games by scores of 5–3, 7–5 and 4–2.

Going into the 1945 season, Falk would not have the services of Boo Ferriss. On February 24, 1945, Ferriss received a medical discharge as a result of a severe asthma attack and being hospitalized for four months. By the time of spring training, Ferriss had recuperated, reported to the Boston Red Sox camp and made the roster.

Still, with Walter Nothe on the mound the Ramblers went on to win the league title. Bibb Falk was due be discharged soon, and on May 15, 1945, it was proclaimed Bibb Falk Day at Randolph Field. Falk's players presented him with a wrist watch as a token of their appreciation for his three years of service; then they gave him a win as the Ramblers crushed the Brook Field Ganders, 20–2, to take over first place.

Football was declared "essential" to the war effort as a morale booster, so several military installations fielded intercollegiate football teams during the war. In addition to being the baseball coach, Bibb Falk was the trainer for the Randolph Field football Ramblers. The squad was coached by Frank Tritico and was a powerhouse.

In 1943, the Ramblers were led by "Bullet Bill" Dudley, a former Virginia All-American running back and the NFL's 1942 Rookie of the Year and MVP, edging out Don Hutson of the Green Bay Packers. Also on the 1943 Ramblers squad was former Tulsa All-American running back Glenn Dobbs.

The 1943 Randolph Field Ramblers achieved a 9–1–0 record, losing only to Southwestern Louisiana Institute, and were invited to play in the 1944 Cotton Bowl. On a sloppy, rain-soaked field the Ramblers fought the University of Texas, coached by Dana X. Bible, in a defensive struggle to a 7–7 tie. The Ramblers are the only military institution to play in the Cotton Bowl.

Bibb Falk

During 1944, Glenn Dobbs was transferred to the Second Air Force base at Colorado Springs, where he joined the Superbombers squad coached by Bill Reece. The Second Air Force had defeated Hardin Simmons College in the 1943 Sun Bowl. The Superbombers would have another fine season in 1944, finishing with a record of 11–3. In the final Associated Press poll, the Superbombers ranked 20th.

In 1944, the Randolph Field Ramblers, once led by Bill Dudley and a squad featuring eight other former NFL players and several college stars such as Johnny Stryzkalski of Marquette and Jack Russell of Baylor, still went undefeated, finishing with a 10—0 record and being voted as the number three team in the nation in the final Associated Press (AP) poll of the year, behind number one Army and number two Ohio State.

In the second game of the season, the Ramblers avenged their Cotton Bowl tie with Texas, defeating the Longhorns, 42–6. The closest game in the 1944 season for the Ramblers was a 19–0 win over the Third Air Force Gremlins. The Third Air Force squad had defeated the Second Air Force Superbombers, 14–7.

In December of 1944, the Randolph Field Ramblers would meet the Second Air Force Superbombers in the Treasury Bond Bowl at the Polo Grounds in New York. The game was played in the snow and only 8,536 people were in attendance as the Ramblers won the game, 13–6.

10

Bibb Falk Becomes a Longhorn Legend

Following World War II, Bibb Falk returned to coach the University of Texas baseball team. At the time Austin was a city of about 130,000 inhabitants, and the University of Texas had an enrollment of about 17,000, with 10,000 being male students. In less than a decade, Bibb Falk would become a legend not only in Texas baseball but all of college baseball. While others would follow him and eclipse his record, there would only be one Bibb Falk. By the time he would retire in 1967, Bibb Falk would win 20 Southwestern Conference championships and two national championships.

In 1946, with Bibb Falk back at the helm, the Texas Longhorns won the SWC championship, going undefeated in conference play with a record of 14–0 and 19–2 overall.

Falk's method of coaching was simple. He didn't give pep talks, but before each game he gave his players any information he had about the opposition. "I'm not a college coach," he explained, "I'm strictly a pro coach. I try to handle everything like the pros do. All my coaching is done on the field. You can't teach a boy to play baseball on the blackboard."[1]

Bibb Falk believed that a player could never be too good to learn more about baseball. His model for a major leaguer was a player who is forever learning, seeking advice from veterans and continually working for improvement. While Falk was brash, it was always in a motivational sense. Sometimes his critics believed he was a little off-color in some of his remarks. One of his more famous quotes in regard to developing a team was "You can't make chicken salad out of chicken shit."[2]

Bibb Falk

William "Rooster" Andrews was best known as the student manager of the Longhorns football teams between 1941 and 1946 under coaches Dana X. Bible and Darryl Royal. But Andrews won a letter in football at Texas in 1945 and also two letters in baseball while a part-time player in 1944 and 1945, playing seven different positions.

Andrews graduated with a business degree from Texas and opened a string of sporting goods stores in Dallas. In regard to the bombastic Falk, Andrews remarked that when Falk walked into his sporting goods store on Guadalupe Street, "All our secretaries would cut off their electric typewriters, just so they could hear Bibb cuss. They thought he was so cute. Bibb was one of those crusty old guys who could cuss all day and not offend anyone."[3]

"Crusty" as a description of Falk's personality would be like throwing him a bouquet. There were times when it was impossible to get a straight answer out him. When one interviewer asked how the Longhorns' infield was shaping up, Falk replied, "It's shaping up fine. We could use some dirt around third base. The mound needs a little work done on it."[4]

Bibb Falk did his own player recruiting. He didn't trust anyone else's recommendation. Furthermore, he never gave any player a full scholarship and never insisted on a binding letter of intent from any recruit. He felt if the young man wanted to back out at the last moment, so be it. He believed that college was a great place to embark on a baseball career. Falk believed, "It's better to go to college and mature. A boy would still have to play in the minors. He couldn't very easily go from college to the majors, but he wouldn't have to start as low after playing college ball."[5]

The argument could be made, however, that occasionally Bibb Falk was lax in his efforts to recruit local talent.

In 1949, the first-ever Texas High School State Baseball Championships were being played literally in Falk's backyard in Memorial Stadium, the Longhorns' football field. Playing in that tournament were the Austin High School Maroons, Falk's alma mater. The Maroons, led by star pitcher Jack Brinkley, were so good in 1949 that going into the final game of the high school championships they had outscored their opponents, 50–1. Earlier in the season, Austin High School had defeated the University of Texas freshman baseball team.

The Maroons were miraculously defeated for the state champi-

10. Bibb Falk Becomes a Longhorn Legend

onship, 3–2, by the El Paso Bowie Bears, a team of poor Hispanic players. In a 2011 article *Sports Illustrated* called them a rag tag team from the 2nd ward of El Paso, a community surrounded by a sewage plant, a smelting operation, the stockyards and a meat packing company.

Still, Jack Brinkley had a terrific season in 1949 at Falk's old school, and instead of trying to recruit him Falk stood by idly while the Boston Braves signed him to a $65,000 bonus contract. Unfortunately, Jack Brinkley never made it to the major leagues; but it still begs the question. Because of his enormous success in high school, what level of achievement would Brinkley have accomplished if Bibb Falk had recruited him and nurtured him at Texas?

Nonetheless, when major league scouts in the southwest encountered a high school prospect undecided on whether to sign a contract with the club they represented or to go to college, more often than not the scout would encourage the youth to go to the University of Texas, where he could get big league preparation from coach Bibb Falk.

In 1944, one of the most colorful characters in Texas Longhorns sports history would arrive on the Forty Acres in the presence of Bobby Layne. He would become both a football and baseball legend at Texas. Coach Blair Cherry would in a single season convert Layne from a single wing tailback to a T-formation quarterback, and the Longhorns would quickly become a major force in SWC football.

In the 1946 Cotton Bowl, won by Texas, 40–27, over the Missouri Tigers, Layne completed 11 of 12 passes, scored four touchdowns and was involved in every one of the Longhorns' 40 points by passing, running or kicking. He also completed a 57-yard pass on a "Statue of Liberty play" to future major league infielder Ransom Jackson. Layne played his last college game on January 1, 1948, as the Longhorns defeated Alabama, 27–7, in the Cotton Bowl.

By the end of his college career, Bobby Layne had set numerous records at the University of Texas that would stand for many years. Those marks included: most pass attempts, 400; most completions, 210; most interceptions, 31; most passing yards, 3,145; most touchdown passes, 25; most combined yards rushing and passing, 3,990; total yards, 4,789; and the longest pass play, an 80-yard touchdown to Jim Canady in 1946. In addition, Layne equaled several other records including most touchdowns scored in a game, four vs. Oklahoma State in 1946.

Bobby Layne was chosen in the first round of the 1948 professional

Bobby Layne

football draft by Pittsburgh of the All-American Conference and traded to the Chicago Bears.

At the time, Bears owner and head coach George Halas thought that quarterback Sid Luckman, who had led the Bears to their legendary 73–0 thumping of the Washington Redskins in the 1940 NFL championship game, was about to retire. Halas had Johnny Lujack waiting in the wings to take over, and the acquisition of Bobby Layne provided the Bears with a quality back-up quarterback.

However, Luckman decided to keep playing, causing a dilemma for

10. Bibb Falk Becomes a Longhorn Legend

George Halas. So it was odd man out and he traded Bobby Layne to the New York Bulldogs. Halas, explaining the trade to Layne, told him, "Bobby, I can't afford to keep three quarterbacks, and I can't make Sid retire. He's Jewish, which means more season tickets, and you're a Baptist from Texas."[6] In addition, Halas told Layne that because Johnny Lujack had attended Notre Dame that also meant more season tickets in Chicago than having a quarterback from Texas.

So Bobby Layne was traded to the New York Bulldogs, owned by singer Kate Smith. Later Layne was to remark, "Every time Kate Smith got a sore throat we were worried about it, getting paid. If she couldn't sing '*God Bless America*' there wouldn't have been any checks."[7]

In 1950, the New York Bulldogs traded Bobby Layne to the Detroit Lions. Layne would go on to become one of the biggest stars in the NFL during the 1950s, alongside such legends as Jim Brown, Otto Graham, Norm Van Brocklin, Ollie Matson, Lou Groza, Raymond Berry and Johnny Unitas.

Layne would lead the Detroit Lions to four Division titles, in 1952, 1953, 1954 and 1957, and consecutive NFL titles in 1952 and 1953. While the Lions would also win the NFL title in 1957, Layne sustained a broken jaw after being hit by a forearm of Chicago Bears tackle Ed "Country" Meadows and had to sit out the championship game. Tobin Rote started at quarterback and led the Lions to a 59–14 victory over the Cleveland Browns.

Bobby Layne wound up his professional football career with the Pittsburgh Steelers in 1962 and was elected to the Pro Football Hall of Fame in 1967. He was the first Texas Longhorn to enter the Hall.

Bobby Layne was also a star pitcher for the Texas Longhorns, and Bibb Falk rated him as the best pitcher he ever coached at Texas. "He never lost a college game," said Falk. "Trouble with him, though, he was crazy as hell."[8] According to Falk, Layne pitched games on his own terms. If you gave him a five- or six-run lead, he would win the game, 10–6. But if the Longhorns were winning by a score of 1–0, Layne would pitch a shutout. In 1946, he pitched a no-hitter against Texas A&M, beating them, 2–1. But he was liable to have been out playing 18 holes of golf that morning.

Bibb Falk had a rule to never disclose his starting lineup prior to a game. Therefore opponents never knew who the starting pitcher was going to be.

Bibb Falk

Rooster Andrews was Bobby Layne's roommate and close friend. Recalling Layne's no-hitter against Texas A&M on May 4, 1946, Rooster Andrews said that the game was played at College Station and the Longhorns needed a win to keep pace for the 1946 SWC championship. Bobby Layne was scheduled to pitch the critical game for Texas. Although Layne had cut his foot two nights before in a rough-housing incident, he was determined to pitch. Bibb Falk did not know about Layne's injury. Layne got the foot stitched, swore his friend Andrews to secrecy and enlisted his assistance.

During games it was Bibb Falk's habit to sit at one end of the bench. As Rooster Andrews was a part-time player, he was usually on the bench the whole game. So Bobby Layne got him to occupy the other end of the bench. Layne gave Andrews some money and told him to go buy a six-pack of beer. Andrews purchased the suds and, between each inning, Layne would slip behind the bench out of Falk's sight line and chug a bottle of beer. "He was doing pretty good," Rooster recalled, "and as he came to the seventh inning, he gave me some more money to go buy some more beer."[9] In the end, Layne had pitched a no-hitter.

All during the game at College Station, a snare drum accompanied Layne's wind-ups and a base drum thumped when the ball went into the catcher's mitt. In regard to the shenanigans of the Aggies fans, Layne stated that the percussion wasn't problematic when he was pitching, but what irritated him was the drum keeping time when he walked to the bench between innings.

Bobby Layne pitched his last game for Texas on May 14, 1946, beating Texas A&M. He was so good a college baseball pitcher that he never lost a Southwest Conference game in four years at Texas, including two years which he played under Falk. His overall record was 39–7, including 27 consecutive wins in SWC play. In 1946, Layne pitched two no-hitters and had 84 strikeouts, a SWC record that stood for 39 years. His first no-hitter of the season came on March 28, 1946, when he beat Southwestern, 7–0. Layne's career pitching record for Texas included working 378⅔ innings (241⅓ in SWC games), allowing 273 hits (66 in SWC games) and totaling 381 strikeouts (241 in SWC games). But the most compelling aspect of Bobby Layne's pitching at Texas was that he was never taken out of a game with his team behind.

The eternal saying is that "everything in Texas is bigger." That

10. Bibb Falk Becomes a Longhorn Legend

cliché could also be applied to the elephantine egos of the SWC opponents from Rice, Texas A&M, Baylor, TCU and Houston that faced Bobby Layne during his days on the mound for the Longhorns. Although Layne consistently baffled his opponents while on the mound, most of them maintained that he didn't have anything on the ball and was more lucky than brilliant as a pitcher.

The criticism of Bobby Layne's pitching success at Texas was reminiscent of that heaped upon Bucky Walters of the Cincinnati Reds in the late 1930s and early 1940s. When the Reds won the National League pennant in 1939, Bucky Walters had a record of 27–11, and in 1940, when the Reds won the World Series, Walters was 22–10. Still, Walters' critics in the National League called him "Lucky Bucky" and maintained that he didn't have anything. But the fact was that Walters' sinking fast ball was getting batters out.

When Bobby Layne was asked what his best pitch was, he replied, "Just trying to win—that was my best pitch."[10]

Hokie Garcia was a former Texas League pitcher turned umpire in the circuit. Garcia liked what he saw in Bobby Layne as a pitcher. He said that Layne had a good fastball and savvy on the mound. When Layne pitched in Houston, Garcia caught up with Bibb Falk and asked him about Layne, thinking perhaps that Falk had rested him for about ten days. Falk replied, "About three or four days is all the rest he's had. I worked him six innings about four days ago."[11]

That was proof enough to Hokie Garcia that Layne's stuff was natural, not just a fluke or due to a long rest between starts. Garcia was convinced that Layne could pitch in the Texas League immediately or even beyond.

Although scouting reports on Layne stated that he telegraphed his pitches, several major league teams expressed interest in signing him, including the Boston Red Sox, New York Giants and St. Louis Cardinals, but he came to the conclusion that he had a better chance of playing at the highest level of competition quicker in football.

"I liked baseball all right," said Layne. "But football was always the main thing. Now if I could have been a hitter, I might have gone to baseball. Pitching got to be too much like work for me. I didn't get a kick out of it, like hitting."[12]

The 1946 Texas Longhorns finished with a collegiate record of 19–2 and a SWC record of 14–0. The team featured five All-SWC players; in addition to pitcher Bobby Layne, the selections included infielders Ransom Jackson and Chuck Zomlefer, and outfielders Hobbs Williams and Bob Ferguson.

In the 1947 non-conference schedule, Texas defeated Hardin-Simmons and McMurray, split a series with Brooks Medical Center of San Antonio, swept two games from Oklahoma, and lost to Beaumont of the Texas League.

Between 1946 and 1947, Falk's Longhorns won 28 conference games in a row before being defeated by the Baylor Bears, 6–2, to end the streak. The 1947 and 1948 Longhorns lost only one game each season, both to Baylor at Waco. Since returning to Texas following the war, Falk's teams had established a conference record of 41–2 in three seasons.

Once again in 1947, Bobby Layne led the Longhorns on the mound, finishing with a SWC conference record of 8–0. In addition, with freshmen eligible to play in 1947, pitcher Murray Wall joined the team. Wall, from Dallas, was 20 years old and married, a Navy vet; he had pitched in 1946 for the Corpus Christi Naval Station. He would go on to become one of the best pitchers in Longhorns history and went 3–0 in 1947 SWC play.

In order to crown a national champion in college baseball, the College World Series began in 1947 as the NCAA Baseball Championship. The format for the first College World Series was eight teams divided into two four-team, single-elimination tournaments. The two winners would meet in a best-of-three final series for the championship.

The first NCAA Baseball Championship was played at the 2,500-seat Hyames Field at Western Michigan College in Kalamazoo, Michigan. Texas finished third, eliminated by eventual champion California, 8–7, in the second round after defeating Oklahoma, 10–9. The Golden Bears were led by pitcher/outfielder and later three-time All-Star outfielder with the Boston Red Sox, Jackie Jensen and outfielder Lyle Palmer, who went on to have a six-year minor league career. California went on to defeat Yale, 17–4 and 8–7, for the championship. Playing first base for the Yale Bulldogs was slick-fielding but weak-hitting, future 41st President of the United States, George "Poppy" H. W. Bush.

While attendance had been sparse, 3,792 for the two days the games were played, with some fans simply watching the games from behind a fence in the outfield, a tradition had been born and the College World Series would become an annual event.

10. Bibb Falk Becomes a Longhorn Legend

In 1948, Bibb Falk's Longhorns had another fine season, winning the SWC crown and finishing with a collegiate record of 18–1 and a SWC record of 13–1. Although Texas qualified for the NCAA Baseball Championships, they declined to participate.

As the College World Series format evolved in 1948, changes were made with the four-team playoffs being changed to double elimination tournaments. But the finals remained a best-of-three contest.

The 1948 NCAA Baseball Championship was once again played at Hyames Field in Kalamazoo. With Texas deciding to stay home, the SWC was represented by the Baylor Bears, who were eliminated in the third round by USC, 16–3. The Trojans then advanced to defeat Yale for the championship, winning two out of three games.

In 1949, Texas continued to dominate winning the SWC championship with a conference record of 12–3 and an overall record of 23–7. The Longhorns were led by two All-Americans, pitcher Murray Wall and first baseman Tom Hamilton, the first University of Texas players to receive the honor.

For the season, Hamilton hit .426 with 12 home runs and had a slugging percentage of .848. Frank Womack, a pitcher converted to an outfielder, never had a homer during the season but hit .405. On May 14, 1949, Murray Wall pitched a two-hitter against Texas A&M to win the SWC championship. The 1949 NCAA Tournament Region C playoffs were held at Clark Field in Austin with Texas sweeping Oklahoma A&M, 3–2 and 7–3.

Once again in 1949, changes in the format for the NCAA Baseball Championship were implemented. The final was expanded to a four-team, double-elimination format. Eight teams began the playoffs, with the four finalists decided by a best-of-three district format.

Bibb Falk was not sure if he wanted to take the Longhorns to the NCAA Baseball Championship. Five players had graduated and others were talking about attending summer school. Asked if the Longhorns would participate in the NCAA tournament, Falk responded, "Why should we take a ragout team up there and get beat first crack out of the box."[13]

But the Longhorns did advance to the 1949 finals along with USC, St. John's and Wake Forest, and with their star players.

After the NCAA Baseball Championship lost money being played in Kalamazoo in 1948, it was moved to Wichita, Kansas, in 1949, and

Bibb Falk

was played in Lawrence Dumont Stadium, which had a seating capacity of 7,635. The Texas Longhorns were crowned national champions in the tournament as they defeated St. John's, 7–1, then Wake Forest, 8–1 and 10–3 as Jim Ehrler got the victory in the championship game. In fact, Jim Ehrler and Charles Gorin yielded only five runs in 27 innings for Texas on the mound.

The Longhorns' Tom Hamilton hit three home runs in the series and was named Most Outstanding Player. It was the first year that the award was presented.

But as Bibb Falk quickly pointed out, a lot of credit for the Texas success needed to be given to Frank Womack. A pitcher converted into an outfielder, Womack did a great job leading off. He opened Games One and Two with singles, then went on to score. Over the course of the series, Womack led off the inning with a single six times and scored four times.

Culminating in the Longhorns' victory in the 1949 College World Series, the 1940s had been a decade of remarkable success for sports at the University of Texas. Within a four-year span following World War II, Texas had captured national attention as the Orange and White had placed teams in the highest level of competition in every major sport.

In football, Texas had more success than such powerhouse programs as Penn State, Georgia, Alabama and Penn. The Longhorns' football record in the 1940s was 78–21–3, which was surpassed only by Notre Dame and Michigan.

Of course, standing just a little taller in success during the 1940s at Texas had been the extraordinary baseball teams coached by Bibb Falk, and the golden age of Longhorns baseball was only beginning.

Texas began the defense of its national championship in 1950 by losing two exhibition games against Dallas and Houston of the Texas League, before sweeping a series with the AAA Milwaukee Brewers of the American Association and heading into collegiate competition.

While the Longhorns had lost games to Dallas and Houston, neither team scored an earned run off Murray Wall. The talented 1950 Longhorns team included the best college pitching staff in the nation, featuring right-handers Wall and Jim Ehrler, along with southpaws Charlie Gorin and Frank Womack.

While Big Tom Hamilton had gone on to the professional level, he was replaced by a very capable, hard-hitting first baseman in Kal

10. Bibb Falk Becomes a Longhorn Legend

Segrist. Center field Bob Brock, the leading hitter on the team, returned from the 1949 squad. Playing shortstop was Ben Tompkins, who was also the Texas Longhorns' quarterback who would guide the Longhorns to a 9–1 record in the 1950 football season, losing only to national champion UCLA.

Once the collegiate season began, the reigning national champion Texas Longhorns showed no signs of slowing down, finishing with an outstanding record of 27–6.

Texas began their drive to a second consecutive national title when they faced Arizona at Clark Field in a best two out of three-game series in the NCAA regional playoff series. Arizona had won the first game, 6–2.

In the second game, played on June 7, the Longhorns were trailing Arizona, 5–3, in the sixth inning. With two men on base, Irving Waghalter, a weak-hitting infielder, came to bat. As Waghalter grabbed his bat and started toward the plate, Bibb Falk grabbed him and put a hand on his shoulder. Looking Waghalter square in the eyes, Falk said, "I don't care where you hit, Wag, just so you knock it out of here."[14] Waghalter doubled up in laughter. He had never hit a home run at Clark Field and hardly expected to hit one. To his own amazement, on the first pitch Waghalter hit the ball over the right field fence to give Texas a 6–5 lead. The Longhorns went on to win the game and the following day defeated Arizona, 7–3, to advance to the College World Series.

The 1950 College World Series used an eight-team, double-elimination format. This format would remain in effect until 1988. The selection committee chose one team from each of eight NCAA districts to compete in the College World Series. This procedure would continue until 1954.

As the NCAA continued to seek a more suitable and more profitable site for the College World Series, in 1950 the tournament was moved to Omaha, Nebraska, where it would be played in the brand-new 9,165-seat Omaha Municipal Stadium. At the time the stadium was the home field for the St. Louis Cardinals Triple-A team.

After losing their opening game in the 1950 series on June 15 to Rutgers, 4–2, Texas came back, winning five straight games to win their second consecutive national championship.

On June 17, Texas began the drive to the title defeating Colorado A&M, 3–1. Next Texas defeated Tufts, 7–0, as Jim Ehrler pitched a no-hitter, the first in the College World Series. The Longhorns proceeded to defeat Washington State, 12–1, and Rutgers, 15–9.

The Washington State University Cougars had taken a train from Pullman, Washington, to Omaha to play in the College World Series. The team featured first baseman Ted Tappe, who would go on to play 34 games in the major leagues for the Cincinnati Reds and Chicago Cubs, and Gene Conley, a 6'8" pitcher who also played on the Cougars' basketball team.

Gene Conley would go on to play both professional baseball and basketball. He would pitch for the Boston/Milwaukee Braves and become a forward on the Boston Celtics. Conley holds the distinction of being the only professional athlete to play on both a World Champion MLB team (Milwaukee Braves 1957) and a World Champion NBA team (Boston Celtics 1959, 1960, 1961).

In the 1950 season, the WSU Cougars finished with a 29–4 record and defeated Stanford in the West Coast playoffs to earn a berth in the NCAA series. Ted Tappe hit .372 (16-for-43) in conference play while Gene Conley posted a 5–2 record and hit .417 (5-for-12) in conference action. Notwithstanding their loss to Texas in the Series, the Cougars reached the finals by defeating Alabama, 2–1, and Rutgers, 3–1.

In the championship game, played on Friday evening, June 23, before 2,384 spectators at Municipal Stadium, Texas defeated the Washington State Cougars, 3–0, to become the first team to win back-to-back national championships. The start of the game was delayed 30 minutes when a cloudburst occurred that left the field wet with surface water that had to be swept away by park attendants with brooms.

Jim Ehrler, fresh off his no-hitter against Tufts, squared off against Washington State left-hander Rod Keogh. The first five innings were a pitcher's duel, with Texas ahead, 1–0, before Texas got to Keogh for two runs in the sixth.

In the Texas half of the sixth inning, Keogh began by fanning Jim Ehrler. Frank Womack singled and Irv Waghalter drew a base on balls. A fine play by Cougars third baseman Don Paul retired Ben Tompkins for the second out. Keogh issued an intentional walk to Kal Segrist, loading the bases. It was the 12th walk issued by Keogh. This brought Bob Brock, the Longhorns' leading hitter, to the plate. Brock would set a record in the 1950 College World Series for total bases that would stand for several years. Brock got a hit when the Cougars' third base-

10. Bibb Falk Becomes a Longhorn Legend

Texas players greet Kal Segrist after his three-run homer—1950 College World Series (reprinted with permission from *The Omaha World-Herald*).

man, Don Paul, moved out of position towards shortstop. Womack scored on the play. Frank Kana followed with a single, scoring Waghalter, making the score 3–0 Texas. At this point Gene Conley was summoned to the mound and finished the inning by striking out Gus Hrncir.

Although Jim Ehrler allowed only seven Cougars base runners in seven innings, Bibb Falk, sensing victory was at hand, began to have concerns that Ehrler was tiring. So when Ehrler got a single in the bottom of the seventh inning, Falk sent in a pinch-runner. Murray Wall took the mound in the eighth inning and had no trouble continuing to get Washington State batters out. Texas won the game, 3–0, for their second consecutive national championship. Bob Brock went 2-for-5 with an RBI for the Longhorns. For the second straight year, Jim Ehrler got the victory in the championship game.

Murray Wall had a record of 8–2 in the 1950 season and was again named to the College All-America Team. Also named to the 1950 All-America Team was Nebraska outfielder Bob Cerv, who achieved an incredible slugging percentage of .878 during the season. Cerv hit 22 singles, ten doubles, three triples and nine home runs for 87 total bases.

Bibb Falk

Bob Cerv would go on to play 12 years in the major leagues and play in three World Series with the New York Yankees. In 1958, he would hit 38 home runs for the Kansas City Athletics.

Although the College World Series had been moved to Omaha in 1950 with high hopes of making it a profitable enterprise, once again the tournament failed financially. Total attendance for the tourney was 17,185, far below expectations. But part of the problem had been that bad weather had ruined several gates. The NCAA had been protected from the loss by an agreement made with the organizing committee in Omaha that had underwritten the expenses. The agreement was that all ticket revenue, after taxes and guaranteed minimums, would be split 50/50 between the College World Series committee and the NCAA.

Going into the 1951 season, the reigning two-time national champion Texas Longhorns had a 50-game conference home winning streak at Clark Field. The streak dated back to April 10, 1943. Texas had won 90 of the last 100 collegiate games, 58 of 60 at home, losing only to Ohio State in 1949 and Oklahoma in 1950. The Longhorns continued to dominate such teams as Alabama, LSU, Tulane, Minnesota, Oklahoma and Iowa.

In 1951, the Texas Longhorns failed to make the NCAA playoffs when the Texas A&M Aggies tied for the SWC championship and won the right to represent the conference based on having a 2–1 record vs. Texas.

One of the setbacks suffered by Texas in the 1951 season was the loss of pitcher Jim Ehrler, who hurt his arm. Ehrler was replaced in the Longhorns rotation by Luther Scarborough, who had come to Texas on a basketball scholarship.

The Aggies were eliminated in the third round of the 1951 College World Series by Utah, 15–8. Underdog Oklahoma won the national championship. The Sooners had begun the season with six consecutive losses before gaining momentum and going on to win the Big Seven Conference title. In the College World Series, Oklahoma went undefeated, toppling Ohio State, Springfield, USC and Tennessee.

The 1952 Longhorns were considered a long shot to win the SWC title. Still, they won the conference championship with an 11–4 record, then upset favored Arizona to reach the NCAA tournament where they were eliminated in the third round by eventual champs Holy Cross. The Longhorns' success in 1952 was due in part to the superb pitching

10. Bibb Falk Becomes a Longhorn Legend

of Luther Scarborough, who was credited with nine of the Longhorns' 11 conference victories. Scarborough won eight straight games and tied Bobby Layne's record with nine wins in a SWC season.

The man who would become Bibb Falk's successor as Texas coach, Cliff Gustafson, was a middle infielder on the team and batted .286. However, Gustafson went to bat only seven times with two hits in the season as a result of breaking his leg sliding into second base against Oklahoma.

Shortstop Joe Tanner led the team in hitting with a .378 average. Tanner would be signed by the Boston Red Sox but never graduated to the major league level.

Bibb Falk commanded respect from his players. Some of Falk's players believed that he never praised them in an attempt to have them prove him wrong. In 1953, when All-American center fielder Travis Eckert hit a home run over the center field wall, he was greeted in the dugout by Falk, who told him, "You're gonna' learn to pull the ball one of these days."[15]

In the late 1940s, after the Longhorns made several errors and lost a game to TCU, Falk instructed the team bus driver to high-tail it all the way back to Austin with no stops to eat or use the bathroom. In the days before interstate highways, the trek from Fort Worth to Austin was a test of endurance. As the bus rolled down the highway, Falk berated the bonehead play of his players against TCU, rambling and raving that they missed signs, threw to the wrong bases, and the cut-off men were never in the right place. He scolded his players, telling them that no big leaguer would have played like they did today. It was the ultimate disgrace for Bibb Falk that his players had not performed like big leaguers.

As the level of discomfort became intense among the players, Bob Brock, an outfielder from Houston, spoke up. Looking Falk straight in the eyes he stated, "Remember that not all of us have big league bladders."[16] With that, the crusty coach grinned and told the bus driver to stop at the next rest stop.

Billy Disch had been ailing for well over a decade when he died on February 3, 1953, at the age of 78. The University of Texas and many of Disch's friends, in recognition of his long term of service to the athletic department, decided to establish a memorial committee for him. D. C. "Bobby" Cannon, Bibb Falk's teammate on the 1920 Longhorns, who had played center field and was elected team captain by the other players, was named chairman of the Disch Memorial Committee.

Bibb Falk

Funds poured in from all over Texas to support the funding for the memorial. A small check was sent by Bibb Falk's brother, Collie, who had moved to San Antonio. Bibb Falk's father, Gus, had moved to San Antonio to live with Collie following the death of his wife Christina in 1952 at the age of 87. Billy Disch had also moved to San Antonio and was buried there in the cemetery near the grave of Christina Falk.

Like Billy Disch, Gus Falk was a devout Methodist. Gus had always been extremely grateful for the guidance and opportunity that Billy Disch had provided to two of his sons, Bibb and Chet. Enclosed with his check, Collie Falk had written a short note to Bobby Cannon that stated, "Mr. Disch was buried about ten yards from my mother who died a couple of years ago. I was out to the cemetery last Saturday and after we watered the flowers on our grave, Pop watered the new grass planted on Mr. Disch's grave. He takes care of theirs like he does ours. He was eighty-four the other day."[17]

The University of Texas was eternally grateful to Billy Disch as well. Although he had officially stepped down as head coach of the Longhorns in 1940 when he contracted cardiac problems, he still retained the title of head coach until 1952, and each year his name appeared in the Texas media guide ahead of Bibb Falk's. Although Bibb Falk had been the actual functioning head coach since 1940, with time out for service in World War II, and was directing the team while winning two national titles, his official title was Field Coach. But Falk knew who he was and never complained about being ceremoniously upstaged by the Longhorns legacy of Billy Disch.

Regardless of the fact that the record book contradicted him, at the start of every season Bibb Falk expressed his perpetual pessimism and predicted that his team would finish in last place. As the 1953 college baseball season approached, Falk was asked by the *Dallas Morning News* what the prospects for the Longhorns were. Falk replied that they were gloomy. The Longhorns had experienced the loss of several key players like shortstop Joe Tanner, pitcher Luther Scarborough and others to graduation, military service and professional baseball. Nevertheless, the 1953 Longhorns started strong with four straight victories and finished in a tie with SMU for the SWC championship with a record of 25–7–1. Travis Eckert hit .357 for the season and Paul Mohr .353.

Although Texas had a superior season record of 2–1 over SWC co-champion SMU, they still had to win the final two games against

10. Bibb Falk Becomes a Longhorn Legend

Texas A&M to win the right to represent the SWC in the College World Series.

The Longhorns won the first game, played in the rain, 1–0. In the second game, also played in the rain, the game was tied 1–1 in the ninth inning with two outs. Then two Longhorns reached base. This brought power-hitting first baseman Paul Mohr to bat. Coach Falk called time and told Mohr that if the Aggies attempted to issue an intentional walk to him, to take a swing at the ball if it came in range. As expected, the Texas A&M pitcher and catcher lined up to issue the intentional pass to Mohr in order to set up a force play at any base.

Mohr became over-anxious, swung at the first pitch wide outside, and hit a high pop-up to left field. According to Travis Eckert, who was sitting alongside Falk, the coach jumped up from the bench and began shouting at Mohr, mildly cursing at him, telling him he was supposed to be a line drive hitter. But the ball got up in the wind, sending the Aggies' left fielder and center fielder to the wall, where instead of making an easy catch, they watched the ball just barely drop over the fence for a three-run home run to give Texas a 4–1 win. According to Eckert, Falk began shouting, "he did exactly what I told him to do!"[18]

Texas then won two out of three from the University of Arizona in the NCAA District 6 Playoff Series to reach the College World Series.

Once again the struggling College World Series was to be played at Omaha's Municipal Stadium, so the Omaha Cards of the Western League, the stadium's regular tenants, turned over the facility to the collegians for a week and hit the road.

Texas started strong in the Series, defeating Duke, 2–1, and Lafayette, 7–3, before being defeated by Michigan, 12–5. Texas rebounded, defeating Michigan, 6–4. This left three schools in the tournament with one loss, Texas, Lafayette and Michigan. A drawing was held to determine which school with one loss would draw a bye into the championship game. Michigan drew the bye. Texas defeated Lafayette, 13–3, for the right to play Michigan in the title game.

Michigan had reached the title game by defeating Stanford, 4–0, Boston College, 6–2 and Texas, 12–5, before losing to the Longhorns, 6–4.

Ray Fisher was head coach of the Wolverines and in his 33rd season at Michigan. He had been at the job since being banned from organized ball by Judge Kenesaw Mountain Landis in 1920 following

Bibb Falk

a contract dispute with the Cincinnati Reds. Fisher had followed Carl Lundgren as Wolverines coach, and Lundgren had followed Branch Rickey.

The 1953 College World Series championship game took place on Tuesday evening, June 16, at Omaha's Municipal Stadium with 5,303 fans in attendance. Michigan's southpaw ace, Marvin Wisniewski, started the game against the Longhorns' Tom Jungman and went eight innings.

Bibb Falk's selection of Jungman to start the game was a total surprise to all. Jungman had a season record of 0–0 and an ERA of 7.60, and had only been to bat six times in the 30 games that the Longhorns had played. But Falk's mound core lacked depth and he was gambling that Jungman could last three or four innings. Then he would use every other pitcher he had if necessary. When Michigan got to Jungman for two runs in the third inning, he was soon replaced by Don Reifler, another seldom used pitcher.

Texas came back to score two runs in the fourth inning on a home run by Ron Spradlin with one man on and tie the score, 2–2. Reifler was replaced in the fourth inning by J. L. Smith, a strong stopper. The Wolverines took a 5–2 lead into the seventh inning when Texas scored twice to make the score 5–4 Michigan. Michigan scored two more runs in the eighth when the Longhorns committed a couple of errors and Dan Cline lined the ball over center fielder Travis Eckert's head. There was some concern by the Michigan base runners about whether Eckert was going to make the catch, and they hesitated, resulting in a couple of them grouped up at second base. The official ruling was that one run had scored and one base runner was called out for passing the runner ahead of him.

Michigan, with Marvin Wisniewski still on the mound, took a 7–4 lead into the top half of the ninth inning. Texas threatened to turn the tide when Tom Snow tripled and Roy Kelly doubled to drive Wisniewski from the hill and make the score 7–5. Jack Corbett came on for Michigan and proceeded to fill the bases with Longhorns. Coach Fisher sent Jack Ritter, a left-hander, in to pitch. It was a good strategy. With one out and the bases full, Ritter faced Paul Mohr, a left-handed batter, and struck him out on sweeping curve balls. At that point, Coach Falk sent Randolph Blesenbach up to pinch-hit for Smith. Blesenbach slashed a ball past first base. He thought it was foul so he didn't run

10. Bibb Falk Becomes a Longhorn Legend

very fast. But the ball was ruled fair, was fielded, and became the game-ending out. Bibb Falk took the defeat in stride.

J. L. Smith, Texas relief ace, was selected the Most Outstanding Player in the 1953 College World Series, the second Longhorn to win the title.

No one called Falk Bibb—he was perpetually referred to as "Coach," unless someone did it behind his back. However, Falk commonly called his players "mullets and goons." Following the Longhorns' 7–5 loss to Michigan in the 1953 College World Series that deprived them of a third national championship, Falk's players gave him an engraved cigarette lighter with the inscription "To the big leaguer from the Mullets and Goons."

Despite his supposed pessimistic and cantankerous persona, or as one sportswriter called him, "the Captain Bligh of college baseball," Bibb Falk had a caring and generous streak about him. For years he made it his practice to take two secretaries who worked in the University of Texas athletic department to lunch at the exclusive Austin Club on their birthdays. During World War II at Randolph Field, he became aware of the fact that his newly assigned and newly wedded publicist was having trouble making ends meet on a second lieutenant's salary. So he went into his pocket and handed the man five dollars, telling him to take his wife out to dinner. Stories of Falk's caring and generosity abound, but have been more often than not sidetracked in favor of chronicling his gruff behavior in regard to matters on the diamond.

Going into the 1954 season, Texas had several experienced letterman on its team such as center fielder Travis Eckert, first baseman Paul Mohr, left fielder Tommy Snow and pitcher Boyd Linker, who had a record of 10–3 with an ERA of 2.30 in 1953.

The 1954 Longhorns won the SWC championship again with a collegiate record of 15–7–2 and a SWC record of 10–2–1. But they didn't make it back to the College World Series. Since 1950, the baseball committee of the NCAA had been choosing one team from each of the eight districts to compete in the College World Series. That changed in 1954, when District playoffs were conducted to determine the eight teams to participate in the College World Series. Subsequently, in the District 6 playoffs, Texas lost two of three games to Oklahoma State, 3–6, 16–12, 6–7, and was eliminated in the tournament.

For the next two seasons, hard times would fall upon the diamond at Clark Field as the nadir of Longhorns baseball would occur. Texas

Bibb Falk

A&M (1955) and SMU (1956) seized the moment and won SWC titles. In 1955, the Texas Longhorns finished with a losing record for the first time in decades. They stumbled home with a 10–13–1 collegiate record and were 7–8–1 in conference play. It was the first time that the Texas Longhorns had failed to win more games than they lost since 1910 and only the second time (also in 1898) since there had been a baseball program on the campus. In 1956, matters only got worse as Texas finished with a collegiate record of 5–13 and a dismal conference record of 3–11.

Finally, in 1957, happy times returned to the Forty Acres as Bibb Falk put together a team of heavy-hitting Longhorns the likes of which had not been seen in Austin since 1953. Falk's corps of hard-hitting Longhorns was led by third baseman Max Alvis, who also played halfback on the 1956 Longhorns football team, but after hitting .403 in 1957 SWC play, Alvis began to concentrate on baseball.

Max Alvis (ten doubles, one triple, four home runs, 59 total bases), along with center fielder Roy Menge (five doubles, two triples, six home runs, 57 total bases) and left fielder Wayne McDonald (ten doubles, two triples, three home runs, 56 total bases) formed a monster trio of hitters in the middle of the Texas lineup. In fact, after the first two hitters in the Longhorns lineup, opposing pitchers faced seven straight hitters that were capable of bouncing the ball off the fence at Clark Field. Furthermore, second baseman Woody Woodman, not considered a power hitter, ranked fourth on the team in total bases with 41 and hit .402. At one point, Woodman hit safely in 18 straight games.

In 1957, the powerful Longhorns lineup averaged 8.5 runs per game and they reached double digits in runs in ten out of 24 games. In winning 19 games with 5 losses, the Texas lineup had 397 total bases.

Falk also had two quality pitchers on the 1957 Longhorns. Both would sign major league contracts before their eligibility expired. One was Howie Reed, an All-American who went on to pitch for ten years in the major leagues for the Kansas City Athletics, Los Angeles Dodgers, California Angels, Houston Astros and Montreal Expos. The other was Harry Taylor, who had a cup of coffee with the Kansas City Athletics in September 1957.

Still, as good as Howie Reed and Harry Taylor were, the two hurlers, along with the powerful hitting of Alvis, Menge, McDonald and Woodman, were not enough to carry Texas to their third National Championship.

10. Bibb Falk Becomes a Longhorn Legend

The 1957 Longhorns finished the season with a colligate record of 19–5 and a SWC record of 12–1 while winning the Southwest Conference baseball championships for the 31st time in 42 years. Still, Bibb Falk seemed curmudgeonly about taking the SWC title. Chomping on a cigar, Falk snarled, "It's a five out team. Five men don't get on base enough to count."[19]

Nonetheless, Texas advanced to the District 6 playoffs and quickly dispatched Arizona, 7–1 and 2–0. Returning to the College World Series in Omaha for the first time since 1954, Texas won its first game, defeating Connecticut, 3–0. In the second round, the heavy-hitting Longhorns' bats went cold and they were beaten by Penn State, 4–1. They were eliminated in the third round by Notre Dame, 9–0.

The University of California gave up only two runs in four games and went undefeated in the 1957 College World Series, defeating Penn State, 1–0, in the final. It was the second national championship for the Bears.

In the late 1950s, Bibb Falk was referred to in *Sport* magazine as "The Dean of College Baseball Coaches." The 1958 season was Bibb Falk's 17th year as coach at Texas, and with the power pack of hitters including Max Alvis, Ray Menge and Woody Woodman returning, the Longhorns won the SWC championship for the 32nd time with collegiate record of 18–5 and a SWC record of 13–2. By contrast, SMU finished second in the SWC with a conference record of 9–6 and a collegiate record of 11–11.

While the 1958 Longhorns may have not been the best overall team that Bibb Falk coached at Texas, it was without a doubt the hardest hitting team he piloted, finishing the conference schedule with a team batting average of .316. Six players hit over .300 in conference play; Max Alvis hit .403 to lead the SWC in hitting, followed by left fielder Woody Woodman at .333, center fielder Ray Menge at .321, first baseman Jerry Good at .314, pitcher George Myers at .306, and catcher Johnny Elam at .300. Alvis led the conference not only in hitting but also with 37 total bases, 25 hits, and seven doubles.

But the Longhorns had a pitching deficit and failed to make it back to the College World Series when they were eliminated in the District 6 playoffs, losing two out of three games to Arizona by scores of 14–3, 4–16, and 2–5.

In the 1959 campaign, the Longhorns were hampered by the loss

Bibb Falk

of three outstanding players: third baseman Max Alvis, the SWC's leading hitter, who signed a professional contract with the Cleveland Indians after being taken in the amateur free agent draft; first baseman Jerry Good; and former third-team All-American outfielder Roy Menge, who was scholastically ineligible. As a result, the Longhorns turned out to be a mediocre team, finishing with a collegiate record of 13–7 and a SWC record of 9–5 while losing the SWC title to Texas A&M. .

The Aggies were coached by Tom Chandler and featured pitcher Rollie Sheldon, who would go on to pitch for five years in the major leagues for the New York Yankees, Kansas City Athletics and Boston Red Sox.

In 1960, the Texas Longhorns rebounded and won the SWC championship with a collegiate record of 19–3 and a conference record of 13–2. But Texas failed to make it back to the College World Series, being eliminated in the District 6 playoff at Clark Field by Houston, 4–2.

Still, it should be mentioned that in the 1960 College World Series won by Minnesota, Jim Wixson of Oklahoma State threw a no-hitter against North Carolina. It remains the last no-hitter in the College World Series.

As the 1960s began, long-overdue honors for Bibb Falk started to occur. On December 30, 1961, in ceremonies held at the Sheraton-Dallas Hotel, he was inducted into the Texas Sports Hall of Fame. Falk was introduced by fabled retired football coach Dana X. Bible, who was serving as athletic director at Texas. In 1962, Bibb Falk was inducted into the University of Texas Hall of Honor.

Bibb Falk never talked about the National Baseball Hall of Fame, and it is doubtful that he ever visited Cooperstown. Eugene Converse Murdock stated that when he conducted an hour-long taped interview with Falk in 1974, he was reluctant to talk about the Hall of Fame. It is likely that Bibb Falk felt his body of work in major league baseball could stand on its own without over-aggrandizement. It is also likely that Falk's ego was bruised just a little by never getting the call from Cooperstown.

In 1961, Texas won 20 games for the first time since 1953, finishing with a collegiate record of 20–5–2 and a SWC record of 11–3–2. At one point in the season, the Longhorns won 17 games in a row. The longest winning streaks in Texas history were 23 in a row, accomplished by the 1914 and 1923 teams. The 1961 Longhorns were led by All-

10. Bibb Falk Becomes a Longhorn Legend

American outfielder Chuck Knutson, the first Texas All-American since Murray Wall in 1950.

Another player who made significant contributions to the 1961 Longhorns was Pat Rigby, a junior. His father, Lloyd "Rabbit" Rigby, had played third base for Bill Disch's Longhorns in the mid 1930s and was captain of the team his senior year.

For the 1961 campaign, Bibb Falk moved Pat Rigby to third base from second base, where he played in the 1960 season, and he proceeded to hit .333. In mid–April, when Texas was on a hot, 12-game winning streak, Rigby was hitting .358. After graduating from Texas in 1962, Rigby played minor league ball for four years in the Chicago White Sox organization.

In the 1961 District 6 playoffs at Clark Field, Falk's Longhorns quickly dispatched Arizona, two games to none. But after advancing to the College World Series, the Longhorns wasted no time in being eliminated by USC, 8–6, and Western Michigan, 8–2. USC went on to win the College World Series and become the first team to win three national titles.

The 1962 Longhorns were even better than the year before, leading the SWC in hitting with a team .278 average and in fielding with a .961 average while finishing with a collegiate record of 22–7 and taking the SWC title with 12–2 record. The Texas resurgence was led by four key players. Pat Rigby, who had been moved back to second base and was chosen as a unanimous SWC first team selection and an All-American, hit .382. Chuck Knutson, although a first team SWC selection, was passed over as a repeat All-American while hitting .354. Ed Kasper, a utility infielder, hit .303 and was named to the SWC first team. On the mound, Tom Belcher, also a unanimous SWC first team selection, did the heavy lifting, winning eight of the 12 Longhorns' conference victories with 54 strikeouts and finishing with an overall record of 12–2. Belcher also contributed at the plate, hitting .296.

The game that won the SWC championship for Texas in 1962 is considered the greatest comeback in Longhorns baseball history. The game between Texas and Texas A&M was played on May 10, 1962, at Clark Field. After three and a half innings, the Longhorns were trailing the Aggies, 9–2. But Texas kept chipping away at the deficit and by the ninth inning the score stood at 10–10.

In another of his uncanny moves, Bibb Falk inserted Buddy New,

Bibb Falk

a little-used player, in the lineup against Texas A&M. Falk reasoned that New, a left-handed hitter, could hit the Aggies pitcher, a right-hander, because he wasn't striking anyone out. Falk was convinced that New was going to hit him, and he did. After New stroked a double with two out in the tenth inning, catcher Gary London stroked another double to score New and win the 1962 SWC championship for Texas. As New crossed the plate with the winning run, the pragmatic Bibb Falk was unimpressed with New's performance, quietly stating that sometimes they come through and sometimes they don't.

The Longhorns went on to play in the 1962 College World Series and lost to Michigan in the first round game, 3–1. But the Longhorns rebounded in their second game and soundly trounced Northern Colorado, 12–2, then eliminated Ithaca, 3–1. Next the Longhorns faced Michigan again and shut out the Wolverines, 7–0.

This left three teams in the running for the championship game: Texas, Michigan and Santa Clara. As had been the custom in the Series, a drawing was held to determine which team with one loss would draw a bye and automatically advance to the championship game. Once again, just as in 1953, luck was with the Wolverines as they drew the bye.

Consequently, Texas squared off against the Santa Clara Broncos for the right to play Michigan in the championship game. Texas was leading, 2–1, in the third inning and had the bases loaded. Broncos coach John Paddy Cottrell called on 210-pound, 6'4" right-hander Bob Garibaldi to enter the game.

Garibaldi had already been a workhorse in the Series for Santa Clara. He had started and pitched seven innings in the Broncos' opening game win over Florida State, then pitched in relief in the Broncos' wins over Missouri and Florida State.

After Garibaldi issued a walk to increase the Texas lead to 3–1, he closed the door on the Longhorns, shutting them out for the next seven innings as the Broncos fought back and eventually defeated Texas, 4–3, in ten innings, eliminating them from the Series.

The following day, Santa Clara met Michigan in the championship game with 7,395 fans at Municipal Stadium in Omaha. In the sixth inning, with the score tied 3–3, Santa Clara starter Charles Marcenero was hit in the hand by a line drive. For the third straight day, Coach Cottrell brought Bob Garibaldi into the game. There were no outs and two men on base. Garibaldi struck out the next two batters and got the

10. Bibb Falk Becomes a Longhorn Legend

third out on a comebacker. The game went into extra innings as Garibaldi held the Wolverines hitless for the next eight innings. However, in the end, at 20 minutes before midnight, Michigan prevailed, rallying for two runs in the 15th inning to win its second national championship, defeating Santa Clara, 5–4.

Santa Clara Broncos coach John Cottrell was in his second year. Later Cottrell would leave the school with a 193–53 won-lost record and become the chief scout for the Philadelphia Phillies for ten years.

Santa Clara's Bob Garibaldi and Texas' Tom Belcher were chosen the pitchers for the all-tournament team. Garibaldi had set three pitching records in the 1962 College World Series that still stand: most innings pitched (five games), 27 2/3, most wild pitches, six, and most strikeouts, 38. Signed by the San Francisco Giants on July 4, 1962, for a $150,000 bonus, Garibaldi would pitch in parts of four seasons for the Giants between 1962 and 1969, appearing in 15 games, but never would be credited with a major league win.

Michael "Pinky" Higgins graduated from high school in Dallas in 1926 and went on to play college baseball for Billy Disch at the University of Texas before embarking on a 14-year big league career with the Philadelphia Athletics, Boston Red Sox and Detroit Tigers in which he would get 1,941 hits and play in two World Series.

In the spring of 1930, Higgins' senior year at Texas, the powerful New York Yankees team of Babe Ruth, Lou Gehrig, Earle Combs, Tony Lazzeri and Bill Dickey came to Austin to play the Longhorns at Clark Field. The Yankees just got by the Longhorns when Gehrig hit a two-run home run over the right field fence in the scoreboard area that bounded up Red River Street to give New York an 8–6 victory.

Following his playing days, Higgins would manage the Boston Red Sox from 1955 to 1962. Later Higgins would serve as a vice president and general manager for the Red Sox.

During his tenure as Red Sox manager, Pinky Higgins let Ted Williams know that their relationship was asymmetrical, and he kept him on a short leash. Just because "The Splendid Splinter" was a superstar, it gave have him no extra leverage with the manager.

On August 7, 1956, the New York Yankees and Boston Red Sox were locked in a scoreless tie in the bottom of the 11th inning when Boston loaded the bases. This brought Ted Williams to the plate. Yankees pitcher Tommy Byrne walked Williams, sending the winning run home. But Williams was angry. He felt the walk was an indignity, hurled his bat 30 feet into the air, and acted momentarily as if he was going to go back to the dugout rather than touch first base.

It was a classic case of Williams showboating, and Higgins took notice. He confronted Williams in the clubhouse and told him in front of the team, "Kid, that the lousiest thing I've ever seen in baseball."[20] Higgins conferred with Red Sox owner Tom Yawkey, who had been listening to the game on the radio. Williams was fined $5,000. Only Babe Ruth had been fined more by an owner.

In 1963, Pinky Higgins made a visit to the University of Texas Austin campus and met with Bibb Falk, whom he always had great respect for as a judge of talent. During their conversation, Falk told Higgins he couldn't make the Texas team today, "because you've got to be able to read and write to get into this school now."[21]

Mike "Butch" Thompson was a native Texan born in Dallas, who grew up in Roswell, New Mexico. Thompson had wanted to play ball for Bibb Falk since he was six years old. His father and grandfather had impressed two things on him while he was growing up in Roswell; get a college education and play baseball for Bibb Falk at Texas. According to Thompson, "When I was real young, my father and grandfather coached me—and all they talked about was Coach Falk. Even after we moved to New Mexico when I was six, I wanted to come to Texas and play for him."[22]

Butch Thompson did enroll at Texas and in 1962, playing for the Longhorns' freshman team, he hit .439 with two home runs and 15 RBI in 11 games.

During the summer of 1962, Thompson played semi-pro ball in the fast-paced Basin League in Rapid City, South Dakota, and hit .274 after a slow start.

Finally, in 1963, Butch Thompson got his chance to play for Bibb Falk on the varsity and in the Longhorns' first 21 games, he hit .408. For a left-handed pull hitter, Clark Field seemed like a natural environment for Thompson with its 300-foot right field line. But often the wind blew in from right, cutting down on a left-hander's natural advantage. Falk, recognizing the disadvantage it put Thompson under, taught him to hit to left when the wind was bad. Hitting to the opposite field resulted in several key hits for Thompson. Still, in 1963 Thompson hit seven home runs over the right field wall at Clark Field, including a

10. Bibb Falk Becomes a Longhorn Legend

couple over the 375-foot mark in the power alley with plenty of room to spare, while driving in 35 runs in 21 games.

While Thompson played first base, he actually preferred to catch. A scout had told him that catching was his best chance to get to the majors. In 1963, the Longhorns' catcher was going to be senior Gary Loudon, but Bibb Falk had assured Thompson that he would get behind the plate the following season.

For the 1963 season, Butch Thompson hit .409 while talented shortstop Bill Bethea hit .364. Both were selected as All-Americans. Bethea was chosen as the All-American first team shortstop over Florida State third-team All-American shortstop Woody Woodward, who had gotten the attention of a lot of big league scouts with his slick fielding.

The most sought-after All-American named on the 1963 team was Rutgers catcher Jeff Torborg, who hit a phenomenal .537 for the season and was signed by the Los Angeles Dodgers for $100,000. Torborg went on to play ten years in the major leagues as a back-up catcher for the Dodgers and California Angels, finishing with a .214 lifetime batting average. He caught three no-hitters that were pitched by Sandy Koufax, Bill Singer and Nolan Ryan. Torborg later managed for 11 seasons between 1977 and 2003 with the Cleveland Indians, Chicago White Sox, New York Mets, Montreal Expos and Florida Marlins. His lifetime managerial record was 634–718.

The Texas Longhorns had a very good season in 1963, finishing with a collegiate record of 21–7–1 and a SWC record of 12–3, but not good enough to win the SWC title outright as they finished in a tie with TCU, which was led by All-American pitcher Lance Brown, who compiled an 11–1 record.

Having large scholarship programs had allowed Texas and Texas A&M to dominate the SWC for a long time. But by the 1960s, SWC championships were becoming more challenging. Now other schools such as Baylor, TCU and Rice began to catch up, making the conference more balanced. In fact, SMU had gone from no baseball scholarships to eight.

The Longhorns were automatically selected to represent the SWC in the 1963 College World Series. In Texas' first game in the Series, they defeated the eventual champion, USC, 8–3. In their second game, the Longhorns fell to Missouri, 3–2. Rebounding in the third game, Texas defeated Penn State, 6–4, before being eliminated by Arizona, 10–8.

Bibb Falk

In the 1963 championship game, played before 8,682 fans, USC defeated Arizona, 5–2, for the Trojans' fourth national championship. A new attendance record had been set in 1963 for all games in the College World Series of 52,757.

Since its inception in 1914, the Southwestern Conference athletic programs had been racially segregated as were the schools' academic programs.

On June 5, 1950, the U.S. Supreme Court ruled that the University of Texas must integrate its graduate and professional schools. Two days later, John S. Chase, an African American, enrolled at the University of Texas to study architecture. Thus Texas became the first university in the South to enroll an African American. Starting in 1956, Texas began to admit black undergraduate students.

But the sports teams at Texas and in the SWC remained segregated. Memorial Stadium, the Longhorns' football facility in Austin, had segregated seating areas, segregated restrooms and segregated water fountains. Although the U.S. Supreme Court had outlawed segregation in public schools with its Brown vs. Topeka Board of Education case in 1954, there was a lot of foot-dragging towards integrating southern schools at all levels.

In the SWC, a gentlemen's agreement was in existence among the coaches and they were slow to act. It wasn't just Darrell Royal, the football coach at Texas, who was slow about recruiting blacks. It was all the coaches in the Texas athletic department, including Bibb Falk, who absolutely showed no interest in seeking out black players.

On November 19, 1963, in a surprising move, the University of Texas Board of Regents overturned a rule that had prohibited black athletes from playing on the school's various intercollegiate teams. To that end, three black men—James Means, Oliver Patterson and Cecil Carter—became members of the Longhorns' track team the following year.

In 1964, the dorms at Texas were integrated. But the football, basketball and baseball teams remained all-white.

In 1967, Don Baylor, a gifted black athlete in football and baseball, graduated from Stephen F. Austin High School, Bibb Falk's alma mater. While Falk was retiring that year, he nonetheless showed no interest in Don Baylor and made no attempt to recruit him for his successor.

Darrell Royal did offer Don Baylor a scholarship to play football at Texas. But when Baylor became the second choice of the Baltimore

10. Bibb Falk Becomes a Longhorn Legend

Orioles in the 1967 amateur draft, he signed for $7,500. Later Baylor enrolled at Blim Junior College in Brenham, Texas. In 1979, Don Baylor would be chosen the American League MVP after leading the league in runs with 120 and RBI with 139, while hitting 36 home runs with a batting average of .296.

The SWC broke the color barrier in football in 1966 when two black athletes began play: Jerry LeVias, a halfback/receiver at SMU, and John Westbrook, a running back at Baylor.

In 1969, the University of Texas Longhorns would be the last all-white football team to win a national collegiate football championship. That year a football scholarship had been offered to Leon O'Neal, a black athlete from Killeen, Texas, but he flunked out of school.

In 1970, Julius Whitter, from San Antonio, a back-up offensive lineman, would become the first black player to play varsity football at Texas.

Texas claims to have shared the national title with Nebraska for 1970. But that assertion is controversial as Texas lost the Cotton Bowl to Notre Dame on New Year's Day, 1971, while the only blemish on the Cornhuskers' record was a tie with USC during the regular collegiate season.

The following year, in 1971, the Texas basketball team would be integrated. But the baseball squad continued to be an all-white institution, either by design or happenstance. As late as 1983, Texas won a national title with an all-white baseball team coached by Cliff Gustafson that included future major leaguers Roger Clemens and Calvin Schiraldi.

By the end of the 1970s, Texas would have its first black All-American football player in running back Earl Campbell, who would shatter most of the existing Longhorns rushing records and be named the winner of the 1977 Heisman Trophy. Two decades later, Campbell would see most of his records eclipsed by another Longhorns black running back, two-time All-American and 1998 Heisman Trophy winner Ricky Williams.

The breakthrough team in bringing black players to college baseball was Arizona State, which has produced some outstanding African American players such as Reggie Jackson, Ken Landreaux and Hubie Brooks.

Today, institutional discrimination has been eliminated from collegiate sports. Still, there is a de facto component in college baseball being comprised of mostly white players because black athletes today, unlike in the 1950s and 1960s, have choices in collegiate athletics and choose not to play college baseball in favor of basketball, football and track.

In 1964, the Texas Longhorns were dethroned for the SWC baseball title by Texas A&M. Texas, with a collegiate record of 16–7–1 and a SWC record of 10–5–1, finished in a tie for second place with Baylor. Part of the problem for Texas in 1964 was that the team failed to score runs. In their seven losses, Texas scored only one or two runs in five of them.

Butch Thompson took over behind the plate for the Longhorns in 1964, but failed miserably at the plate, hitting just .253 with two home runs. The Longhorns were led in hitting by sophomore first baseman Buddy Young from Houston, who hit .379.

The final series of the year, with Texas playing Texas A&M, was like old times at Clark Field. The first game, played on May 7, attracted 3,000-plus fans. However, the game ended in 5–5 tie when it was called due to darkness.

The following day, on May 8, a doubleheader was scheduled to bring an end to the collegiate season. An overflow crowd of 4,240-plus turned out at Clark Field. The bleachers were full, special chair rows had been set up along both foul lines, there were fans standing along the lines, and some were sitting on top of the fence. Also, about 100 observers were looking on from atop Memorial Stadium, where a UIL State track meet was in progress.

Texas won the first game, 3–2, after they had entered the seventh inning, the final inning, trailing, 2–1. In the second game, Texas A&M clinched the SWC title with a 5–2 win when the Aggies' first baseman, Frank Stark, hit a bases-loaded double with two out in the final inning. In the final series of the season with Texas A&M, the Longhorns' Buddy Young went 5-for-9.

Texas A&M advanced to the 1964 College World Series and was eliminated in the second round, losing to Seton Hall, 14–5.

In 1965, Texas won the SWC championship, finishing with a collegiate record of 18–7 and a conference record of 11–4. The 1965 Southwest Conference race was its 50th, and the 40th time that Texas had been champions, including four co-championships. For Bibb Falk it was his 18th SWC championship, including three co-championships.

10. Bibb Falk Becomes a Longhorn Legend

The Longhorns won the SWC crown because they were tough in the clutch. Five of their 11 conference wins came by one-run margins. In all five of those games, the opposition had the tying and/or winning run on base in the ninth inning.

Texas clinched the SWC title on the next-to-last day of the SWC season, Friday, May 7, when they scored four runs in the top of the ninth to defeat Texas A&M. The Aggies finished second in the SWC with a record of 10–5.

One of the players that Bibb Falk was looking to turn things around for Texas in 1965 was junior left fielder Joe Hague. As a sophomore in 1964, Hague had hit .308 with one home run in 26 at-bats before he broke a bone in his hand. In 1965, Hague hit .343 and led the Longhorns in home runs with five and RBI with 23. For a while Hague was leading the nation in doubles, home runs and RBI.

First baseman Buddy Young started the 1965 season in a terrible slump. But Bibb Falk stayed with him because of his fine glove. As the season progressed, Young started to hit and wound up hitting .283.

The 1965 season was Butch Thompson's senior year at Texas, and it got off to a tragic start. In a humiliating 12–4 loss to Texas A&M on March 13, Thompson was hit by a Steve Hillhouse pitch, and the ball fractured the smallest of two bones in the forearm an inch above the wrist.

Prior to 1965, major league scouts had offered Butch Thompson bonus contracts. Suddenly a new world evolved for signing players, both collegiate and non-collegiate. The major league draft had been implemented, and now about the only thing scouts would do is tell players their team was interested in them and turn their names in with a recommendation for the draft.

Following the 1965 season, catcher Butch Thompson was signed by the St. Louis Cardinals as a free agent draft choice and assigned to the Raleigh Class A club. Although he had showed much promise at Texas, Butch Thompson never made it to the major leagues.

Texas won the SWC in 1965 because of two very good pitchers, senior right-hander John Collier (ERA 1.45) and sophomore left-hander Gary Moore (ERA 2.93). The two started all 15 of Texas' SWC games with Collier going 7–1 and Moore 4–2.

The Longhorns were given an automatic selection to the College World Series because the selection committee determined that no suitable candidate could be found to play them in the District Six tournament.

Trinity University of San Antonio had finished with a record of 20–4, but their roster included eight freshmen and two fourth-year seniors who were ineligible by NCAA rules. That left the team with only eight to ten eligible players.

Without having a tune-up, Texas entered the 1965 College World Series at Omaha and was quickly eliminated after losing to Washington State, 12–5, and Florida State, 3–2.

The winner of the 1965 College World Series was Arizona State, managed by Bobby Winkles and led by future Oakland A's stars Rick Monday and Sal Bando.

As the 1966 SWC season started, everyone, including Bibb Falk, was picking Texas A&M to win the conference title. Falk was very direct in his opinion of the Aggies: "They'll win. They're loaded. They have hitting pitching and fielding—a good all round team."[23] Falk actually predicted that TCU would finish second and the rest of the teams in the SWC would scramble for what was left.

Joe Hague had passed up his last year of eligibility to sign a contract with the St. Louis Cardinals, and Bibb Falk said the loss of Hague would be a key factor in the Longhorns not repeating as champions.

Still, Falk had some veterans returning in pitcher Gary Moore, first baseman Buddy Young, outfielder Joe Gideon and Forrest Boyd.

Doing the catching now for Texas was James Scheschuk, a fine defensive receiver. The Cincinnati Reds had liked Scheschuk's catching style, but wouldn't offer him a contract because of his low batting average. In fact he had never hit over .200.

When the smoke cleared in the tight 1966 SWC race, four teams had finished in a tie for the championship. The Longhorns finished with a collegiate record of 21–9–2 and a conference record of 9–6. Texas advanced to the College World Series on a coin toss with Texas A&M, Baylor and TCU.

In the College World Series, after defeating Arizona, 5–1, in their first game, the Longhorns were eliminated by loses to St. John's, 2–0, and Oklahoma State, 6–1.

Oklahoma State would advance to the finals, where they lost to Ohio State, 8–2, with a record College World Series crowd of 10,507 in attendance.

10. Bibb Falk Becomes a Longhorn Legend

On August 1, 1966, the University of Texas campus would be rocked by a heinous crime unparalleled in the history of American universities, and the incident would be the catalyst for police departments all over America creating SWAT teams.

That morning, Charles Whitman, a 25-year-old architectural engineering student and ex–Marine, climbed to the top of the University of Texas Tower with three rifles, two pistols and a sawed-off shot gun and, just before noon, began to fire down upon the pedestrians below. Before ascending the tower, Whitman had already murdered his mother and wife.

The shooting spree lasted 96 minutes. Forty-three people were shot, 13 died, and the incident was witnessed by hundreds of students, professors, tourists and store clerks, before Whitman was finally gunned down by the Austin police in the sunny shadows of the early afternoon atop the tower.

The shooting incident was the most tragic and painful day in the University of Texas history, and the lasting memory still lingers over the Forty Acres.

The 1967 baseball season would be the last for Bibb Falk, bowing out after 50 years in the game as a player, manager, coach and scout.

Just because the end was near, Falk never stopped being Falk. Jimmy Raup was a relief pitcher on the 1967 Longhorns. In a game against Oklahoma that year, Falk brought Raup into a game against Oklahoma with the bases loaded and nobody out. Raup proceeded to strike out the side, getting the third out on a high breaking ball.

Immediately, Raup went strutting off the mound, feeling cocky and self-assured. Then he saw Bibb Falk coming out toward him. He was expecting adulation, such as "nice job," from the coach. But Falk looked straight at him and said, "How long do you expect to get away with that shit?"[24]

As a swan song for Bibb Falk, the Texas Longhorns went on to win the SWC title in 1967 with a collegiate record of 17–11 and a SWC record of 10–5.

Bibb Falk coached his last game at Texas on May 19, 1967, in the NCAA District 6 championship. In the ninth inning, Houston staged a four-run rally to take a 4–3 victory and close Falk's coaching career. Houston had scored all four runs in the ninth inning on two singles, a

Bibb Falk

double, a walk and a triple. All that Falk said that day was "Some days you try something and it works. Some days it doesn't."[25]

Bibb Falk had taken over from his mentor, Billy Disch, in 1940 and continued the Texas tradition to the fullest. For 25 years at the Texas Longhorns helm, Falk's won-lost record was a remarkable 477–177, and his teams had won outright or tied for 20 SWC championships.

SWC publicity director Wilbur Evans had once said, "Bibb is so dedicated to baseball that until a week or so ago he thought the verse in the Bible said, 'In the big inning God created heaven and earth.'"[26]

A lot of persons connected to Falk thought he might become a scout again, but he was clearly through with baseball. He told a sports reporter from the *Austin American Statesman*, "I'll probably be hanging around the drug store this time next year."[27]

There were always rumors circulating that Bibb Falk had become a millionaire through stock market investments, but he quickly downplayed such talk as nonsense. "Why do they think I waited until I was 68 to retire?" asked Falk. "I was going as long as I could to build up a big enough pension to live on. I didn't get started on it until 1950."[28]

11

Looking Back

In many ways Bibb Falk was a kind, caring person who just did not know how to show it. But on the ball field he was a perfectionist. Travis Eckert played for Bibb Falk in the early 1950s. In a 1989 interview in the *Austin American Statesman*, Eckert remarked that Falk coached one way—his way.

"If your personality suited his way of coaching, he could make you into a great ballplayer. If your personalities didn't mesh, though, he could destroy you. I found it best to be easy and just roll with the punches."[1]

Jimmy Raup was a relief pitcher for the Longhorns in the early 1960s. He stated that Bibb Falk made you furious when you played for him—that was his method of motivation. Raup said that in 1989, shortly before Falk died, he saw Falk at the Houston/Texas doubleheader. Falk asked him how his curve ball was. "I told him I was coaching Little Leaguers and getting those 10 year olds out pretty consistently. He said, 'Well you're finally in the right league.'"[2]

Perfectionist, bombastic, tough, forthright, a man of few words; however one chose to describe Bibb Falk's coaching style, the fact remains that during his long tenure at the University of Texas, his teams produced many big league ball players. In fact, 18 of Falk's players went on to play in the major leagues and scores of others had minor league careers. Some were quality players with long and distinguished major league careers, others marginal big leaguers, while the experiences of some amounted to having a cup of coffee in the big leagues. But Bibb Falk was proud of them all, and the wall of his office in Gregory Gym was covered with All-American certificates and pictures of players and outstanding Texas teams he had coached.

The players who went through their careers at Texas under Falk's direction could be separated into three groups: first, the ones who went on to play major league baseball; second, the ones who were sure things to play big league ball, but for one reason or another failed to make it to the next level; and finally, the what ifs—those players who concluded their baseball careers wearing the orange and white of the Longhorns that may have been able to play at a higher level.

Among the first group is Murray Wall, who was an All-American at Texas and pitched the Longhorns to successive national championships in 1949 and 1950. Wall pitched in relief for four years in the major leagues for the Boston Braves (1950), Boston Red Sox (1957–1959) and Washington Senators (1959). Sadly, on October 8, 1971, in Lone Oak, Texas, Murray Wall would take his own life at the age of 45 with a self-inflicted gunshot blast.

Ransom (Handsome Ransom) Jackson got a B. S. degree in Business Administration from the University of Texas, then played third base for ten years (1950–1959) in the major leagues with the Chicago Cubs, Brooklyn/Los Angeles Dodgers (World Series 1956) and Cleveland Indians. He finished his big league career with 835 hits, including 103 home runs, and a batting average of .261.

Jackson's odyssey to the Forty Acres was a result of several detours in his personal goals after the onset of World War II. Following graduation from high school in Little Rock, Arkansas, Jackson enrolled in an officers' training program at the University of Arkansas. When the program was cancelled, he transferred to TCU and once again enrolled in an officers training program.

As a result of wartime restrictions on travel, the high school Jackson had attended shut down its athletic programs. So he had not played either high school baseball or football. Still, he was recruited to play on the Horned Frogs' 1944 football team. Although the squad had only 16 players, TCU won the SWC title. However, they were defeated in 1945 Cotton Bowl, 34–0, by Oklahoma.

In early 1945, when the officers' training program at TCU was cancelled, Jackson enrolled at the University of Texas. Immediately, he was recruited by Longhorns coach Dana X. Bible to join the Texas football program.

11. Looking Back

In 1945, Texas finished with a record of 10–1 and was invited to play in the 1946 Cotton Bowl, in which Jackson caught a couple of key passes from Bobby Layne.

That spring, Ransom Jackson joined Bibb Falk on the Texas baseball team and led the SWC in hitting for three years.

In 1948, Jackson was signed by the Chicago Cubs for $6,000 and assigned to their Class A Des Moines club in the Western League, where he hit .322 with 156 hits, including 31 doubles, had 76 RBI and scored 100 runs. After spending 1949 with Los Angeles of the Pacific Coast League and Oklahoma City of the Texas League, Jackson spent the 1950 season with Springfield of the International League, where he hit .315 with 20 home runs and 68 RBI.

Later that season he was called up by the Chicago Cubs, where he would eventually play third base in an infield that included Ernie Banks, Gene Baker and Dee Fondy, one of the best infields in Cubs history. Playing for the Cubs from 1953–1955, Ransom Jackson would hit 19, 19, and 21 home runs, and was selected to play in the 1954 and 1955 All-Star Games.

On December 9, 1955, the Cubs traded Ransom Jackson along with pitcher Don Elston to the Brooklyn Dodgers for third baseman Don Hoak, pitcher Russ Meyer and outfielder Walt Moryn.

Although the Brooklyn Dodgers had just won their first World Series title in 1955, the front office was becoming concerned that Jackie Robinson was nearing the end of his career and decided that they needed a capable replacement at third base, so they acquired Jackson. As it turned out Robinson played in 117 games in 1956, 72 at third base, then retired.

The 1957 season was the Dodgers' last in Brooklyn before the franchise transferred to Los Angeles. In their last game as the Brooklyn Dodgers played on September 28, 1957, they defeated the Philadelphia Phillies 11–8. In the game Ransom Jackson hit the last home run in Brooklyn Dodgers history.

During the 1957 season, Jackson suffered a serious knee injury and never played regularly again. During the 1958 season, the Los Angeles Dodgers sold Jackson to the Cleveland Indians. In 1959, he was traded back to Chicago Cubs, where his career had started and where it would end.

Third baseman Max Alvis was one of the most talented players

Max Alvis—Cleveland Indians (National Baseball Hall of Fame Library Cooperstown, New York).

ever to play for Bibb Falk at Texas. After being signed by the Cleveland Indians following his selection in the 1958 amateur free agent draft, Alvis played four seasons in the minors, two with the Indians' AAA affiliate in Salt Lake City, where in 1962 he hit .319 with 25 home runs, which earned him a late-season call-up to the majors, where he appeared in 12 games.

11. Looking Back

Max Alvis went on to play in 1,013 games for the Cleveland Indians and Milwaukee Brewers over nine years (1962–1970), and was a two-time All-Star (1965 and 1967).

In his rookie season with the Indians in 1963, Alvis had his best year with 165 hits, 32 doubles, 22 home runs, 67 RBI and a .274 batting average. While he was passed over for "Rookie of the Year" honors in favor of Chicago White Sox pitcher Gary Peters, who finished with a record of 19–8 and an American League-leading ERA of 2.33, Alvis finished 17th in the American League MVP vote.

In the 1964 season, Alvis contracted spinal meningitis and missed a third of the season but still managed to hit 18 home runs with 53 RBI. He would return full-time in 1965 and hold down the Tribe's third base position until 1969, when he split the position with Lou Klimchock.

Over the winter of 1969–1970, the Indians acquired Graig Nettles from the Minnesota Twins, who proceeded to beat out Alvis for the third base job in spring training. As a result, the Indians traded Alvis to the Milwaukee Brewers right before the start of the 1970 season, and in his final season in the big leagues, he played in 62 games and hit .183.

While Max Alvis was overshadowed at the hot corner during his career in the American League by Clete Boyer and Brooks Robinson and was never in contention for a Gold Glove Award, he was a steady performer, playing 971 games at third base and one inning at shortstop (on May 11, 1969). He finished his nine-year major league career with 111 home runs, 373 RBI and a batting average of .247.

Alvis went back to his home town of Jasper, Texas, and became a banker. He joined the First National Bank of Jasper in 1977 and worked his way up the position of Vice President before retiring in 2013.

Another notable Longhorn who went on to the big leagues was Grady Hatton, who was the team captain in 1943. He played under both "Uncle Billy" Disch and Bibb Falk before going on to play the hot corner for 12 years in the big leagues for six teams (Cincinnati Reds, Chicago White Sox, Boston Red Sox, St. Louis Cardinals, Baltimore Orioles and Chicago Cubs).

Grady Hatton was discovered as a big league prospect by the Cincinnati Reds while playing for an Army team. But when Hatton was discharged in February 1946, he could have signed with any one of 15 major league teams. The only major league club that did not make an offer to Hatton was the Boston Braves. With so many teams wanting

Hatton, the Reds had to pay top dollar and signed him for a $25,000 bonus, a handsome sum when it is considered that the Reds also signed Ted Kluszewski that same spring off the campus of Indiana University for only a $15,000 bonus.

According to Hatton, "I would not have been able to go straight to the major leagues had it not been for the fundamentals taught me by Uncle Billy and Bibb. Those guys made a lot of money for me."[3] Hatton was an All-Star third baseman for the mediocre post-war Cincinnati Reds (1946–1954). In 1952, Hatton led all third basemen in the National League in fielding with a .990 mark.

Hatton's career with the Reds had some tense moments when fellow Texan Rogers Hornsby was named manager in late 1952. At spring training in Tampa, Florida, in 1953, Hornsby was irritated because Hatton, despite the fact that he was already in Tampa, didn't report for the first day of practice. Hatton became agitated when Hornsby left him behind with the second team squad for the final exhibition in Tampa while the first team started making their way north to start the season, playing a series against Washington. Although Hatton had been the Reds' regular second baseman during 1952, Hornsby benched him in 1953 in favor of weak-hitting utility infielder Rocky Bridges.

The relationship between Hatton and Hornsby was further complicated by the fact that Hatton was the Reds' player representative in dealing with management. On June 11, 1953, Hornsby left Reds starting pitcher Clarence "Bud" Podbielan in a game against the Brooklyn Dodgers at Ebbets Field so long as to become humiliated, being battered for nine runs.

Following the game, Earl Lawson, a reporter for the *Cincinnati Times-Star*, rushed into the clubhouse to ask Hornsby why he had left Podbielan in the game so long. Hornsby read the riot act to Lawson and called him a "second guessing son of a bitch."[4] Then he banned him from the Reds clubhouse. Nonetheless, Grady Hatton assured Lawson that there was no way that Hornsby could prohibit the players from talking to him.

Hornsby had a managerial history of not being liked by his players. When he was managing the St. Louis Browns, Bill Veeck, Jr. had remarked that he had to fire Hornsby before the players whacked him.

Now Hornsby was in disfavor with his players in Cincinnati. Grady Hatton was asked by his teammates to approach Reds general manager

11. Looking Back

Grady Hatton—Cincinnati Reds (National Baseball Hall of Fame Library Cooperstown, New York).

Bibb Falk

Gabe Paul with a complaint that Hornsby was urinating in the clubhouse shower room. Paul's response was to have a placard printed with the message on it, "Please don't urinate in the shower."[5]

On September 17, with eight games to go in the 1953 season, Rogers Hornsby was fired by Gabe Paul. On April 18, 1954, the Reds traded Grady Hatton to the Chicago White Sox, who promptly packaged him with $100,000 cash after he had played in just 13 games and traded him to the Boston Red Sox for future Hall of Fame third baseman George Kell.

In 1959, Grady Hatton played for the Houston Buffs, who had left the Texas League to become a member of the American Association. The team featured future Hall of Famers Ron Santo and Billy Williams. For a while Hatton managed the team.

Grady Hatton wrapped up a 12-year major league career in 1960, playing 28 games for the Chicago Cubs. He retired with 1,068 hits and lifetime batting average of .254.

Following his playing career, Grady Hatton became manager of the fledgling Houston Astros (1966–1968), who had in their first four years of existence never finished higher than eighth place. In Hatton's first year as manager in 1966, the Astros, led by a group of young players such as second baseman Joe Morgan, shortstop Sonny Jackson and outfielders Jimmy Wynn and Rusty Staub, were finally on the verge of being competitive. Then Morgan broke his kneecap and Wynn dislocated his elbow running into the center field wall at Connie Mack Stadium in Philadelphia. The Astros took a dive and finished again in eighth place with a record of 72–90.

By 1972, Grady Hatton was serving as a scout with the Houston Astros. Prior to the 1972 season, the Astros put together an extensive goodwill tour with a number of players participating. Among those players were Tommy Helms and Jimmy Stewart, just acquired from the Cincinnati Reds, and Dave Roberts, acquired from the San Diego Padres, along with Jimmy Wynn, Norm Miller and Larry Dierker.

When the Astros' goodwill tour reached Austin, Hatton decided to look up his old coach and friend Bibb Falk. He told Falk that he was along "as chaperone to control the players." Falk, always direct in his responses, looked at Hatton and said, "How in the hell can you control them? You couldn't control them when you were managing."[6]

Of course it was a just a case of luck and fate that there were some "can't miss" players scattered among Bibb Falk's Longhorns alumni that

11. Looking Back

turned out to be disappointments at the professional level and either never made it to the big leagues or didn't last long. Many of Falk's players who signed with major league teams never wore a big league uniform for even one game. Other players' major league experiences amounted to a late-season call-up and never returned.

One of the most surprising disappointments among Falk's players at the major league level was Tom Hamilton, a multi-talented athlete who excelled in both basketball and baseball.

As a 15-year-old freshman at Arkansas City, Kansas, Tom Hamilton made the all-state basketball team. Then his family moved to Dallas, where he enrolled in Crosier Tech and twice made all-state honors. He was signed by scout Hap Morse to a major league contract with the Philadelphia Phillies. However, commissioner Kenesaw Mountain Landis nullified the contract on a technicality.

So after graduating from high school, Tom Hamilton enlisted in the U.S. Army and attained the rank of lieutenant. Discharged from the Army in 1946, Hamilton enrolled in the University of Texas, where his college roommate would be future Dallas Cowboys legendary coach Tom Landry.

Standing 6'4" inches and weighing 213 pounds, Hamilton made the basketball team and during the 1946–1947 season was a substitute player on the Texas team that won third place in the 1947 NCAA tournament.

In the spring of 1947, Tom Hamilton joined the Longhorns baseball team and played first base under Bibb Falk from 1947 to 1949. In his first year on the team, he was selected as an All-SWC player, hitting .333.

The following year he hit .305, prompting Bibb Falk to intervene. According to Falk, Hamilton was hampered by two circumstances. First, as a result of playing post-season basketball, he didn't join the team until March 2. Then Falk worked with Hamilton and got him to spread out a little at the plate. This kept him from lunging at pitches and gave him better use of his wrists.

As a result, in the Longhorns' national championship season of 1949, Hamilton had 12 home runs and hit .417 with a slugging average of .848. That year, Tom Hamilton was a first team All-American, first team SWC, and was voted the College World Series Most Outstanding Player in the first year the award was given.

Bibb Falk

At the same time, Hamilton continued to excel in basketball and became the first player in Texas history to score 1,000 points in his career. He was an All-SWC team player in 1950, and overall earned four letters in baseball and three in basketball during his collegiate career.

Signed by the Philadelphia Athletics, Tom Hamilton played in 67 games in 1952–1953, mostly as a pinch-hitter. Although Hamilton was one of the best college distance hitters of his generation, he never hit a major league home run in 66 at-bats.

Tom Hamilton's major league legacy is that on December 16, 1953, he was involved in an 11-player trade between the Philadelphia Athletics and New York Yankees that saw the A's send Hamilton, along with Harry Byrd, Eddie Robinson, Carmen Mauro and Loren Babe to the Yankees for Don Bollweg, John Gray, Jim Robertson, Jim Finigan, Vic Power, and Bill Renna.

Following his playing days, Hamilton managed in the New York Yankees farm system for a while. In 1960 he returned to Austin and became the baseball coach at St. Edward's University. Eventually Hamilton became the athletic director at the school and oversaw an ambitious building program that included construction of new facilities for baseball, track and field, tennis and handball. Tom Hamilton also served on the U.S. Olympic Basketball Committee.

Inducted into the University of Texas Hall of Honor in 1971, Tom Hamilton died on November 29, 1973, at the age of 48 of complications associated with a cerebral hemorrhage.

Ben Tompkins was another one of those "can't miss" players of Falk's. Actually Tompkins was better known as a quarterback on the Texas Longhorns' 1950 SWC championship squad. But Tompkins was also a pretty fair infielder; he could play second, third and shortstop. He played on Falk's 1950 National Championship team and in January 1951, while he was still in his junior year in college, the Philadelphia Phillies shelled out $50,000 to sign him to a contract and assigned him to their Class B farm club in Wilmington, Delaware, of the Interstate League.

Hap Morse, a Phillies scout in Dallas, was sensitive to the fact that Tompkins was a valuable asset to the Texas athletic programs. "I want it definitely stated that we did not go after Tompkins but that he called the scouts in and talked contract. I don't want anybody to start saying we raided the campus,"[7] said Morse.

Phillies owner Bob Carpenter considered Tompkins a great

11. Looking Back

prospect and approved the bonus for him, which was slightly less than the $65,000 he had paid to sign left-handed pitcher Curt Simmons. However, Simmons would pitch for 20 years in the major leagues and win 193 games (115 for the Phillies). Two days after Tompkins signed his contract with the Phillies, he was drafted into the U.S. Army. Following his hitch with Uncle Sam, Tompkins returned to baseball and in 1953 hit .316 playing for Terra Haute, but he would never play one game in the big leagues.

When the "what if" Texas players are considered, one name stands out far above all others—Bobby Layne. Athletes who have played both major league baseball and professional football simultaneously are rare. One of the first was Jim Thorpe, who played for the New York Giants and the Canton Bulldogs. More recently in the 1980s and 1990s there were Bo Jackson and Deion Sanders. But as the quintessential competitor, Bobby Layne could have excelled in both sports at the same time.

For many, Bibb Falk's assessment of Bobby Layne that he was "crazy as hell" would be an understatement. Whether Layne was playing horseshoes, dominoes, baseball or football, he did not just want to win—he had to win. After playing golf for less than a year, Layne shot consistently in the '70s and even had a hole-in-one to his credit. He liked to gamble, too. Early one morning in 1959, he got into a $100-a-game gin rummy session. The action eventually escalated into an all-day poker session with some pots reaching $10,000. At the end of the day, Layne had won $20,000.

According to Doak Walker, who roomed with Bobby Layne when they played for the Detroit Lions and followed him into the Professional Football Hall of Fame at Canton, if Layne was in Safeway, he had to be the best shopper in the store. "Bobby never lost a game," said Walker. "Time just ran out on him a few times."[8]

Layne actually tried professional baseball for one season, playing at Lubbock in the West Texas-New Mexico League in 1948. He appeared in a few games, but with mediocre success. Following 1948 he never attempted to play baseball again. "I played at Lubbock for two reasons," said Layne. "Somebody wrote I was afraid to play, and the owner of the club was a good friend of mine. He made me a deal that I could drive back to Lubbock when I wasn't pitching." Layne lived in Lubbock with his wife Carol, who was from there. The two had met while students at Texas.

Bibb Falk

While Bobby Layne went on to have a Hall of Fame career in professional football, he also established himself as a titan when it came to frolicking. He slept only three or four hours a night, loved his Jim Beam, three fingers potions, as they say in Texas, and for many years, according to his own account, smoked upwards of four packs of cigarettes a day. Layne liked to stay out all night until dawn. He had a custom of leaving $100 tips in hole-in-the-wall cafes.

Yale Lary, another Hall of Fame teammate of Layne's in Detroit, said of him, "When he said block, you blocked. And when he said drink, you drank."[9]

One tale of Bobby Layne's forays into the wee hours has it that one night following a pre-season game in Detroit; he headed for a bar with linebacker Joe Schmidt in tow. When Layne was unable to find a parking spot, he pulled his car onto the sidewalk under a canopy. About a half-hour had passed when a policeman entered the establishment and began to inquire who might be the driver of the illegally parked car. Layne quickly fessed up to the violation and took the officer aside, spoke with him and quickly befriended him.

When it came time for Layne, Schmidt and their acquired entourage to leave the bar, the officer was waiting outside. With his patrol car lights flashing and the siren wailing, he led Layne and his merry band of frolicsome followers to the next saloon.

Inside, as the party settled in and ordered a round of drinks, Layne recognized a portly gentleman seated at the end of the bar. So he went over and asked him to join him and his friends for a drink. It was Henry Ford II, and without hesitation, he immediately joined in the merry-making.

Paul Bean was a business associate of Layne's in Lubbock and was able to put his popularity in a down-to-earth ethos. "We'd forget how Bobby belonged to the world," said Bean. "In Lubbock, he'd be one of the guys. In Detroit, he was god."[10]

In regard to his legendary free-spirit life-style, Layne said, "I hope I'm not remembered for all that publicity that I was supposed to be a big hell-raiser. I did some of it, but I don't think I'd have been able to play fifteen years of pro football if I'd have done all that I was supposed to have."[11]

Bobby Layne continued to live in the fast lane nearly to the end. In 1983, he gave up cigarettes following surgery for throat cancer. On November 17, 1986, he began to hemorrhage in his lower esophagus,

11. Looking Back

a condition associated with a liver problem. Layne drove himself to the hospital in Pontiac, Michigan, where surgery to stop the bleeding was performed. A few days later he was released from the hospital and, accompanied by a private nurse, flew back to Lubbock.

Bobby Layne died on December 1, 1986, of cardiac arrest. He was 59 years old. At the wake held in Layne's honor, the atmosphere was upbeat. Whisky was consumed with three fingers of Jim Beam for everyone there.

Bibb Falk's retirement years were an exercise in solitude. He continued to live in Austin in the house on Avenue D and occasionally attended Texas baseball games. He spent a considerable amount of time autographing old photos of himself and baseball cards. His productivity in this endeavor is manifest by the extensive and diverse amount of signed memorabilia available today on eBay.

In late May 1989, Bibb Falk came down with pneumonia and was taken to Brackenridge Hospital in Austin. On June 8, 1989, he died at the age of 90. Falk was buried in Austin Memorial Park.

Two days later, the Wichita Shockers denied Bibb Falk a last hoorah from above when they defeated Cliff Gustafson's Texas Longhorns, 5–3, in the final game of the 1989 College World Series. Several of the Shockers went on to have major league careers, including Eric Wedge, Mike Lansing and Pat Forbes.

Bibb Falk had been the last surviving member of the infamous 1920 Chicago White Sox. Currently Falk ranks fourth in all-time batting average among Chicago White Sox players. His career average of .315 with the White Sox ranks him behind Joe Jackson's .340, Eddie Collins' .331 and Zeke Bonura's .317. Also he currently ranks 14th all-time in extra-base hits in White Sox history.

In 1968, Cliff Gustafson replaced Bibb Falk as the head baseball coach at Texas. Gustafson is one of only a few college coaches who has both played in the College World Series and coached in it.

Cliff Gustafson grew up near Kenedy, Texas. His father, a cotton farmer, died when he was only five years old. Along with his mother and brother, they continued to pick the cotton crop. On the farm Cliff use to throw a tennis ball against a barn in imaginary games that had him pitching for the New York Yankees against the Boston Red Sox.

By the time Gustafson had reached his teens, his mother had moved the family to San Antonio. It was there that Cliff began to play

Bibb Falk

basketball, football and baseball on an organized level. Eventually his interest and skills in sports took him to the University of Texas, where he played on Bibb Falk's SWC championship team in 1952. The year before, he broke his leg sliding into second base against Oklahoma and the injury ended the season for him. Still, Gustafson finished his playing career at Texas with a .308 batting average.

For a brief moment on a spring day in the early 1950s, an iconic moment took place at Clark Field where three men who would lead and guide the University of Texas Longhorns baseball team for 80 years were on the field together.

Cliff Gustafson saw Bibb Falk talking to an old man in a wheelchair. Somebody whispered, "That's Mr. Disch."

"I started to go over and meet him, but I didn't," Gustafson recalled. "I have always regretted it. When Bibb used to come to the ball park after he retired, I always encouraged our players to go over and talk with him. I didn't want them to make the same mistake I did."[12] Cliff Gustafson never met Billy Disch.

After graduating from the University of Texas, Cliff Gustafson played for a while for the Plainview Ponies in the now defunct West Texas-New Mexico League. One day, he asked for three days off and went for an interview for a high school teaching job.

When Falk retired following the 1967 season, people started to encourage Gustafson to apply for the Texas job. Gustafson had been coaching baseball at South San Antonio High School in San Antonio. His teams had won seven state titles and he was content. He liked coaching high school kids and aspired to becoming a principal. He simply told those persons pushing him toward the Texas job that Darrell Royal, the Texas athletic director, could hire any coach in the world. So Gustafson was thunderstruck when he received a call from Royal, so discombobulated in fact that he hung up on Royal, thinking it was a crank call. However, upon making contact with the Longhorns' athletic director, Gustafson accepted the job, taking a pay cut from $11,500 per year to $11,000.

The hiring of Gustafson turned out to be a win-win situation for both him and Texas. Gustafson would take the Longhorns to the College World Series a record 17 times and win national titles in 1975 and 1983, the Longhorns' third and fourth. When Gustafson retired after 28 years in 1996, he had won more games at Texas than Billy Disch and

11. Looking Back

Bibb Falk combined with a record of 1466–377–2. At that time he was the winningest college coach in history.

During Cliff Gustafson's tenure at Texas, 35 of his players would go on to play major league baseball, including such standouts as Keith Moreland, Roger Clemens, Greg Swindell, Spike Owen, Calvin Schiraldi, Burt Hooton, Dennis Cook and Shane Reynolds. When Gustafson was reminded of the large contingent of his players that reached the majors, he remarked, "I'm proud of that, but I'm just as proud of coaching three orthopedic surgeons."[13]

In the case of Roger Clemens coming to Texas, Cliff Gustafson did not recruit him out of Spring Woods High School in Houston. Clemens was being pursued by the professional scouts, but he felt that he wasn't ready for the pros. So he enrolled at Jacinto Junior College and pitched on the school's team for two years before Gustafson approached him about coming to Texas.

In two seasons as a Longhorn, Roger Clemens had a record of 25–7 and was a key player on the Texas 1983 National Championship team that was unbeaten in the College World Series.

Toward the end of Bibb Falk's tenure at Texas, he was concerned about how many West Coast teams were going to the College World Series. The West Coast formula for success was simple—they played more games each season than the SWC teams. When Cliff Gustafson took over at Texas in 1968, he began to advocate for more games. By the 1969 season, the SWC, which previously had limited teams to a 30-game schedule, began to allow 42 games with the addition of doubleheaders.

Despite a strong recruiting drive by Gustafson, his scholarships were whittled away by the NCAA. Falk was amazed at Gustafson's success at achieving a winning record with fewer and fewer scholarships. "When I gave the program to him," said Falk, "I had 21 scholarships. Now all he has is 13."[14] Falk submitted that Gustafson had to do a lot of juggling with just 13 scholarships.

In 1992, Cliff Gustafson was named to the College Baseball Coaches Hall of Fame. Despite the fact that accolades for Gustafson were slow in coming at Texas in light of his enormous success leading the baseball program, he harbored no resentment towards either of his predecessors, Billy Disch and Bibb Falk.

Although completed in 1975, Disch-Falk Field wasn't dedicated

Bibb Falk

until April 19, 1995. The ceremony took place after the first game of a doubleheader with TCU to honor the University of Texas' two legendary baseball coaches, "Uncle Billy" Disch and Bibb Falk. Immediately there were dozens of Cliff Gustafson's former players calling for the university to add his name to the field along with those of Disch and Falk.

When informed of Bibb Falk's death, Cliff Gustafson remarked, "Legendary is not a good enough word for him. He surpassed that. Unique. Sharpest baseball mind I've ever been associated with.[15]

In 1981, the College of Fine Arts at the University of Texas opened a new performing arts building on the site of Clark Field, the old baseball stadium where Bibb Falk, and before him Billy Disch, had plied their trade pushing, prodding and sometimes pulling their Longhorns teams toward victory on the diamond. It was a fitting setting for the new venue in that the work of Bibb Falk on that real estate was just what one expects from a good play—excitement, drama and excellence.

Today, The University of Texas at Austin has an enrollment of 50,000-plus students and is funded by a $20 billion, system-wide endowment fund that attracts some of most talented academics in the nation and beyond.

The SWC is gone now, disbanded in 1996 after a glorious 82-year history. The demise of the conference was hastened by cheating scandals in football, loss of revenues from expanding television coverage which did favor the regional markets of the SWC teams, and loss of a large fan base due to the goliath that professional football had become in Houston and Dallas. The SWC teams are now scattered throughout several conferences, including the SEC, Conference USA, and the American Athletic Conference. Texas, along with Baylor and Oklahoma A&M (now Oklahoma State), TCU and Texas Tech, are now members of the Big 12 Conference.

Cliff Gustafson resigned in 1996 and was replaced by Augie Garrido, who quickly established himself as the latest Longhorns baseball coaching legend.

Augie Garrido played in the College World Series in 1959 with Fresno State. Following college, he signed a contract with the Cleveland Indians and played for six seasons in the minor leagues, reaching the AAA level with Portland of the Pacific Coast League. His head coaching career began in 1969. Garrido came to the Forty Acres after having a

11. Looking Back

successful coaching career at San Francisco State, Cal-Poly, Illinois and California State-Fullerton, where his teams won three College World Series in 1979, 1984 and 1995.

Under Garrido's leadership, the Longhorns have added two more College World Series titles, their fifth in 2002 and sixth in 2005, to the Texas legacy.

On the afternoon of April 29, 2011, at the now-named UFCU Disch-Falk Field with 7,334 fans looking on, the Texas Longhorns defeated Oklahoma, 5–0. Augie Garrido became the first Division I coach in college baseball to reach 1,800 career victories.

Entering the 2015 season, Augie Garrido is now the career leader in college baseball wins with 1,920. Recently Garrido signed a contract extension to coach the Texas Longhorns through the 2017 season.

Afterword: College Baseball Coaches; No Ticket to the Show

College baseball, like college football and basketball, has had its share of great coaches past and present. But college baseball and its head coaches don't get the same level of media attention in their respective athletic departments that their high-profile, revenue-producing colleagues in the football and basketball programs get.

Jonas Ramsey, who served as sports information director at the University of Texas in the early 1970s, offered this insight into the focus of the Longhorns athletic department: "There are two sports at Texas; football and spring football."

When the topic of all-time great college coaches comes up, college baseball coaches are never considered. Most often the names of legendary college football coaches such as Knute Rockne, Glenn "Pop" Warner, Woody Hayes, Paul "Bear" Bryant and others are mentioned. If it's not football coaches, then basketball coaches take center stage and names such as Adolph Rupp, John Wooden, Bobby Knight, Mike Krzyzewski are offered into the conversation. College baseball coaches aren't even an after-thought.

The names of great college baseball coaches—and there have been many—are considered abstract, and one almost gets the notion that in terms of historical significance, being a college head baseball coach is a thankless endeavor. Although Bibb Falk had a magnificent career at the helm of the Texas Longhorns baseball team and developed winning

Afterword

teams and many major league-caliber players during his tenure on the Forty Acres, if one mentioned his name outside of Austin, Texas, or the SWC, the reply was most likely to be—Bibb who?

Of course, Bibb Falk's baseball anonymity goes farther than the college level. Very few baseball authorities and self-appointed historians even realize that it was Falk who replaced Shoeless Joe Jackson in left field in the Chicago White Sox lineup.

Major league baseball has traditionally relied on developing its managers at the minor league level, and it is an accepted fact among college coaches that no matter how successful your program is, no big league general manager is going to be knocking on your door when there is a job open. If a college coach does aspire to moving up to the big leagues, it is certain that he will have to leave his program's success on the campus in the past and begin a long and rigorous apprenticeship in the minor leagues. In 2001, only nine out of 199 coaches (4 percent) in the major leagues had coached in college.

On the other hand, many college coaches who would be great candidates for major league jobs prefer to remain at the collegiate level because of the job security as well as the camaraderie experienced on the campus. Job security at Texas was a key factor in Bibb Falk's decision to remain at the college level and not seek a major league post.

One of the most famous college baseball head coaches to rise to the major league level was Branch Rickey. But like others who followed such a career path, Rickey's major league experiences eclipse his college participation in a biographical sense.

Branch Rickey's odyssey in becoming one of the most famous baseball executives of all time was a long journey that started at the college level. In 1899, Rickey was playing semi-professional baseball in Ohio for the Lucasville team. After graduating from Ohio Wesleyan College in 1904, where he had been a catcher on the baseball squad, Rickey became the baseball coach at Allegheny College for a brief time. From 1905–1907 Rickey was an unsuccessful back-up catcher in the American League for the St. Louis Browns and New York Highlanders. Following his brief stint in the major leagues, Rickey continued to play ball in semi-pro leagues. By 1910, Rickey was attending law school at the University of Michigan and coaching the baseball team.

Future Hall of Fame member George Sisler played for Branch Rickey at Michigan and had a brilliant college career. As a freshman,

Afterword

Sisler struck out 20 batters in seven innings. Following graduation from Michigan, George Sisler would be the subject of considerable controversy.

After completing high school, George Sisler signed a contract with Akron of the Class C Ohio-Pennsylvania League. But Sisler decided to attend college instead. While he was attending college, Akron sold Sisler's contract to Columbus of the American Association, from which it was purchased by Pittsburgh Pirates owner Barney Dreyfuss. Upon Sisler's graduation from Michigan, Dreyfuss laid claim to Sisler, but the National Commission (baseball's three-man ruling body at the time) awarded Sisler to the St. Louis Browns, who were now being managed by none other than Branch Rickey.

Rickey converted George Sisler from a pitcher to a first baseman, and he would go on to become one of the all-time greats of the game, hitting over .400 twice and being voted into the Hall of Fame in 1937.

In 1918, Rickey would move over to the St. Louis Cardinals, become general manager and build the most extensive farm system in major league baseball that was the anchor of the successful Cardinals teams from the 1920s through the 1940s.

In 1926 although the St. Louis Cardinals had won the National League pennant, the first in the franchise's history, and defeated the powerful New York Yankees in the World Series, Cardinals owner Sam Breadon was not happy and neither was the Cardinals' star player, Rogers Hornsby. The Series had not only been one of the most dramatic of all time, but also the most profitable World Series with gate receipts of $1,207,864.

Sam Breadon was at odds with Rogers Hornsby over several issues, including Hornsby's gambling activities. Hornsby, a player-manager, was upset over what he considered the meddling of Branch Rickey over on-field matters and over his salary. Although Breadon offered Hornsby a one-year contract calling for $50,000, he wanted a three-year contract calling for $150,000. Hornsby also didn't like it that Branch Rickey had received a $25,000 bonus for the 1926 season. But Rickey's contract called for the bonus if he won a pennant.

Sam Breadon reached the conclusion that enough was enough and instructed Rickey to trade Rogers Hornsby to the New York Giants. So on December 20, 1926, Rickey traded Hornsby for Frank Frisch and pitcher Jimmy Ring. The trade was controversial when it was made,

Afterword

with Frisch replacing the hard-hitting Hornsby, who had won six consecutive National League batting titles from 1920–1925, hitting over .400 in three of those seasons. But the trade would be a long-term benefit to the Cardinals as Frisch would be a key element of the teams that would become known as the "Gas House Gang," winning pennants for St. Louis in 1928, 1930, 1931 and 1934.

Of course, Branch Rickey is best known today for integrating the major leagues with the signing of the Jackie Robinson in 1946 to a contract with the Brooklyn Dodgers.

Prior to being signed by Rickey, Jackie Robinson had been a multi-sport great at UCLA, playing football, baseball, basketball and track. Following service in the U.S. Army during World War II, Robinson played one season in the Negro Leagues with the Kansas City Monarchs.

Another notable college coach who reached the major league level was Dick Howser, who managed the New York Yankees and Kansas City Royals.

Dick Howser was born in Miami, Florida, in 1937 and was a two-time All-American shortstop at Florida State University. As a sophomore in 1956, he set a school record with a batting average of .422. Signed by the Kansas City Athletics, Howser played for eight years in the American League with Kansas City, Cleveland and New York from 1961–1968.

During the 1977 season, Yankees owner George Steinbrenner wanted to fire manager Billy Martin. He asked general manager Gabe Paul to recommend a replacement, and Paul stated that Yankees coach Dick Howser was his preference. But Howser turned the job down. Nonetheless, when Martin was fired the following year in July, Howser managed the Yankees for one game while waiting for Bob Lemon to assume the helm.

In 1979, Dick Howser left the New York Yankees and managed the Florida State University team to a record of 43–17–1.

In late 1979, after Billy Martin was fired again after punching out a marshmallow salesman in a Minneapolis hotel bar, Dick Howser was selected by George Steinbrenner to take over as manager of the New York Yankees for the 1980 season.

Dick Howser's Yankees won the American East Division Championship in 1980, finishing with a record of 103–59, but were swept by the Kansas City Royals in the American League Championship Series.

Ironically, in 1981 Howser took over as manager of the Kansas City

Afterword

Royals, and in 1984 his team won the American League West Division championship. The following season, Howser guided the Royals to another league championship and ultimately to the franchise's only World Championship, defeating the St. Louis Cardinals in the 1985 Word Series.

Unfortunately, Dick Howser died in 1987 at the age of 51 of cancer. To honor Howser, in 2005 Florida State named its renovated stadium in his honor.

Bobby Winkles, a graduate of Illinois Wesleyan (1952) was the manager of the California Angels (1973–1974) and Oakland Athletics (1977–1978). He also was a coach for several big league teams, including the California Angels, Oakland Athletics, San Francisco Giants, Chicago White Sox and Montreal Expos.

Before arriving in the big leagues, Bobby Winkles had been a huge success as the head baseball coach at Arizona State University. Winkles became the first baseball head coach at ASU in 1959 and built the program up from scratch. During his tenure as the Sun Devils' head coach, Winkles' teams won three national titles in the span of five years (1965, 1967, and 1969), and he had a career record of 524–173. In 2001, Packard Stadium, the Sun Devils' home field, was renamed Bobby Winkles Field in his honor.

Several of the players that Bobby Winkles coached at ASU went on to have outstanding major league careers, including, Reggie Jackson, Sal Bando, Rick Monday, Larry Gura, Floyd Bannister and Craig Swan. In fact, over the history of their programs both Arizona State University and the University of Texas have each sent 102 players to the majors.

Another former college coach who reached the majors was John Boles, manager of the Florida Marlins (1996, 1999–2001). Earlier in his career, Boles had been head coach at St. Xavier University and Louisville.

In 2015, the only major league manager with previous college coaching experience is John Farrell of the Boston Red Sox, who was an assistant coach at Oklahoma State from 1997–2001.

Many college baseball head coaches are legendary in the sport but are invisible in the annals of baseball history.

J. F. "Jack" Coffey played two seasons of big league ball with the Boston Braves (1908) and the Detroit Tigers and the Boston Red Sox (1918). In fact, Coffey is the only player to have been a teammate of Ty Cobb and Babe Ruth in the same year.

Afterword

During his playing career and after, Coffey became the head baseball coach of Fordham University, serving for 44 seasons between 1909 and 1958 with breaks in 1918, 1922 and 1944. During his tenure at Fordham, notable players on Coffey's teams included Frank Frisch, "The Fordham Flash," and Vin Scully, an outfielder who went on to become a legendary broadcaster with the Brooklyn/Los Angeles Dodgers.

Jack Coffey built a huge tradition of winning at Fordham, and through the 2013 season, the Rams lead all college baseball teams in wins with 4,298. Texas is second in wins with 3,246 and USC is third with 2,698. Coffey Stadium at Fordham was named in his honor.

When Ray Tanner was promoted to athletic director at the University of South Carolina in July 2012, he completed a college baseball coaching career in which his teams at North Carolina State and South Carolina won two national baseball championships and 1,133 games. But no one outside of the South has heard of him and he remains virtually unknown by baseball fans, sportswriters or commentators.

Bibb Falk's successor as head coach at the University of Texas, Cliff Gustafson, led the Longhorns to the College World Series 17 times and won two national championships. He retired in 1996 with 1,427 wins. At that time, it was the most wins ever by a college Division I coach, yet Cliff Gustafson's name is rarely mentioned in the press outside of Austin.

Clint Evans was the head baseball coach at the University of California from 1930–1954. During Evans' tenure, his Bears had a record of 547–256 and won the first College World Series in 1947. Several of Evans' players went on to play major league baseball, including Sam Chapman (also a football All-American), and Jackie Jensen. In 1964, the Bears' home field was renamed Evans Diamond.

The story of legendary University of Southern California (USC) Trojans baseball coach Raoul "Rod" Dedeaux's is unparalleled. Dedeaux's Trojans teams won 1,342 games and 11 College World Series titles (1948, 1958, 1961, 1963, 1968, 1970–1974, and 1978) during his 45 years at the school.

Dedeaux was born in New Orleans but grew up in southern California. He was a protégé of Casey Stengel, who spotted him playing ball at Hollywood High School. After Rod Dedeaux graduated from USC in 1935, Stengel, then manager of the Brooklyn Dodgers, signed him for a $1,500 bonus. Dedeaux had a cup of coffee in the major

Afterword

leagues, playing two games with the Dodgers in 1935 before an injury forced him to retire as a player.

In 1966, Dedeaux attempted to talk USC outfielder Mike Garrett into playing his senior year with the Trojans. Garrett, a star running back with the USC football team, had just won the Heisman Trophy. Dedeaux wanted Garrett to evaluate the possibilities of whether a better future in professional sports for him was in football or baseball. While Garrett was drafted by the Pittsburgh Pirates in the 41st round of the 1965 amateur draft, when the Kansas City Chiefs drafted Garrett and offered him $300,000 to sign a contract, he wisely took the money and ran. Still, while playing in the NFL Garrett was drafted three more times over the ensuing years by MLB teams. Garrett would play nine years in the NFL for Kansas City and San Diego and later become the Athletic Director at USC.

The list of USC players during Dedeaux's tenure at USC who went on to have distinguished major league careers includes Bill Lee, Tom Seaver, Randy Johnson, Fred Lynn, Ron Fairly, Mark McGwire, Steve Kemp, Roy Smalley and Dave Kingman. Also, Sparky Anderson was a bat boy for USC under Dedeaux, and the future Hall of Fame manager played close attention to Dedeaux's management style.

A footnote to the career of Ron Dedeaux is that he was called by some the "greatest part-time coach" in college baseball because of his outside business interest and entrepreneurship. While coaching at USC, Dedeaux also built a trucking business in California with assets and holdings in the excess of $4 million, which prompted him to accept a normal salary of $1 a year to coach the Trojans.

While it is a rare occurrence for a college baseball head coach to be hired as a major league manager, the number of former major league players who following their playing days became college baseball head coaches is extensive and impressive. A few others besides Bibb Falk are briefly mentioned here.

Charles "Bunny" Hearn, a southpaw, pitched six years in the major leagues from 1910–1920 for Boston, St. Louis and New York in the National League and Pittsburgh in the Federal League. In 1917 and 1918, Hearn filled in as coach of the University of North Carolina baseball team during World War I. He would return as coach for 14 more years from 1932–1946. Overall, Hearn's teams would win 214 games, lose 133 and tie two, while winning ten conference titles. Bunny Hearn

Afterword

is regarded as one of the most colorful college coaches ever and one of the most quoted. He is credited with first making the statement in one way or another that you "win some, you lose some and some are rained out."

Harry Wolter both pitched and played the outfield for seven years in the major leagues (1907, Cincinnati Reds, Pittsburgh Pirates, St. Louis Cardinals; 1909 Boston Red Sox; 1910–1913 New York Highlanders/Yankees; 1917 Chicago Cubs) and had a lifetime record as a pitcher of 4–6 with a .270 batting average.

In 1916, Wolter became the head baseball coach at Stanford, then returned to the major leagues for the 1917 season. Following a few more years playing minor league ball on the West Coast, in 1923 Wolter became head coach at Stanford and held down the helm until 1943. He would return for his third stint as head coach from 1946–1949.

In 1931, Stanford was the California Inter-Collegiate Baseball Association champions with a record of 18–5. In 26 years of coaching at Stanford, Harry Wolter's team's compiled 277 wins.

Ray Fisher was a graduate of Middlebury College. He pitched in the major leagues for ten years between 1910 and 1920, with a brief interruption in 1918 for military service in the Army during World War I. With the New York Yankees and Cincinnati Reds, he compiled a career record of 100–94.

Acquired on waivers in March 1919, Fisher went 14–5 for the Reds during the season and was selected by manager Pat Moran as the starting pitcher for the Reds in Game Three of the 1919 World Series against the White Sox, allowing three runs and seven hits in seven innings. The Reds lost the game, 3–0, as White Sox starter Dickie Kerr handcuffed them with a superb curve and excellent control. While Ray Fisher pitched a pretty decent game, he may have actually thrown the game away with a wild throw into center field on a bunt by Ray Schalk that eventually led to two Chicago runs.

Following the 1920 season, Cincinnati Reds president Garry Herrmann wanted to cut Fisher's salary by $1,000. Herrmann was using Fisher as trade bait with the Philadelphia Phillies in hopes of acquiring left-hander Eppa Rixey.

Fisher was dissatisfied with the terms of his contract and requested his release. When he didn't report to spring training, there were rumors that Fisher intended to jump his contract and play for an independent

Afterword

team in Franklin, Pennsylvania. When the Reds refused to modify his contract, Fisher quit and accepted the position of freshman football coach and baseball coach at the University of Michigan. In an unprecedented move, Commissioner Kenesaw Mountain Landis banned Fisher for life from organized ball.

The entire scenario involving Ray Fisher, his dissatisfaction with his contract, the snub by the Reds, and his ban by Landis seemed bizarre. But in the end it worked out satisfactorily for Fisher. He became the baseball coach at Michigan and went on to have a highly successful collegiate coaching career, winning a national championship in Michigan's first trip to the College World Series in 1953. Overall Fisher won 15 Big Ten Championships while establishing a record of 637–294–8 during 38 seasons at Ann Arbor. A side note to Fisher's tenure at Michigan is that one of the players he coached on the freshman football squad was Gerald R. Ford, who went on to become the 38th president of the United States.

In 1980, baseball commissioner Bowie Kuhn reinstated Ray Fisher to major league baseball as a player in good standing.

Upon receiving his sheepskin from St. Mary's College in 1907, Harry Hooper was signed by the Boston Red Sox in 1908 and played 17 years in the American League. Hooper played in the outfield with Bibb Falk on the Chicago White Sox from 1921 to 1925. Like Falk, he received a degree in civil engineering. In 1971, Harry Hooper was elected to the Hall of Fame.

Harry Hooper was always slightly offended by the stereotype advanced by some historians, sportswriters and uniformed fans that the ball players of his era were a bunch of uneducated rowdies and drunkards. Hooper was quick to point out that when he joined the Boston Red Sox in 1909, there were several players on the roster with college backgrounds. The starting catcher, Bill Carrigan, had gone to Holy Cross. First baseman Jake Stahl had gone to the University of Illinois, and third baseman Larry Gardner to the University of Vermont. Red Sox outfielder Duffy Lewis was another St. Mary's alumnus. Pitcher Marty McHale, another civil engineering graduate, had gone to the University of Maine. In addition, Chris Mahoney had graduated from Fordham and Ray Collins from the University of Vermont.

Harry Hooper was appointed as head coach at Princeton University on September 25, 1930. He coached for the 1931 and 1932 seasons,

Afterword

compiling a record of 22–29–1. He resigned when the university, facing financial difficulties as a result of the Depression, cut his salary.

"Smoky Joe" Wood played in the American League for 11 years and had one of the best fastballs in major league history. In 1911, Wood pitched a no-hitter against the St. Louis Browns. During the Boston Red Sox's World Championship season of 1912, Wood had a record of 34–5 with 258 strikeouts. In the 1912 World Series, he had a record 3–1.

Following an arm injury, Wood was sold by the Red Sox to the Cleveland Indians in 1917 and converted to an outfielder. Consequently, Smoky Joe Wood and Babe Ruth are the only two players to have both pitched and played outfield in World Series games. On May 24, 1918, Wood hit a home run in the 19th inning to give Cleveland a 3–2 victory over the New York Yankees at the Polo Grounds. It was Wood's second home run in the game.

Smoky Joe Wood finished his major league career in 1922 with the Cleveland Indians. In 1923, Wood was named head coach at Yale. When Wood was contacted by Yale and offered the same salary that he had been offered by the Indians for the 1923 season, he accepted. Smoky Joe Wood went on to coach the Yale baseball team for 15 years and finish with a record of 283–228–1. During his tenure at Yale, he coached his son, Joe Wood, who would have a brief stint in the major leagues with the Boston Red Sox in 1944, pitching in three games.

The fact that Smoky Joe Wood is not in the Hall of Fame may be due to the fact that he was implicated in a game-fixing scandal in late 1926, more than having borderline qualifying career statistics.

In 1919, it was the policy in major league baseball that part of the World Series revenues went to the clubs that finished in second and third place in the American and National Leagues.

In 1926, pitcher Dutch Leonard alleged that between games of September 24 and 25, 1919, he, Detroit Tigers teammate Ty Cobb, and the Cleveland Indians' Tris Speaker and Smoky Joe Wood had met under the stands to discuss how it might be arranged for Detroit to finish in third place. Cleveland already had a lock on second place. In short, according to Leonard they agreed to fix the game played on September 25 for Detroit to win, allowing the Tigers to clinch third place. The players also allegedly discussed placing bets on the game, and evidence showed that Wood had done so on behalf of himself and Leonard. While

Afterword

it was alleged that Cobb had offered to put up $2,000 and Speaker $1,500, neither came through with the money. The game was won by Detroit, 9–5. But the Tigers finished out of the money in fourth place, one-half game behind the New York Yankees.

The incident may have been forgotten, but Dutch Leonard had saved two letters related to the incident that he received from Smoky Joe Wood and Ty Cobb. In late 1926, Leonard turned over the letters to American League president Ban Johnson, who gave them to Commissioner Landis for investigation. It was also reported that Leonard had actually sold the letters to Johnson for $20,000. The letters became public and were printed in newspapers all around the country. Cobb, Speaker and Wood called Leonard's charge false in regard to a fix, but were vague in regard to admitting any betting on the game.

In an attempt to sort the matter out, Judge Landis summoned Cobb, Speaker and Leonard to his office in Chicago for a hearing. Leonard declined to attend, which agitated Landis because he would not confront the men he was accusing.

By that time, Smoky Joe Wood was coaching at Yale, and Dutch Leonard was out of baseball and living in California. With allegations of a fix swirling about, suddenly both Ty Cobb and Tris Speaker decided to leave major league baseball and threatened to sue to clear their names. Then the fans started to show strong support for Cobb, Speaker and Wood. In a surprising move, Judge Landis castigated the press for spreading rumors, swept the entire matter under the rug, and cleared both Ty Cobb and Tris Speaker, stating that there was not sufficient evidence to convict either player.

Smoky Joe Wood was not included in Landis's decision because he was no longer associated with organized ball. Wood had told Landis that he never had any conversation with Cobb on September 24 or 25. He said that after the game on September 25, Cobb had come up to him and asked, "How much did you bet on the game today?" Wood asked him why and he said, "Leonard asked." Thinking it was none of his business, Wood gave him a vague answer.[1] Furthermore Wood said he never spoke to Speaker about a bet on the game.

Wood also remarked to Landis that while betting on a game was not exactly a practice, it was not uncommon for players to bet on a game even in the middle of the season. "I recall one instance when the whole Washington team went broke, that is, they lost all their cash

Afterword

they had with them on a ball game that I pitched and beat Walter Johnson. They won it back the next day, when Bob Groom beat our team."[2]

Long after his coaching days at Yale were over, Smoky Joe Wood never stopped loving the game. Author Roger Angell has written about sitting with Wood when he was 91 years old during a game played between Yale and St. John's in 1981. The opposing pitchers that day were future major leaguers Ron Darling for Yale and Frank Viola for St. John's. The game went 12 innings before St. John's won. Throughout the game Smoky Joe Wood viewed it enthusiastically.

On March 25, 1985, four months before Smoky Joe Wood passed away at the age of 95, he was presented with an Honorary Doctorate of Humane Letters by Yale president and future major league baseball commissioner, A. Bartlett Giamatti.

Although John "Stuffy" McInnis was just 5'9½" tall and weighed about 165 pounds, he was the first baseman in Connie Mack's famous "Hundred Thousand Dollar Infield" (McInnis 1B, Eddie Collins 2B, Jack Barry SS and Frank Baker 3B). McInnis played major league baseball for 19 years and played in five World Series. Although he is not in the Hall of Fame, McInnis had a brilliant career, finishing with a batting average of .307 with 2,405 hits, while compiling a lifetime fielding average of .993 at first base.

In 1927, Stuffy McInnis played in one game for the Philadelphia Phillies while managing the team to a last-place finish with a record of 51–103. Soon after he joined the college ranks and became head coach at Norwich University, the Brooks School and Cornell for the next 14 years.

In 1948, Stuffy McInnis filled in for the ailing coach, Paul Eckley, at Amherst College and his team finished with a 10–1 record, winning games over Eastern Intercollegiate League powers such as Dartmouth, Holy Cross and Colgate. Amherst also lost, 4–3, to league champion Yale. McInnis was so popular on the Amherst campus that the student body voted him an honorary member of the Class of 1948.

The following year, McInnis was hired to coach the Harvard Crimson baseball team. He remained at Harvard through the 1954 season, when ill health forced him to resign.

Pitcher Jack Coombs was another notable former major league player who went on to coach at the college level after hanging up his

Afterword

spikes. A teammate of Stuffy McInnis on the great Philadelphia Athletics teams of the early 1910s, Coombs played for 14 years in the major leagues, winning 158 games. In 1910, Coombs went 31–9, and the following year went 28–12.

He pitched in three World Series, for the Philadelphia Athletics in 1910 and 1911, and the Brooklyn Robins in 1916. In the 1910 World Series, won by the Athletics four games to one over the Chicago Cubs, Jack Coombs won three games, all complete games.

After leaving major league baseball in 1920, Jack Coombs went on to become the head baseball coach at Duke. Between 1929 and 1952 Coombs' teams compiled a record of 383–171. Forty-seven of Coombs' players reached the major leagues, including Ace Parker, Crash Davis, Eric Tipton and Dick Groat.

In 1945, Jack Coombs' book, *Baseball—Individual Play & Team Strategy*, was published by Prentice Hall. The book became a must-read handbook not only for college coaches, but at all levels. The baseball stadium at Duke, built in 1931 and renovated several times, is named Jack Coombs Field.

Another Philadelphia Athletics player who went on to be a notable college head baseball coach was Jack Barry. The shortstop in Connie Mack's $100,000 infield, Barry was signed by the Athletics manager off the campus of Holy Cross for a $500 signing bonus.

Barry would play in the major leagues for 11 years with time out while serving in the U.S. Navy in 1918. He would play on five World Series-winning teams: the Philadelphia Athletics in 1910, 1911, and 1913 and the Boston Red Sox in 1915 and 1916. Barry also managed the Boston Red Sox to a second-place finish in 1917 with a record of 90–62.

In 1921, Jack Barry became the head coach of the Holy Cross baseball team and served in the position for 40 years until he died at the age of 73 in 1961. Barry's lifetime college record was 619–147, and 28 of his players would reach the major leagues.

In 1952, his Holy Cross team had a season record of 15–2 and won the College World Series, outscoring larger schools such as Texas, Missouri, Western Michigan and Penn State, 52–17, in seven games. After defeating Western Michigan, 5–1, in their opening game, Holy Cross lost to Missouri, 1–0. But they rebounded, defeating Bibb Falk's Texas team, 2–1, eliminating the Longhorns from the tournament, and went on to win the next four games and defeat Missouri, 8–4, in the final.

Afterword

Jerry Kindall played nine years in the major leagues with the Chicago Cubs, Cleveland Indians and Minnesota Twins (1956–1958, 1960–1965). While he was weak at the plate, finishing with a career batting average of .213 in 2,057 at-bats, Kindall was a smooth-fielding shortstop-second baseman.

Jerry Kindall became the first former player on a College World Series championship team (University of Minnesota, 1956) who also would be a head coach of a championship team in the Series (University of Arizona, 1976). Also, in the 1956 College World Series Kindall became the only Series player to hit for the cycle.

In Jerry Kindall's first trip to the College World Series as a coach in 1976, his Arizona Wildcats won the title. His Arizona squads also won the Series in 1980 and 1986. For 24 years at Arizona, Kindall's overall record in the College World Series was 36–24, and his career college coaching record was 860–580–5. In 2004, the University of Arizona renamed its field in honor of Jerry Kindall.

Thirty-one players who played for Jerry Kindall's Arizona Wildcats went on to the major leagues, including Kenny Lofton, Ron Hassey, Craig Lefferts, Joe Magrane, Casey Candaele, and Gilbert Heredia. Another of Kindall's players was Terry Francona, who not only went on to play major league baseball with several teams, but has become a highly successful big league manager with the Philadelphia Phillies and Boston Red Sox (World Series Champions in 2004). Francona is currently the skipper of the Cleveland Indians.

While college baseball has had a long tradition over the past century and produced some remarkable head coaches, players and teams, the college game has long suffered from a lack of media exposure, both print and electronic. But one can't completely fault the media; rather the game has been low on the list of priorities for promotion in college athletic departments across the nation. While college football has a tradition of bowl games going back over 100 years, there wasn't even a College World Series until 1947.

What's ironic is that the first sporting event to be televised was a college baseball game. On May 17, 1939, with Bill Stern calling the play-by-play, the second game of a doubleheader between Princeton and Columbia at Baker Field was televised.

The Rose Bowl predates the major leagues' World Series. On January 1, 1902, then billed as the Tournament of Roses football game, the

Afterword

first Rose Bowl game was played with Michigan defeating Stanford, 49–0.

In the 1920s, the Rose Bowl became a national event when the first transcontinental broadcast of the game from Pasadena took place in 1927. The game was carried by WEAF in New York, the flagship station of NBC, with Graham McNamee calling the play-by-play. The first Rose Bowl to be televised nationally occurred on January 1, 1952, with baseball broadcasters Mel Allen of the New York Yankees and Jack Brickhouse of the Chicago Cubs doing the play-by-play. In addition, the first color telecast of the Rose Bowl took place in 1962.

Starting in 1953, both ABC and CBS grabbed part of the New Year's Day audience with ABC broadcasting the Sugar Bowl, while CBS broadcast the Cotton Bowl and Orange Bowl. Today the ESPN stations broadcast 34 bowl games.

Popular championship tournaments in college basketball got started in the late 1930s with the NAIA (1937), NIT (1938) and NCAA (1939). However, college basketball was a little slow on getting on the gravy train that television broadcasting would become.

In 1961, Eddie Einhorn, future co-owner of the Chicago White Sox, bought the television rights to the NCAA basketball tournament for just $6,000. However, when he attempted to find stations interested in carrying the championship game between Ohio State and Cincinnati, Einhorn couldn't find any stations outside of Ohio and Kentucky that were interested in showing the game.

But Einhorn was persistent, and in 1968 he coordinated what is considered the first nationally televised college basketball game. Billed as the "Game of the Century," Einhorn put together a spectacular showdown between UCLA, featuring Lew Alcindor, and Houston, featuring Elvin Hayes, in the Astrodome that was watched by millions of fans.

The NCAA men's basketball tournament continued to grow in popularity through the 1970s, 1980s and 1990s. In 2010, CBS and Turner Sports signed a 14-year, $10.8 billion contract to broadcast the men's tournament.

Now the tournament is a must-watch event across the nation, generates hundreds of millions in advertising revenue, and is responsible for millions being bet in office pools. Even President Barack Obama nationally announced his bracket picks for the 2013 tournament.

Even the Little League World Series has had a longer tradition of

Afterword

television coverage than the College World Series. The first championship Little League World Series game to be televised occurred on ABC in 1953. The Birmingham, Alabama, team defeated the squad from Schenectady, New York, 1–0.

In was in that Little League World Series championship game of 1953, from Williamsport, Pennsylvania, that Howard Cosell launched his sports broadcasting career, calling the play-by-play on ABC radio.

Finally, in 1980, the College World Series came to television, broadcast by ESPN. Now in its 34th year of broadcasting the Series, ESPN, ESPN2, ESPNU and ESPN3 carry 153 games each year. Since 2003, for the final, best three out of five championship series, Mike Patrick has done the play-by-play along with several color commentators. In 2013, the color commentators were Orel Hershiser and Kyle Peterson. Others who have assisted Patrick over the last decade include Robin Ventura and Harold Reynolds.

While the competition in college baseball today is keen, some fans consider college baseball a fundamentally different game with the introduction in the 1970s of aluminum rather than wooden bats that tend to make the games offensive battles more than defensive battles.

In addition, college baseball has a complex and bifurcated designated hitter rule. NCAA Rule 7 (2) (b) states that the DH hitting for the pitcher is not mandatory. Therefore the pitcher can be used in the lineup as both the pitcher and designated hitter (P/DH) and can be moved to another position if removed from the mound, because the pitcher is not considered a defensive position for substitution purposes. The rule also allows for the insertion of a new DH if a pitcher (P/DH) moves to a defensive position or a DH moves to a defensive position, a pinch-hitter, after batting for someone, comes in to pitch, or a defensive player comes in to pitch. Furthermore, under NCAA Rule 7 (2) (1), if a P/DH is ejected he can be replaced by two players, a pitcher and a DH, or by one player, a P/DH. Such nuances in the college game turn the heads of baseball purists.

Over the years, college baseball has not received the same respect for its student/athletes by professional teams as that received by college basketball and football players, and many college players, regardless of their class standing, are just a signature away from a major league contract. The major leagues have traditionally and continue to raid the college baseball teams for their stars without any regard for age or their

Afterword

class standing, and it has caused some problems in retaining continuity in the game.

Take the case of Sandy Koufax, who immediately after graduating from Lafayette High School in Brooklyn, arrived on the campus of the University of Cincinnati on a basketball scholarship in the fall of 1953.

Head coach Ed Jucker's Cincinnati Bearcats basketball teams would win back-to-back NCAA tournament titles in 1961 and 1962, When Sandy Koufax arrived on the University of Cincinnati campus in the fall of 1953, Jucker was the coach of the freshman basketball team. So Koufax played freshman basketball for him in the 1953–1954 season. Jucker was also the head coach of the Cincinnati Bearcats baseball team and invited Koufax to try out for the squad. "I didn't even know he could pitch," said Jucker. "At the end of the basketball season, he told me to come over to the gym to take a look at him. I was amazed. It was almost like the wonder man. It struck me in such a fashion. The way he could throw—the speed and the curve—you just didn't see that."[3]

Koufax threw so hard that only one teammate could catch him, Danny Gilbert. While Koufax was having some trouble getting the ball over the plate, that did not preclude major league scouts from pursing him. They knew his potential with his 90 mph-plus fastball, and the Brooklyn Dodgers and Pittsburgh Pirates wanted him. Bill Zinser, a Cincinnati native working for Brooklyn as a scout, signed Koufax to a $14,000 bonus contract with his hometown Dodgers.

The unfortunate aspect of this situation was that the raid on Koufax denied him the chance to develop into a star as a college player before becoming a major leaguer and to achieve even a higher level of greatness in his professional career. The existing bonus rule in major league baseball denied Koufax any minor league experience and forced him to languish on the bench of the Dodgers for two years before getting the opportunity to grow as a hurler. And of course, the early signing of Koufax by the Dodgers denied both the University of Cincinnati and college baseball of the opportunity to showcase a huge star in the game.

In contrast, the NBA had a four-year rule in regard to recruiting or drafting players until 1971, when in a 7–2 vote the U.S. Supreme Court allowed Spencer Haywood to be drafted by the Seattle Supersonics of NBA three years into college. Previously Haywood had been playing in the ABA for the Denver Rockets. In 1996, the NBA instituted

Afterword

a rule change that mandates that players be at least one year removed from high school to be drafted.

The NFL currently has a policy that no player can be drafted until he is three years out of high school. That policy was challenged by talented Ohio State running back Maurice Clarett in 2003 after he was suspended from the Buckeyes following his freshman year, in which he helped Ohio State win a national championship. Clarett's suit went all the way to the U.S. Supreme Court, unsuccessfully.

College baseball continues to be the stepchild of varsity sports, and its talent is diluted annually by the MLB draft. Still, with growing exposure by ESPN and with the MLB Network starting to come on board, college baseball and the College World Series are now a profitable venture for the NCAA. Hundreds of reporters and thousands of fans now travel to Omaha, Nebraska, each year for the finals, tickets are getting harder to get, and the Series appears to have an optimistic future. The sport and event are positioned for growth in popularity. With the growth in popularity in college baseball perhaps, finally, the long-overdue recognition for the college baseball head coaches will follow, and more of them will wind up in major league dugouts.

Appendices

Appendix A

Bibb Falk Major League Career Batting Record

Year	Club	G	AB	Runs	Hits	2B	3B	HR	RBI	Ave.
1920	Chicago (A)	7	17	1	5	1	1	0	2	.294
1921		152	585	62	167	31	11	5	82	.285
1922		131	483	58	144	27	1	12	79	.298
1923		87	274	44	84	18	6	5	38	.307
1924		138	526	77	185	37	8	6	99	.352
1925		154	602	80	181	35	9	4	99	.301
1926		155	566	86	195	43	4	8	108	.345
1927		145	535	76	175	35	6	9	83	.327
1928		98	286	42	83	18	4	1	37	.290
1929	Cleveland (A)	126	430	66	133	30	7	13	94	.312
1930		82	191	34	62	12	1	4	36	.325
1931		79	161	30	49	13	1	2	28	.304
Totals 12 years		1354	4656	656	1463	300	59	69	785	.314

Appendices B, C, D

Appendix B

Bibb Falk Professional Baseball Managerial Record

Year	Team	League	Record	Finish
1932	Toledo Mud Hens	American Association	87–80	4th
1933	Cleveland Indians	America League	1–0	

(Note: Interim manager between Roger Peckinpaugh and Walter Johnson)

Appendix C

Comparative Statistics of Bibb Falk and Shoeless Joe Jackson as Chicago White Sox Players

Name	Yrs.	Games	AB	Runs	Hits	2B	3B	HR	RBI	BA	SA
Bibb Falk	9	1067	3874	526	1219	245	50	50	627	.315	.442
Joe Jackson	6	648	2439	396	829	139	79	30	426	.340	.499

Appendix D

University of Texas Longhorns Football Scores During the Years Bibb Falk Was a Player

1919
Record 6–3–0

Date	Home / Away		vs.
9/27	H	Texas 26	Howard Payne 0
10/4	H	Texas 39	Southwestern (Texas) 0
10/11	H	Texas 0	Phillips 10
10/18	H	Texas 7	Oklahoma 12 (@ Dallas, TX)
10/25	A	Texas 29	Baylor 13
11/1	H	Texas 32	Rice 7
11/8	H	Texas 35	Arkansas 7
11/13	A	Texas 13	Haskell 7
11/27	A	Texas 0	Texas A&M 7
		181	63

Bibb Falk, Tackle, All-Southwestern Conference

Appendix E

1918
Record 9-0-0

Date	Home / Away		vs.
9/28	H	Texas 19	Texas Christian 0
10/13	H	Texas 25	Penn Radio School 0
10/27	H	Texas 22	Penn Radio School 7
11/3	H	Texas 26	Ream Field 2
11/10	H	Texas 27	Oklahoma State 5
11/13	H	Texas 22	Camp Mabry 0
11/16	A	Texas 14	Rice 0
11/23	H	Texas 32	Southern Methodist 0
11/28	H	Texas 7	Texas A&M 0
		194	14

SWC Co-Champion (Oklahoma)

1917
Record 4-4-0

Date	Home / Away		vs.
10/6	H	Texas 27	Trinity (Texas) 0
10/13	H	Texas 35	Southwestern (Texas) 0
10/20	H	Texas 0	Oklahoma 14 (@ Dallas, TX)
10/27	H	Texas 0	Rice 13
11/3	A	Texas 0	Baylor 3
11/10	H	Texas 7	Oklahoma State 3
11/20	A	Texas 0	Texas A&M 7
11/29	H	Texas 20	Arkansas 0
		89	40

Appendix E

Southwestern Conference Baseball Championships During the Years Bibb Falk Was Field Coach/ Head Coach at the University of Texas

Year	SWC Champions
1940	Texas
1941	Texas
1942	Texas A&M

Appendix E

Year	SWC Champions
1946	Texas
1947	Texas
1948	Texas
1949	Texas

Note: Texas National Champions

1950	Texas

Note: Texas National Champions

1951	Texas/Texas A&M

Note: Texas A&M advanced to theCollege World Series based on a 2–1 record vs. Texas

1952	Texas
1953	Texas/SMU

Note: Texas advanced to the College World Series based on 2–1 record vs. SMU

1954	Texas
1955	Texas A&M
1956	TCU
1957	Texas
1958	Texas
1959	Texas A&M
1960	Texas
1961	Texas
1962	Texas
1963	Texas/TCU

Note: Texas advanced to College World Series based on a 2–1 record vs. TCU

1964	Texas A&M
1965	Texas
1966	Four-way tie, Texas, Texas A&M, Baylor, TCU

Note: Texas advanced to the College World Series on a coin toss

1967	Texas/TCU

Note: Texas advanced to the College World Series based on 3–0 vs. Texas A&M

Appendices F, G

Appendix F

Coaching Records of Billy Disch, Bibb Falk & Cliff Gustafson at the University of Texas

Coach	Years	(All) W—L	(Collegiate) W—L	(SWC) W—L	Ties
Disch	29	512–180	461–111	281–68	20
Falk	25	477–177	439–152	278–84	20
Gustafson	29	1466–377	1005–225	461–152	2

Appendix G

Major League Players Who Were Coached by Bibb Falk at the University of Texas

Name	Years at Texas	Major League Team(s)	Debut in MLB
Grady Hatton	1941–1943	Cincinnati (N), Boston (A), St. Louis (N), Baltimore (A), Chicago (N), Chicago (A)	April 16, 1946
Mel Deutsch	1939–1941	Boston (A)	April 21, 1946
Pete Layden	1939–1941	St. Louis (A)	April 20, 1948
Randy Jackson	1946–1947	Chicago (N), Brooklyn (N), Los Angeles (N), Cleveland (A)	May 2, 1950
Murray Wall	1947–1950	Boston (N), Boston (A), Washington (A)	July 4, 1950
Kal Segrist	1950	New York (A), Baltimore (A)	July 16, 1952
Tom Hamilton	1947–1949	Philadelphia (A)	September 4, 1952
Charlie Gorin	1948–1950	Milwaukee (N)	May 29, 1954
Mack Burk	1954–1955	Philadelphia (N)	May 25, 1956
Harry Taylor	1956–1957	Kansas City (A)	September 17, 1957
Howie Reed	1957	Kansas City (A), Los Angeles (A), California (A), Houston (N), Montreal (N)	September 13, 1958
Max Alvis	1958–1958	Cleveland (A), Milwaukee (A)	September 11, 1962
Wayne Graham	1956	Philadelphia (N), New York (N)	April 10, 1963
Bill Bethea	1961–1963	Minnesota (A)	September 13, 1964
Bart Shirley	1960	Los Angeles, N), New York (N)	September 14, 1964

Appendix H

Name	Years at Texas	Major League Team(s)	Debut in MLB
Chuck Hartenstein	1962–1964	Chicago (N), Pittsburgh (N), St. Louis (N), Boston (A), Toronto (A)	September 11, 1965
Joe Hague	1964–1965	St. Louis (N), Cincinnati (N)	September 19, 1968
Gary Moore	1965–1966	Los Angeles (N)	May 3, 1970

Appendix H

First Team All-Americans Who Played for Bibb Falk's Texas Teams

Year	Name	Position
1949	Murray Wall	Pitcher
	Tom Hamilton	Outfield
1950	Murray Wall	Pitcher
1961	Chuck Knutson	Outfielder
1962	Pat Rigby	Second Base
1963	Bill Bethea	Shortstop
	Butch Tompson	First Base

Chapter Notes

Chapter 1

1. Elizabeth A. Moize, "Austin: Deep in the Heart of Texans," *National Geographic*, 177, no. 6 (June 1990).
2. http://archives.starkcenter.org/bitstream/handle/1104817538BASE|
3. Bill Little, "Bibb Falk," *The Longhorn Album*.
4. Jamie Aron, *The Daily Texan*, October 9, 1991.
5. Tom Murray, "To the Big Leaguer—from the Mullets and the Goons," *Alcalde*, June 1964.
6. "Gruff Bibb Falk Kept Busy Denying Baseball Yarns," *Houston Chronicle*, June 18, 1967.
7. Bill Little, "Bibb Falk."
8. MackBrown-TexasFootball.com—Official website of the Texas Longhorns—Texas Football http://www.mackbrown-texasfootball.com/sports/m-footbl/spec-rel/061703aab.html.

Chapter 2

1. Joe Vila, "Are Offering 8 to 5 That Sox Will Win," *Philadelphia Inquirer*, October 1, 1919, 14.
2. John I. B. "Toney" Marsh, "How the Series Looks to Me," *Boston Herald*, September 25, 1919, 14.
3. Hugh Fullerton, "I Recall," *The Sporting News*, October 17, 1935, 5.
4. Lee Allen, *The American League Story* (New York: Hill & Wang, 1962).
5. *Cincinnati Commercial Tribune*, October 1, 1920, 8.
6. Lawrence S. Ritter, *The Glory of Their Times: The Story of the Early Days of Baseball Told by the Men Who Played It* (New York: William Morrow, 1984).

Chapter 3

1. Robert W. Creamer, *Babe: The Legend Comes to Life* (New York: Fireside, 1974).
2. Frank Graham, *McGraw of the Giants* (New York: G. P. Putnam's Sons, 1944).
3. *Philadelphia Inquirer*, September 18, 1920.
4. Grand Jury testimony of Eddie Cicotte from articles published in the *Cincinnati Enquirer* and the *Philadelphia Inquirer*, September 29, 1920.
5. Grand Jury testimony of Joe Jackson from articles published in *The Cincinnati Enquirer* and *The Philadelphia Inquirer*, September 29, 1920.
6. Richard C. Lindberg, *Total White Sox: The Definitive Encyclopedia of the World Champion Franchise* (Chicago: Triumph Books, 2006).
7. *Philadelphia Inquirer*, September 30, 1920.
8. *Cincinnati Commercial Tribune*, September 30, 1920, 1.

Chapter Notes

9. *Cincinnati Commercial Tribune*.
10. "Baseball Probers Ordered to Dig to Bottom of Scandal," *Philadelphia Inquirer*, October 29, 1920, 18.
11. "In a Lifetime Full of Second Chances, Denny McLain Receives His Biggest," *The New York Times*, December 29, 2003, D9.
12. *Total White Sox*.
13. *Cincinnati Enquirer*, September 29, 1920.
14. Bartee Haile, "Ex-Big Leaguer Makes Champions Out of Longhorns," *My Plainview*, http://www.myplainview.com/news/article_65688faa-bf0b-54bb-b541-9f0bda8d6d28.htm.
15. Bill Little, "Bibb Falk," *The Longhorn Album*.
16. Lee Allen, *Cooperstown Corner: Columns from The Sporting News, 1962–1969* (Cleveland: Society for American Baseball Research, 1990).

Chapter 4

1. J. G. Taylor Spink, *Judge Landis and Twenty-Five Years of Baseball* (New York: Thomas Y. Crowell, 1947).
2. "Ask Why Rothstein Was Not Indicted," *New York Times*, August 2, 1921, 28.
3. *Ibid*.
4. *Ibid*.
5. Spink, *Judge Landis and Twenty-Five Years of Baseball*.
6. Edward Burns, "Jackson Loses Fight to Re-Enter Baseball," *Chicago Daily Tribune*, January 20, 1934, 19.
7. *Ibid*.
8. Grantland Rice, *The Cincinnati Post*, October 1919.
9. Lindbergh, *Total White Sox*.
10. Tom Pettey, "Rothstein Dies Without Telling Name of Slayer," *Chicago Daily Tribune*, November 7, 1928, 25.

Chapter 5

1. Lawrence S. Ritter, *The Glory of Their Times*.
2. Jack Gallagher, "Bibb Falk Remembers Casey," *The Houston Post*, May 20, 1962.
3. *Ibid*.
4. "Waite Hoyt's Scrapbook, Thanksgiving in Kobe, Japan," *Greater Cincinnati Sports*, November 1977.

Chapter 6

1. "Collins Deal Hinges on One Man, Says Ruppert," *New York World*, January 31, 1923.
2. Willie Kamm, as told to Ford C. Frick, "Greatest Play I Ever Saw," *New York Evening Journal*, October 20, 1924.
3. Bill Little, "Bibb Falk."
4. Geoffrey C. Ward and Ken Burns, *Baseball: An Illustrated History* (New York: Alfred A. Knopf, 1994).
5. Jimmy Banks, "Bibb Falk Mixes Wit with Baseball," *Austin Bureau of The News* (date unknown).

Chapter 7

1. James E. Elfers, *The Tour to End All Tours: The Story of Major League Baseball's 1913–1914 World Tour* (Lincoln: University of Nebraska Press, 2003).
2. Jack Gallagher, "Bibb Falk Remembers Casey."
3. "Bibb Falk," *The Longhorn Album*.
4. "Abandoned," *Time* magazine, November 24, 1924, 28, http://content.time.com/time/magazine/article/0,9171,719534,00.html#ixzz2e1wbdHDf.

Chapter 8

1. "Falk Not Rated One of Game's Best Outfielders," clipping in the National Baseball Hall of Fame Library archives dated March 1, 1925.
2. "Gruff Bibb Falk Kept Busy Denying Baseball Yarns," *Houston Chronicle*, June 18, 1967.
3. Interview with baseball player Bibb Falk with comments, Eugene Converse Murdock, June 3, 1974, Austin, Texas, Cleveland Public Library, Social Services Dept.

Chapter Notes

Chapter 9
1. Randy Riggs, "Falk Did It His Way: Intense, Demanding, Caring," *Austin American Statesman*, June 11, 1989, 1.
2. "Bibb Falk," *The Longhorn Album*.
3. "Uncle Billy Dies in Texas," *Milwaukee Journal*, February 4, 1957, 7.
4. George Breazeale, "Bibb Falk: A Legend, Followed 'Institution,'" *Austin American Statesman*, July 31, 1970.
5. Leigh Montville, *Ted Williams: The Biography of an American Hero* (New York: Doubleday, 2005).
6. Lawrence Ritter, *The Glory of Their Times*.
7. Thomas Gilbert, *Baseball at War*.
8. Montville, *Ted Williams*.
9. Worth Matthis, "To Make Big Time, Never Stop Improving, Falk Tells Charges," *Dallas Morning News*, March 15, 1953.

Chapter 10
1. *Dallas Morning News*, December 20, 1961.
2. "Ex-Big Leaguer Makes Champions Out of Longhorns."
3. Riggs, "Falk did it his way."
4. Jack Gallagher, *Houston Post*, May 10, 1967.
5. Charlie Holmes, "No Time for Falk," *Dallas Times Herald*, December 24, 1961.
6. Denne Freeman, "Fact or Fiction, Layne's Exploits Fondly Revealed," *University Press*, December 12, 1986, Bobby Layne, University of Texas athletics Media Relations, http://archives.starkcenter.org.
7. Freeman, "Fact or Fiction, Layne's exploits fondly revealed."
8. "Bibb Falk," *The Longhorn Album*.
9. Bill Little, *Stadium Stories—Texas Longhorns* (Guilford, CT: Globe Pequot, 2005).
10. "What Makes Bobby Layne and What Makes a Winning Pitcher," *Houston Press Daily*, May 21, 1946, Bobby Layne, University of Texas athletics Media Relations, http://archives.starkcenter.org.
11. *Ibid*.
12. *Ibid*.
13. Baseball 1949 NCAA Tournment. The H. J. Lutcher Stark Center for Physical Culture and Sports e-Archives, http://archives.starkcenter.org.
14. Banks, "Bibb Falk Mixes Wit with Baseball."
15. Murray, "To the Big Leaguer."
16. Jack Gallagher, *Houston Post*, May 5, 1967.
17. Collie Falk's note to Bobby Cannon. University of Texas Media Relations. The H. J. Lutcher Stark Center for Physical Culture and Sports e-Archives, http://archives.starkcenter.org.
18. Murray, "To the Big Leaguer."
19. "Blame It on the Majors," *Time*, 1957 http://content.time.com/time/magazine/article/0,9171,824964,00.html#ixzz2e1wbdHDf.
20. Leigh Montville, *Ted Williams*.
21. Murray, "To the Big Leaguer."
22. Quote by Mike Butch Thomson. University of Texas Sports News Service, Jones Ramsey-Orland Sims, May 7, 1963. The H. J. Lutcher Stark Center for Physical Culture and Sports e-Archives. htp://archives.storkcenter.org.
23. David Wiessleb, "Falk Digs for Title Nugget as Premier Diamond 'Miner,'" *Daily Texan*, April 1, 1966.
24. Riggs, "Falk Did It His Way."
25. Breazeale, "Bibb Falk: A Legend, Followed 'Institution.'"
26. "They Said It"–12.03.62–SI Vault, http://sportsillustrated.comm.com/vault.
27. George Breazeale, "Longhorns' Falk Announces Retirement," *Austin American Statesman*, May 7, 1967.
28. "Gruff Bibb Falk Kept Busy Denying Baseball Yarns."

Chapter 11
1. Riggs, "Falk Did It His Way."
2. *Ibid*.
3. Murray, "To the Big Leaguer."
4. William A. Cook, *The Baseball Life of Ted Kluszewski* (Jefferson, NC: McFarland, 2012).
5. Earl Lawson, *Cincinnati Seasons:*

Chapter Notes

My 34 Years with the Reds (South Bend, IN: Diamond Communications, 1987).

6. "Astronotes," *The Sporting News*, February 26, 1972, 43.

7. "Phils Pay $50,000 to Sign Tompkins," *New York Times*, February 1, 1951, 32.

8. Blackie Sherrod, "A Long Long Layne A-Winding, Bobby Layne," University of Texas Athletics Media Relations, http://archives.starkcenter.org.

9. Galyn Wilkos, "Layne Is Gone, but His Reputation Lives On," *Star-Telegram*, December 2, 1986.

10. Mark Waugrin, "Goodbye, Bobby Layne," *Austin American Statesman*, Bobby Layne, University of Texas athletics Media Relations, http://archives.starkcenter.org.

11. John McClain, "Bobby Layne: Flamboyant Quarterback, Leader and Winner Reminisces," *Chronicle*, Bobby Layne, University of Texas athletics Media Relations, http://archives.starkcenter.org.

12. "Cliff Gustafson: The Winningest Coach in NCAAA Division 1 Baseball History," University Co-op, Austin, Texas, Gustafson, Cliff, http://archives.starkcenter.org.

13. Tim Kurkjian, "Cliff Gustafson," SI.Com, May 2, 1994.

14. "Bibb Falk" *The Longhorn Album*.

15. Brad Townsend, "Longhorns mourn death of legendary Falk," *San Antonio Light*, June 10, 1989.

Afterword

1. "Ty and Tris Charged with 'Fixing' Game Played Late in 1919," *Philadelphia Inquirer*, December 22, 1926, 22.

2. Ibid.

3. John Bach, *University of Cincinnati Horizons*, May 2000.

Bibliography

Books

Cook, William A. *August "Garry" Herrmann: A Baseball Biography.* Jefferson, NC: McFarland, 2008.

———. *The 1919 World Series: What Really Happened?* Jefferson, NC: McFarland, 2001.

Coppedge, Clay. *Texas Baseball: A Lone Star Diamond History from Town Teams to the Big Leagues.* Charleston, SC: History Press, 2012.

Gilbert, Thomas. *Baseball at War: World War II and the Fall of the Color Line.* New York: Franklin Watts, 1997.

Graham, Frank. *McGraw of the Giants: An Informal Biography.* New York: G.P. Putnam's Sons, 1944.

Lindberg, Richard C. *Total White Sox: The Definitive Encyclopedia of the World Champion Franchise.* Chicago: Triumph Books, 2006.

Madden, W. C., and Patrick J. Stewart. *The College World Series: A Baseball History.* Jefferson, NC: McFarland, 2004.

Montville, Leigh. *Ted Williams: The Biography of an American Hero.* New York: Doubleday, 2004.

Ribowsky, Mark. *Howard Cosell: The Man, the Myth, and the Transformation of American Sports.* New York: W. W. Norton, 2012.

Spink, J. G. Taylor. *Judge Landis and Twenty-Five Years of Baseball.* New York: Thomas Y. Crowell, 1947.

The Baseball Encyclopedia: The Complete and Official Record of Major League Baseball, 8th ed. New York: Macmillan, 1990.

Votano, Paul, *Stand and Deliver: A History of Pinch-Hitting.* Jefferson, NC: McFarland, 2003.

Periodicals

Murray, Tom. "To the Big Leaguer— From the Mullets and the Goons." *Alcalde,* June 1964.

Websites

http://www.myplainview.com/news/article_65688faa-bf0b-54bb-b541-9f0bda8d6d28.html.
http://www.baseballinwartime.com.
http://www.mackbrown-texasfootball.com/sports/m-footbl/spec-rel/061703aab.html.
http://content.time.com/time/magazine/article/0,9171,719534,00.html#ixzz2e1wbdHDf.
http://content.time.com/time/magazine/article/0,9171,824964,00.html#ixzz2e1wbdHDf.
http://www.baseball-reference.com.

Archives

Dolph Briscoe Center for American History, University of Texas at Austin.

Bibliography

National Baseball Hall of Fame and Museum, Inc., Cooperstown, New York.

The H. J. Lutcher Stark Center for Physical Culture and Sports, e-Archives, http://archives.starkcenter.org.

Libraries

The New York Public Library, New York, New York.

Monmouth County Library, Manalapan, New Jersey.

North Brunswick Public Library, North Brunswick, New Jersey.

Digital Recording

Interview with baseball player Bibb Falk, with comments (sound recording), creator Eugene Converse Murdock, 1974, Cleveland Public Library Digital Gallery, http://cdm16014.contentdm.oclc.org/cdm/ref/collection/p4014coll27/id/18.

Index

ABA (American Basketball Association) 180
ABC (American Broadcasting Corporation) 178–179
Acosta, Joe 35
Ahearn, Michael J. 54, 56
Alcindor, Lew 178
Alexander, Grover Cleveland 59
All American Girls Baseball League 106
Allegheny College 165
Allen, Mel 178
Alvis, Max 132–134, 149–151
American Association 27, 49, 61, 101, 122, 154, 166
American Athletic Conference 116, 162
American League 3, 19, 26, 32–34, 36–37, 44, 50–52, 74, 77, 79–80, 87–88, 90, 99–101, 105, 165, 167, 172–173
Amherst College 9, 175
Anderson, Sparky 170
Andrews, William ("Rooster") 114, 118
Angell, Roger 175
Ansonia Hotel 53
Appling, Luke 3
Arizona State University 141, 144, 168
Army (United States Military Academy) 112
Asinof, Elliot (*Eight Men Out*) 19
Associated Press (AP) 112
Astrodome 178
Attell, Abe 20, 22, 26, 36, 42, 52–55
Aulds, Doyle ("Tex") 108
Austin American Statesman 103, 146–147
Austin College 14
Austrain, Alfred 25–26, 40–41, 54–56
Autry, Martin ("Chick") 95
Averill, Earl 97–99

Babe, Loren 156
Baker, Frank ("Home Run") 76, 175
Baker, Gene 149
Baker Field 177
Baltimore Orioles 45–46
Bando, Sal 144, 168
Banks, Ernie 149
Bannister, Floyd 168
Barbour, Lou 94
Barrett, Bill 88, 92
Barry, Jack 175–176
Barry, Ralph 28, 31
Baseball—Individual Play & Team Strategy 176
Basin League 138
Battle of San Jacinto 10
Batts, Matt 108
Baylor, Don 8, 140–141
Baylor University 12, 30–31, 77, 102, 112, 119–121, 141–142, 144, 162
Bean, Paul 158
Beaumont, Ginger 11
Belcher, Tom 135, 137
Bellevue Hospital 63
Belli, Marvin 60
Bennett, Curley 52, 54
Benton, Rube 35–36, 63
Berg, Moe 95
Berry, Raymond 117
Bethea, Bill 139
Bevo I 11–12
Bevo II 18
Bible, Dana X 16, 111, 114, 134, 148
Big Seven Conference 126
Big Twelve Conference 162
Biggio, Craig 34
Bird, Harry 156
Blackburn, Joe 93

195

Index

Blackburne, Leana 92–94
Blankenship, Ted 85–88
Blesenbach, Randolph 130
Blim Junior College 141
Boles, John 168
Bollweg, Don 156
Bonura, Zeke 4, 159
Bosch, Anthony 90
Boston, Myer 63
Boston Braves 115, 148, 151, 168, 170
Boston Celtics 82, 124
Boston College 129
Boston Herald 20
Boston Red Sox 4, 11, 22, 29, 47, 69, 71, 78, 88–89, 94, 101, 104, 108–110, 119–120, 127, 134, 137–138, 148, 151, 154, 159, 168, 171–173, 177
Boudreau, Lou 29
Boyd, Forrest 144
Boyd, Robert 83
Boyer, Clete 151
Brackenridge Hospital 159
Breadon, Sam 166
Brickhouse, Jack 178
Bridges, Frank 30
Bridges, Rocky 152
Brigham, Harry H. 35
Brinkley, Jack 114–115
Brock, Bob 123–125, 127
Brook Field Ganders 111
Brooklyn Dodgers (Robbins) 69, 71, 105, 107, 109, 148–149, 152, 167, 169–170, 180
Brooks, Hubie 141
Brooks Medical Center 120
Brooks School 175
Brown, Jim 117
Brown, Lance 139
Brown vs. Topeka Board of Education 140
Burns, "Sleepy Bill" 21, 23, 27, 36, 41, 50, 53–54, 56
Bush, Barbara 8
Bush, George H.W. ("Poppy"; president) 120
Bush, George W. (president) 8
Bush, Jena 8
Bush, Leslie ("Bullet Joe") 69, 72, 74
Byrne, Tommy 137

The Cactus 32
California Angels 132, 168
California Inter-Collegiate Baseball Association 171
California Polytechnic State University–San Luis Obispo 163
California State University–Fullerton 163
Camp Barkley 4, 108
Camp Mabry 11
Camp Normoyle 108
Campbell, Earl 141
Campbell, William ("Bick") 96
Canady, Jim 115
Candaele, Casey 177
Cannon, D.C. Bobby 13, 15, 17, 28, 31, 127–128
Canton Bulldogs 157
Capone, Al 54, 64
Carpenter, Bob 156
Carrigan, Bill 172
Carter, Cecil 140
Cash, Norm 1
Castle, Dr. M.H. 96
CBS (Columbia Broadcasting System) 178
Cerv, Bob 125–126
Chance, Frank 78–79
Chandler, Tom 134
Chapman, Ray 34
Chase, Hal 35–37, 94
Chase, John S. 140
Cherry, Blair 107, 115
Chicago Bears 94, 116–117
Chicago Cubs 35, 65–66, 69, 75, 78, 107, 124, 148–149, 151, 154, 171, 176–178
The Chicago Tribune 42
Chicago White Sox 1–3, 5, 13–15, 18–28, 32–37, 42–48, 50–53, 64–65, 66–69, 73–75, 77–95, 99–100, 103, 106, 108, 135, 139, 151, 154, 159, 165, 168, 171–172, 178
Cicotte, Eddie 14, 19–24, 33, 35–46, 48, 50–51, 53–55, 59, 78
Cincinnati Reds 2, 18–20, 22–24, 30, 36, 39, 41, 43, 57, 59, 65, 78, 106, 108, 119, 124, 130, 144, 151–152, 154, 171–172
Cincinnati Times-Star 152
Cissell, Chalmer ("Bill") 92
Clarett, Maurice 181
Clark Field (Austin, TX) 31, 121, 123, 126, 131–132, 134–135, 137–138, 142, 160, 162
Clemens, Roger 141, 161
Cleveland Browns 117
Cleveland Indians 2–3, 29, 33–35, 43–44, 47, 57, 64–65, 69, 74, 92, 95–100, 108, 134, 139, 148–149–151, 162, 167, 173, 177
Cline, Dan 130
Cobb, Ty 47–48, 59, 67, 72, 76, 89–90, 100, 168, 173–174
Cochran, Mickey 59
Coffey, J.F. Jack 168–169
Coffey Stadium (Bronx, NY) 169

196

Index

Colgate University 175
College Baseball Coaches Hall of Fame 161
College World Series 179, 181; (1947) 120, 177; (1948) 121, 169; (1949) 122, 155; (1950) 123–126; (1951) 126; (1952) 176; (1953) 129–131, 172; (1954) 123, 131; (1956) 177; (1957) 133; (1958) 169; (1959) 162; (1960) 134; (1961) 135, 169; (1962) 136–137; (1963) 139–140, 169; (1964) 142; (1965) 143–144, 168; (1966) 144; (1967) 168; (1968) 169; (1969) 168; (1970–74) 169; (1975) 160; (1976) 177; (1978) 169; (1979) 163; (1980) 177, 179; (1983) 160–161; (1984) 163; (1986) 177; (1988) 123; (1989) 159; (1995) 163; (2002) 163; (2005) 163
Collier, John 143
Collins, Eddie 4, 14, 33–34, 45–46, 48, 51, 59, 62, 66, 73–74, 76, 78–80, 82, 85–86, 88, 90–91, 100, 104, 159, 175
Collins, Ray 172
Collins, Shano 33, 46–47
Collyer's Eye 22
Columbia University 177
Combs, Earle 137
Comiskey, Charles A. ("The Old Roman") 2–3, 15, 17–23, 25–28, 32, 34, 37, 41–44, 46–48, 50–52, 54, 56, 58, 68, 70, 73–74, 78–82, 84–86, 90–92
Comiskey Park 3, 35, 48, 66–67, 74–75, 77, 88, 90–91
Conference USA 162
Conley, Gene 124–125
Cook, Dennis 161
Cook County Grand Jury Hearing (1919 World Series) 35, 38–40, 42–43, 52–53, 56
Coombs, Jack 175–176
Corbett, Jack 130
Cornel University 175
Corpus Christi Naval Station 120
Cosell, Howard 136, 179
Cosgrove, William Edgar (president, Ireland) 82
Cotton Bowl: (1944) 111–112; (1945) 148; (1946) 115; (1948) 115; (1953) 178; (1971) 141
Cottrell, John "Paddy" 137
Coveleski, Stan 74
Crenshaw, Ben 9
Crim, Cal 23
Cronin, Joe 76, 101
Crosier Tech 155
Cross Harry 83
Crowe, Robert 48–50
Cuellar, Mike 45
Cuyler, Kiki 87

Dallas Cowboys 155
Dallas Football Club 10
Dallas Morning News 128
Darling, Ron 175
Dartmouth College 175
Daubert, Jake 22
Davenport, Lum 46
Davis, Crash 176
Daytona Beach Islanders 86
Dedeaux, Raoul "Red" 169–170
Denver Rockets 180
Detroit Lions 117, 157–158
Detroit Tigers 19, 36, 43, 48, 60, 67, 73–74, 80, 89–90, 99–100, 106, 108, 111, 137, 168, 173–174
Dickey, Bill 98, 137
Dierker, Larry 154
Dillinger, Bob 106
DiMaggo, Dom 110
DiMaggio, Joe 105–106
Disch, William J. ("Uncle Billy") 9, 11–13, 15–16, 28, 102–103, 127–128, 135, 146, 151–152, 160–161–162
Disch-Falk Field (UFCU Disch-Falk Field) 5, 161–163
Disch Memorial Committee 127–128
Dobbs, Glenn 111–112
Dobson, Pat 45
Doerr, Bobby 110
Donahue, Pete 30
Douglas, Astynanax 30
Dowd Report 43
Dreyfuss, Barney 27, 166
Dubuc, Jean 36
Dudley, "Bullet Bill" 111–112
Duke of York 83
Duke University 129, 176
Durbin, Dick (senator) 62
Durocher, Leo 109
Dyer, Eddie 29

Eastern Intercollegiate League 175
Eckert, Travis 127–131, 147
Eckley, Paul 175
Edward VIII (Prince of Wales) 83–84
Ehrler, Jim 122–126
Eight Men Out 19
Einhorn, Eddie 178
Elam, Johnny 133
Eller, Hod 19, 24, 58–59
El Paso Bowie Bears 115
Elston, Don 149
RMS *Empress of Canada* 71
English, Dudley 28–29
English, Red 13, 28
Errante, Marty 108
ESPN 1, 178–179, 181

197

Index

ESPN2 179
ESPN3 179
ESPU 179
Evans, Billy 96, 99, 101
Evans, Wilbur 146
Evers, Johnny 79
The Eyes of Texas 10

Faber, Urban ("Red") 14, 19, 33, 45–46, 48, 50–52, 66, 68, 70, 74, 80, 85
Fain, Ferris 106
Fair Park (Dallas, TX) 17
Fairly, Ron 170
Falk, Arthur 7
Falk, Bibb August 1–5, 7–9, 11, 13–18, 25, 27–35, 44–45, 47–48, 50–52, 57, 64, 66–69, 71–82, 84, 86–89, 91–103, 107–111, 113–115, 117–123, 125, 127, 132–136, 138, 140, 142–152, 154–157, 159–162, 165, 169–170, 172, 176; Boston Red Sox coach 101; burial at Austin Memorial Park 159; Chicago White Sox 15, 32–35, 44, 47–48, 50–52, 57, 64, 66–68, 73–80, 86–87, 89, 91–95, 159; Cleveland Indians 3, 96–101; college baseball coach 102–103, 113–115, 117–123, 125, 127–136, 138, 142–152, 154–157, 161–162, 165, 176; college baseball player 2, 12–16, 25, 27–32; college football player 2, 17–18, 25, 28, 32; European tour 81–82, 84; football trainer 111; Oriental tour 69, 71–73, 82; racial intolerance black players 89, 140; Toledo Mud Hens manager 101; traded to Cleveland 95; World War I 11; World War II 4, 107–111
Falk, Chester ("Chet"; "Spot") Emanuel 7–8, 88, 128
Falk, Christine Falk 7–8
Falk, Collie (christened Carl) 7–8, 128
Falk, Elsie 7–8
Falk, Gustav (Gus) Harald 7–8, 128
Falk, Nellie (Englom) 7
Farrell, John 168
Federal League 81, 170
Feller, Bob 104
Felsch, Oscar ("Happy") 2, 24, 33, 35, 37–38, 40, 44–47, 49, 53, 58–60, 68, 87
Fenway Park 110
Ferguson, Bob 120
Ferrell, Wes 97, 101
Ferriss, David ("Boo") 108–111
Finger, Tom 108
Finigan, Jim 156
Fisher, Ray 19, 129–130, 171–172

Fitzgerald, Howard 28
Florida International League 109
Florida Marlins 139, 168
Florida State University 136, 139, 167–168
Fonseca, Lew 95–98
Forbes, Pat 159
Ford, Gerald R. (president) 172
Ford, Henry II 158
Fordham University 169, 172
Fortune, Irv 108
Fothergill, Fatty 99
Francona, Terry 177
Franklin, Ben 26, 52
Frazee, Harry 20, 68
Freil, Bill 88
Fresno State University 162
Friedman, Richard ("Kinky") 9
Friend, Hugo (judge) 51–52
Frisch, Frank 48, 82, 166–167, 169
Fromberg, Morgan 55–56
Frontier League 60
Fullerton, Hugh 20–21, 24, 26–27, 39

Gandel, Arnold ("Chick") 22, 24, 27, 35, 37–40, 47, 50, 53, 56–57, 60, 94
Garcia, Hokie 119
Gardner, Larry 172
Garibaldi, Bob 136–137
Garrett, Mike 170
Garrido, Augie 162
Garrity, John J. (police chief) 42–43
Gedeon, Elmer 62
Gedeon, Joe 25–26, 41, 44, 52, 62
Gehrig, Lou 59, 76, 93, 98, 137
Geiser, Jack 98
Giacalone, Tony 43
Giamatti, A. Bartlett (commissioner) 175
Gideon, Joe 144
Gilbert, Danny 180
Gillett, Irwin 28–31
Gleason, William J. ("Kid") 13, 19–22, 26–27, 32–34, 46–47, 50–51, 58, 73, 77–78, 86 94
God Bless America 117
Good, Jerry 133–134
Gordon, Joe 106
Gorin, Charles 122
Gorman, George (assistant state attorney) 50
Grabiner, Harry 43, 51, 80, 95
Grabowski, Johnny 91
Graham, Otto 117
Gray, Jim 156
Gray, Pete 105
Green Bay Packers 111
Greenberg, Hank 104

198

Index

Greer, Jimmy 14
Griffith, Bert 69
Griffith, Clark 51–52
Groat, Dick 176
Groh, Heine 24
Grove, Lefty 76, 93, 96
Groza, Lou 117
Gura, Larry 168
Gustafson, Cliff 127, 141, 159–162, 169; college baseball coach 127, 141, 159–161; college baseball player 127, 160

Hague, Joe 143–144
Halas, George 116–117
Hamilton, Tom 121–122, 155–156
Hardin Simmons College (Simmons College) 29, 112, 120
Harding, Warren G. (president) 20
Harris, Bucky 87, 101
Hart, Lamar 13
Hart, Maxey 28
Harvard University 175
Haskel Indians 17
Hassey, Ron 177
Hatton, Grady 151–152
Hayes, Elvin 178
Hayes, Woody 164
Haywood, Spencer 180
Hearn, Charles ("Bunny") 170
Heilmann, Harry 72, 76
Helms, Tommy 154
Herchiser, Orel 179
Heredia, Gilbert 177
Herman, Babe 105
Herrmann, August ("Garry") 24, 26, 57, 171
Herzog, Buck 35
Heydler, John 22–23, 36
Higginbottom, Roswell 29
Higgins, Michael ("Pinky") 137–138
Hillhouse, Steve 143
Hoak, Don 149
Hodapp, Johnny 98
Hodge, Clarence ("Shovel") 35, 46, 68
Hoffa, Jimmy 43
Hoffman, Fred 69
Hollywood High School 169
Holy Cross College 126, 172, 175–176
Hooper, Harry 47, 64, 66, 68, 80, 86, 172
Hooten, Burt 161
Hornfield, Bill 88
Hornsby, Rogers 48, 152, 154, 166
Hotel Ansonia 40
Hotel Sherman 41
Hotel Youree 91
Houston Astros 1, 132, 154
Houston Buffs 154

Howard Payne 17
Howser, Dick 167–168
Hoyne, Marclay (chief prosecutor) 42
Hoyt, Waite 34, 69, 71–74, 93
Hrncir, Gus 125
Hudlin, Willis 98
Hunnefield, Bill 92
Hunter, Herb 69
Huston, Col. Tillinghast 73–74
Hutson, Don 111
Hyames Field (Kalamazoo, MI) 120–121

Illinois Wesleyan 168
Indiana University 152
International League 109
Interstate League 108, 156
Ishimaru, Shinichi 107
Ithaca College 136

Jacinto Junior College 161
Jack Coombs Field 176
Jackson, Bo 157
Jackson, Joe (Detroit sportswriter) 20–21
Jackson, Joe ("Shoeless Joe") 2–3, 21–24, 27, 33, 37, 39–48, 50–51, 54–55, 57–59, 64, 68, 87, 103, 165
Jackson, Kate 58
Jackson, Ransom ("Hansom Ransom"; "Randy") 115, 120, 148–149
Jackson, Reggie 141, 168
Jackson, Sonny 154
Jacobson, "Baby Doll" 45
Jamieson, Charley 79, 95, 99, 101
Jennings, Hugh 34
Jensen, Jackie 120
Johnson, Byron ("Ban") 20, 22–23, 35, 37, 42, 48–49, 53, 56–57, 87, 90, 174
Johnson, Ernie 47, 66
Johnson, Randy 170
Johnson, Walter 59, 75–76, 85, 101
Jolley, Smead ("Smudge") 99
Jones, Sam 73–74
Jucker, Ed 180
Judnich, Walt 106
Juneau, William 11
Jungman, Tom 130

Kamm, Willie 68–69, 75, 85, 88, 91
Kana, Frank 125
Kansas City Athletics 107, 126, 132, 134, 167
Kansas City Chiefs 170
Kansas City Monarchs 167
Kansas City Royals 167–168
Kasper, Ed 135
Kell, George 154
Kellogg, Frank (ambassador) 83

199

Index

Kelly, George 69
Kelly, Roy 130
Kemp, Steve 170
Kennedy, Vern 89
Keogh, Rod 124
Kerr, Dickey 33, 45–45, 48, 51–52, 68, 86, 171
Kindall, Jerry 177
King George V 82–83
Kingman, Dave 170
Klimchock, Lou 151
Kluszewski, Ted 152
Knauff, Benny 37
Knight, Bobby 164
Knutson, Chuck 135
Koenig, Mark 98
Koufax, Sandy 139, 180
Krzyzewski, Mike 164
Kuhn, Bowie 172
Kuns, Oscar 7

Lafayette College 129
Lafayette High School 180
Landis, Kenesaw Mountain (commissioner) 26, 50, 54, 57–58, 60–63, 69–71, 87, 89–90, 94, 129, 155, 172, 174
Landreaux, Ken 141
Landry, Tom 155
Lansing, Mike 159
Larry, Yale 158
Lavin, Dr. John 69
Lawrence Dumont Stadium (Wichita, KS) 121
Lawson, Earl 152
Layden, Pete 103
Layne, Bobby 115–120, 127, 149, 157–159
Layne, Carol 157
Lazzeri, Tony 74, 137
League Park (Dunn Field) 96–99
Lee, Bill 170
Lefferts, Craig 177
Leonard, Dutch 48, 89–90, 173–174
Lessiner, Ferdinand ("Rube") 28–29, 31
Levi, Ben 25–26
Levi, Lou 25–26
LeVias, Jerry 141
Leviathan 84
Lewis, Duffy 172
Liebold, Nemo 44, 47
Linker, Boyd 131
Little League World Series 178–179
Lobert, Hans 82
Lodigiani, Dario 106
Lofton, Kenny 177
Los Angeles Dodgers 132, 139, 148, 169
Loudermilk, Grover 27
Loudon, Gary 136, 139

Louis, Joe 93
Louisiana State University (LSU) 126
Luckman, Sid 116
Lujack, Johnny 116–117
Lungram, Carl 130
Luque, Dolph 19, 30
Lynn, Fred 170
Lyons, Ted 30–31, 77, 80, 82, 85, 89, 91, 93, 101–102

Mack, Connie 12, 77, 90, 175–176
Macon Peaches 109
Maharg, Billy 36, 39, 53
Mahoney, Chris 172
Major League Baseball (MLB) 89
Mangum, Leo 91
Margrane, Joe 177
Marquette University 112
Marsh, John I.B. ("Toney") 20
Martin, Billy 167
Mathewson, Christy 59
Matson, Ollie 117
Mauro, Carmen 155
Mays, Carl 22, 33, 34, 73
McAlpin Hotel 59
McClellan, Harvey ("Little Mac") 27, 51, 85
McCollough, George 28, 31
McCormick, Mike 106
McDonald, Charles (chief justice) 42, 51
McDonald, Wayne 132
McGraw, John 14, 27, 36–37, 70, 81–82, 84
McGwire, Mark 170
McHale, Marty 172
McInnis, John ("Stuffy") 175–176
McLain, Denny 43
McManus, George ("Humpy") 63–64
McMullin, Fred 37–39, 42, 53, 57, 60
McMurray College 120
McNally, Dave 45
McNee, Graham 178
McWeeney, Douglas 68
Meadows, Ed ("Country") 117
Means, James 140
Meehan, Jimmy 63
Meiji Shrine Stadium (Tokyo) 107
Memorial Stadium (Austin) 114, 140, 142
Menge, Roy 132–134
Meusel, Van 82
Meusel, Bob 3, 73–75, 91
Meusel, Emil ("Irish") 3, 69, 82
Meyer, Dutch 111
Meyer, Russ 149
Miami Beach Flamingos 109
Miami Sun Sox 109
Middlebury College 171

Index

Miller, Norm 154
Milwaukee Braves 108, 124
Milwaukee Brewers: AAA 122; MLB 151
Minneapolis Millers 109
Minnesota Twins 177
MLB Network 181
Mohr, Paul 128–131
Monday, Rick 144, 168
Montreal Expos 132, 139, 168
Montreal Royals 109
Moore, Gary 143–144
Moore, Maxey 28
Moran, Pat 171
Morehart, Ray 91
Moreland, Keith 161
Morgan, Joe 154
Moriarty, George 70, 72
Morse, Hap 155–156
Morris, Jim 108
Moryn, Walt 149
Mostil, Johnny 47, 64, 66–67, 80, 83, 88–89, 91
Mulligan, Eddie 47, 66, 68, 89
Murdock, Eugene Converse 89, 134
Murphy, Eddie 34–35, 45
Musial, Stan 86, 105
Myers, George 133

NAIA 178
Naranjo, Rube 108
National Association 109
National Baseball Hall of Fame 82, 134, 166, 173, 175
National Commission 26–27, 57, 166
National League 26, 36, 105, 152, 173
Navin Field 67
Naylor, Rollie 50
NBA 124, 180
NBC (National Broadcasting Company) 178
NCAA 161, 179; basketball tournament 178, 180
Negro Leagues 62, 106, 167
Nettles, Gregg 151
Nevers, Ernie 91
New, Buddy 135–136
New York Bulldogs 117
New York Evening World 26, 40
New York Giants 14, 18–19, 27, 35–36, 48, 65, 69, 71, 79, 81–82, 84, 94, 107, 119, 166, 170
New York Giants (football) 17, 157
New York Herald 42
New York Mets 139
New York Stuyvesant Polyclinic Hospital 63
New York Sun 69

New York Supreme Court 52–53
New York Times 20
New York Yankees (Highlanders) 2, 22, 33–35, 37, 64–65, 67–69, 71, 73–75, 77, 79, 82, 88, 91–93, 97, 98, 105–106, 126, 134, 137, 156, 159, 165–167, 171, 173–174, 178
NFL (National Football League) 117, 181
NIT (National Invitational Tournament) 178
North Carolina State University 169
Northern League 109–110
Norwich University 175
Nothe, Walter 108–109, 111
Notre Dame University 117, 122, 133, 141
Nuxhall, Joe 105

Oakland Athletics 144, 168
Obama, Barrack (president) 62, 178
O'Connell, Jimmy 93
Ohio-Pennsylvania League 166
Ohio State University 112, 126, 144, 178, 180
Ohio Wesleyan College 164
Oklahoma A&M University (Oklahoma State University) 12, 14, 115, 121, 131, 134, 144, 162, 168
Oklahoma All-Stars 17
O'Leary, Charlie 78
Omaha Cardinals 129
Omaha Municipal Stadium 123–124, 129–130, 136
O'Neal, Leon 141
O'Neil, Frank ("Buck") 69–70, 72
Orange Bowl 178
Oriental Hotel 12
Ormsby, Emmett T. 96
Owen, Spike 161
Owens, Steve 17

Pacific Coast League (PCL) 47, 69, 92, 105, 149, 162
Packard Stadium (Bobby Winkles Field) 168
Paige, Satchell 106
Palmer, Jim 45
Palmer, Lyle 120
Park Central Hotel 63–64
Parker, Ace 176
Pass, Samuel L. 53
Patrick, Mike 179
Patterson, Oliver 140
Paul, Don 124–125
Paul, Gabe 154, 167
Payne, Howard 13
Peckinpaugh, Roger 87–88, 91–92, 95–96, 99, 101

201

Index

Penn, Albert 28
Penn Radio School 11
Penn State University 122, 133, 139, 176
Pennock, Herb 69, 74
Peters, Garry 151
Peters, Ron 43
Peterson, Kyle 179
Pfeil, Clarence 108
Philadelphia Athletics 12, 35, 50, 65, 77, 90–91, 93, 96–98, 106, 137, 156, 175–176
The Philadelphia North American 36
Philadelphia Phillies 35, 94, 102, 137, 149, 155, 156, 171, 175, 177
Pittsburgh Pirates 11, 27, 87–88, 105, 166, 171, 180
Pittsburgh Rebels 170
Pittsburgh Steelers 116–117, 170
Plainview Ponies 160
Podbielan, Bud 152
Pollett, Howie 106, 111
Polo Grounds 33–34, 36, 58, 112, 173
Porter, Dick 99
Porter, Lee 96
Power, Vic 156
Prince Henry 83
Princeton University 9, 172, 177
Prindville, Edward (state's attorney) 49, 55
Pro Football Hall of Fame 117, 157

Queen Mary 82, 84

Rainey, Dr. Homer 102
Ramsey, Jonas 164
Randolph Field (twelfth base headquarters and base squadron) 4, 107, 131
Randolph Field Ramblers, Texas 4, 108–110, 112
Rath, Morrie 21, 59–60
Raup, Jimmy 145, 147
Raymond, "Nigger Nate" 63
Reach 1920 Official Guide 58
Reading Chicks 108
Redland Field 21
Redmond, Harry 25, 52, 54
Reece, Bill 112
Reed, Howie 132
Reese, Jimmy 99
Reifler, Don 130
Rena, Bill 156
Replogue, Harley (assistant state attorney) 42
Reynolds, Carl 101
Reynolds, Harold 179
Reynolds, Shane 161
Rice, Grantland 59

Rice, Harry 101
Rice Hotel 12
Rice University 1, 11–12, 29, 119, 139
Richards, Paul 46
Rickey, Branch 130, 165–166–167
Rigby, Lloyd ("Rabbit") 135
Rigby, Pat 135
Ring, Jimmy 30, 166
Risberg, Robert 62
Risberg, Swede 22, 24, 37, 39, 41, 44, 47, 49, 57–59, 60–62, 88–89
Ritter, Jack 130
Riverfront Stadium 43
Rixey, Eppa 30, 171
Roberts, Dave 154
Roberts, Ric 106
Robertson, Charlie 67, 73
Robertson, Jim 155
Robertson, Swanie 14, 28, 31
Robinson, Brooks 151
Robinson, Eddie 156
Robinson, Floyd 89
Robinson, Jackie 149, 167
Rockne, Knute 164
Rodriguez, Alex 89
Roosevelt, Franklin D. (president) 104
Rose, Pete 43
Rose Bowl (Tournament of Roses) 177–178
Rothstein, Arnold 30–21, 26, 35, 41–42, 52, 54–56, 63–64
Roush, Edd 19, 24–25
Royal, Darryl 114, 140, 160
Ruether, Dutch 19, 21
Ruffing, Red 94, 106
Rupp, Adolph 164
Ruppert, Col. Jacob 22, 68, 73–74
Russell, Jack 112
Rutgers (The State University of New Jersey) 9, 123–124
Ruth, Babe 2, 59, 65, 68–69, 75–77, 79, 81, 91, 93, 98, 107, 137–138, 168, 173
Ryan, Nolan 1, 139

SABR (Society for American Baseball Research) 109
St. Edwards University 12, 156
St. Johns University 121–122, 144, 175
St. Louis Browns 8, 25, 28, 41, 44–45, 66, 77, 88, 91–93, 98, 105–106, 108, 152, 165–166, 173
St. Louis Cardinals 19, 27, 29, 48, 69, 86, 105–106, 111, 119, 123, 143–144, 151, 166–168, 170–171
St. Mary's College 172
St. Philips College 17
St. Xavier University—Chicago 168

Index

Sallee, Slim 19
Sally League 109
Samuel F. Austin High School 8–9, 114
San Antonio Aviation Cadet Center (SAAC Warhawks) 4, 111
San Antonio Service Baseball League 108, 110
San Diego Padres 154
San Francisco Giants 137, 168
San Francisco Seals 68
San Francisco State University 163
Sand, Heine 94
Sanders, Deon 157
Santa Clara University 136–137
Santo, Ron 154
Scarborough, Luther 126–128
Schacht, Al 101
Schalk, Ray 14, 46, 50–52, 66–67, 76–78, 90, 92, 94
Schaw, George Bernard 83
Scheschuk, Ray 144
Schiraldi, Calvin 141, 161
Schmidt, Joe 158
Scully, Vin 169
Seattle Mariners 28
Seattle Supersonics 180
Seaver, Tom 170
Second Air Force Base 112
Segrist, Kal 123–124
Selig, Bud 62
Sells, Ken 105–106
Seton Hall University 142
Seton Medical Center 88
Sewell, Luke 69, 95
Shawkey, Bob 74
Shearton-Dallas Hotel 134
Sheely, Earl 66, 80, 85–86, 88–89
Shires, Art ("Art the Great") 93–94
Shocker, Urban 66–67
Silas, Xavier 9
Silvera, Charlie 106
Simmons, Al 93, 101
Simmons, Curt 157
Sinclair, John 10
Singer, Bill 139
Sinton Hotel 20–22, 39, 45
Sisler, George 27–28, 76, 91, 165–166
Slaughter, Enos 106–107, 111
Smalley, Roy 170
Smith, Hoke (senator) 90
Smith, J.L. 130–131
Smith, Kate 117
Snow, Tom 130–131
Southern Methodist University (SMU) 30–31, 103, 128–129, 132–133, 139, 141
Southwest Conference (SWC; Southwest Intercollegiate Athletic Conference) 11–14, 17, 25, 28, 30–31, 77, 102–104, 113, 115, 119–121, 126–128, 131–136, 139–146, 148–149, 161–162, 165
Southwestern Louisiana Institute 111
Southwestern Texas College 17
Southwestern University 10, 12, 118
Speaker, Tris 59, 76, 89–90, 173–174
Spradlin, Ron 130
Spring Woods High School 161
Springfield College 126
SPORT Magazine 133
The Sporting News 20
Sports Illustrated 115
Sports World Magazine 43
Sportsman's Park 91
Stahl, Jake 172
Stanford University 129, 171
The Star-Spangled Banner 72
Stark, Frank 142
Staub, Rusty 154
Steinbrenner, George 167
Stengel, Casey 3, 69, 71–72, 82, 101, 169
Stengel, Edna 82
Stephenson, Riggs 3, 69
Stern, Bill 177
Stewart, Jimmy 154
Stinson Field 108
Strunk, Amos 34–35, 44, 47, 64, 69, 73
Stryzkalski, Johnny 112
Sugar Bowl 178
Sullivan, Ed *(Toast of the Town)* 59
Suszuki, Ichiro 28
Sun Bowl 112
Swan, Craig 168
Swindell, Gregg 161

Tanner, Joe 127–128
Tanner, Ray 169
Tappe, Ted 124
Taylor, Harry 132
Tebbetts, Birdie 106, 108
Terwilliger Wayne 106–107
Texas: Austin 1, 6, 7, 18, 31, 88, 101, 121, 137, 140, 154, 156, 159, 165; Brenham 141; Brownsville 27; College Station 18, 118; Dallas 14, 17, 30, 114, 120, 137–138, 155, 162; Donna 15; El Paso 115; Ft. Worth 29; Georgetown 9; Houston 12, 142, 161–162; Jasper 151; Kenedy 159; Killeen 141; Lone Oak 148; Lubbock 157–158; Marlin 27; San Antonio 4, 27, 107, 120, 128, 141, 144, 159–160; Seguin 74; Taylor 28; Waco 27, 31, 120; Waxahachie 29, 46
Texas A&M University 1, 11, 14–16, 18, 25, 29–31, 104, 117–119, 121, 126, 129, 132, 134–136, 142–144

Index

Texas Central Railroad 8
Texas Christian University (TCU) 1, 11, 14, 29–30, 119, 127, 139, 144, 148, 162
Texas League 1, 13, 29, 102, 105, 119–120, 122, 149, 154
Texas Rangers 1
Texas Sports Hall of Fame 134
Texas Tech 162
Third Air Force Gremlins 112
Thompkins, Ben 123–124, 156–157
Thompson, Clarence ("Titanic") 63
Thompson, Mike ("Butch") 138–139, 142–143
Thorpe, Jim 157
Thurston, Sloppy 75, 80, 85
Time Magazine 81, 84
Tipton, Eric 176
Toast of the Town 59
Tobin, Jack 45
Toledo Mud Hens 101, 109
Toney, Fred 37
Torborg, Jeff 139
Trafton, George 94
Trautman, George 109
Treasury Bond Bowl 112
Trinity University 29, 144
Tritico, Frank 111
Tufts University 123–124
Tulane University 126
Turner Sports 178
Tyrell, John 50

Uhle, George 100
Unitas, Johnny 117
U.S. Olympic Basketball Committee 156
U.S. Supreme Court 140, 180–181
University of Alabama 115, 122, 124, 126
University of Arizona 46, 123, 126, 129, 133, 135, 139, 144, 177
University of Arkansas 11–12, 148
University of California 120, 133
University of California–Los Angeles (UCLA) 123, 167, 178
University of Cincinnati 178, 180
University of Connecticut 133
University of Georgia 122
University of Houston 119, 134, 145, 178
University of Illinois 172
University of Iowa 126
University of Louisville 168
University of Maine 172
University of Michigan 27, 122, 129–130, 136–137, 165–166, 172
University of Minnesota 126, 134, 177
University of Missouri 10, 115, 136, 139, 176
University of Nebraska 141

University of North Carolina 134, 170
University of Northern Colorado 136
University of Oklahoma 11–12, 14, 17, 120, 126, 145, 148, 163
University of Pennsylvania 9, 122
University of Seoul 71
University of South Carolina 169
University of Southern California (USC) 121, 126, 135, 141, 169–170
University of Tennessee 126
University of Texas (Austin; the Forty Acres) 1, 4, 7, 9–13, 15, 17–18, 25, 27–32, 82, 88, 102–103, 107, 111–115, 117–149, 151, 154–157, 159–165, 169, 176; Hall of Honor 4, 134, 156
University of Vermont 172
Utah State University 126

Van Brocklin, Norm 117
Veach, Bobby 85
Veeck, Bill, Jr. 152
Veeck, William, Sr. 35
Ventura, Robin 179
Viola, Frank 175
Voskmik, Joe 3, 99

Waco Field Flyers 108
Waghalter, Irving 123–125
Wagner, Honus 59
Wake Forest University 121–122
Walker, Doak 157
Wall, Murray 120–122, 135, 148
Walsh, Ed 59, 79, 81
Walters, Bucky 119
Waner, Lloyd 105
Waner, Paul 105
Ward, Aaron 73–74, 91–92
Warmouth, Cy 75
Warner, Glenn ("Pop") 164
Warner Hotel 40
Washington Nationals (Senators) 35, 51, 75, 79, 85, 87–88, 94, 97–98, 107, 148, 152, 174
Washington State University 124–125, 144
WEAF 178
Weaver, George ("Buck") 14, 21, 33, 37–38, 40, 45–47, 50, 53–54, 59, 62, 94
Wedge, Eric 159
Weiss, William J. 109
Wembly Stadium (London, UK) 82
West Texas–New Mexico League 157, 160
Westbrook, John Hill 141
Western League 129, 149
Western Michigan University 120, 135, 176, 178

204

Index

Whitman, Charles 145
Whitter, Julius 141
Wichita State University 159
Wilber, Del 111
Wilkinson, Roy 46, 51–52
Williams, Billy 154
Williams, Claude ("Lefty") 19–20, 22, 24, 27, 33, 35, 37–40, 42–43, 45–46, 48, 50–51, 53–55, 58, 60
Williams, Hobbs 120
Williams, Ken 91
Williams, Ricky 141
Williams, Ted 29, 77, 104–105, 110, 137–138
Williams College 9–10
Williamson County Sun 9
Wilson, Woodrow (president) 11
Winkles, Bobby 144
Wisniewski, Marvin 130
Wixson, Jim 134
Wolter, Harry 171
Womack, Frank 121–122, 124
Wood, Joe 173
Wood, Smoky Joe 89, 173–175
Wooden, John 164
Woodman, Woody 132–133
Woodward, Woody 139
World Series: (1903) 11; (1906) 65; (1910) 176; (1911) 176; (1912) 173, 176; (1913) 176; (1915) 176; (1916) 71; (1917) 17, 18–19, 87, 176; (1919) 2–3, 18–26, 34–37, 40–44, 48–49, 52–55, 57–59, 63, 65, 78, 81, 86–88, 171, 173; (1922) 71; (1923) 71; (1924) 81, 87; (1925) 87; (1926) 166; (1940) 119; (1946) 29; (1955) 149; (1956) 148; (1985) 168; (2004) 177
World War I 11, 13, 28, 81, 84, 104, 170–171, 176
World War II 4, 62, 104–112, 122, 131, 148, 167
Wright, Marshall 109
Wrigley, P.K. 105
Wynn, Jimmy 154

Yale University 9, 120–121, 173, 175
Yankee Stadium 75, 110
Yawkey, Tom 138
Young, Buddy 142–144
Youngs, Ross 1

Zelser, David 50, 54
Zimmerman, Heine 35–37
Zinser, Bill 180
Zomlefer, Chuck 120
Zork, Carl 50, 52, 55

www.ingramcontent.com/pod-product-compliance
Ingram Content Group UK Ltd.
Pitfield, Milton Keynes, MK11 3LW, UK
UKHW021845140426
5217IPUK00022B/1604